CRITICAL REGIONALISM AND CULTURAL STUDIES

Cheryl Temple Herr

CRITICAL REGIONALISM AND

UNIVERSITY PRESS OF FLORIDA
GAINESVILLE TALLAHASSEE TAMPA BOCA RATON
PENSACOLA ORLANDO MIAMI JACKSONVILLE

CULTURAL STUDIES

From Ireland to the American Midwest

01 00 99 98 97 96 6 5 4 3 2 1

Library of Congress Cataloging-in-Publication Data

Herr, Cheryl.
Critical regionalism and cultural studies: from Ireland to the American Midwest /
Cheryl Temple Herr.
    p. cm.
Includes bibliographical references and index.
ISBN 0-8130-1466-2 (alk. paper)
1. Iowa—Rural conditions. 2. Ireland—Rural conditions. 3. Ireland—Emigration
and immigration. 4. Iowa—Emigration and immigration. 5. Irish-Americans—Iowa.
6. Farm life in literature. 7. Farm life in motion pictures. I. Title.
HN79.I8H47   1996
307.72—DC 20   96-16257

Frontispiece: Country Road near Corcomroe Abbey, County Clare. Copyright 1986 by
Hanno Hardt.

Paul Durcan's poem, "Loosestrife in Ballyferriter," reprinted herein by permission of
the author, was originally published in *Daddy, Daddy* (Belfast: Blackstaff Press, 1990) and
was reprinted in Paul Durcan, *A Snail in My Prime* (New York: Penguin, 1995).

Excerpt from James Joyce's "The Dead" is reprinted herein by permission of the Estate
of James Joyce.

The University Press of Florida is the scholarly publishing agency for the State
University System of Florida, comprised of Florida A & M University, Florida Atlantic
University, Florida International University, Florida State University, University of
Central Florida, University of Florida, University of North Florida, University of South
Florida, and University of West Florida.

University Press of Florida, 15 Northwest 15th Street, Gainesville, FL 32611

For Gary
who knows from farming

and for John
who prefers an indoor job

CONTENTS

THIS BOOK DEVELOPS a rationale for a cross-regional methodology for cultural studies through exploration of recurrent rural crisis. The work draws on history, sociology, economics, anthropology, cinema, and literature. The readership that I address includes practitioners of Irish studies, of midwestern American studies, of rural studies, and of cultural studies in general. I believe that the text can be used with benefit by advanced undergraduates, graduate students, and professional scholars as well as by the general reader. Although my immediate audience is necessarily composed of American readers for whom sociological and literary issues in Irish studies are often occluded—a circumstance that is, in my experience, immensely underestimated by Irish scholars—I believe that many Irish readers may also find something of value here. In any event, research for this project has often taken me to Ireland, and the book draws on work done in Ireland over the past fifteen years.

Those who have generously responded to all or part of the manuscript for this book include Terence Brown, Teresa Brown, Marlena Corcoran, Seamus Deane, Kathleen Quinn, Garrett Stewart, Carol Tyx, and Geetha Varadarajan. I have benefited enormously from all responses; however, I accept full responsibility for everything here. Special thanks to Zack Bowen for his characteristic boundless encouragement; he remains for me a model of scholarly generosity. I am grateful to Gary Peter Ellingson for assiduously scanning a wide variety of Irish and British newspapers for contemporary responses to agri-issues and the global economy. In regard to my argument in chapter 2 about James Joyce's "The Dead," I must note that as this book goes to press a lecture by W. J. McCormack entitled "Entertaining Theory: Joyce, 'The Dead,' and the Famine" has been advertised for a session at the 1995 meeting in Cork of the International Association for the Study of Anglo-Irish Literature. I do not know if our arguments overlap in any way; I want merely to document my argument's independence from Dr. McCormack's lecture.

My thanks to the University of Iowa's Faculty Scholar Program, the University of Iowa's Center for Advanced Studies (directed by Jay Semel, ably assisted by Lorna Olson), the Institute for Irish Studies at Queen's University in Belfast, and the Guggenheim Foundation: some of the research for this book emerged from work on another project specifically funded by the Guggenheim Foundation. My work on this book owes much to the inspiration offered by Desmond Bell; I value his suggestion, predating but also aligning with the programs put forward by Michael D. Higgins and with the film criticism of Martin McLoone, that Irish studies and Irish culture might benefit from a social and aesthetic theory based in the critical regionalism of Kenneth Frampton. On this architectural note, I express my sincere thanks to Mark Haukos, whose drawings appear in chapter 2. I am also grateful to Paul Durcan for allowing me to quote his poem "Loosestrife in Ballyferriter" and to the estate of James Joyce for allowing me to quote from "The Dead." John Kelleher amiably provided wonderful background resources for the study of *Eat the Peach*. Finally, I thank Walda Metcalf of the University Press of Florida for her expert guidance.

Cultural Studies and Critical Regionalism

We can only struggle among assemblages.
JACQUES DELEUZE

THIS BOOK IS about recurrent rural crisis in Ireland and in the American Midwest; I undertook this project because the 150th anniversary of the mid-1840s Irish famine searingly reminds us of family farmers' increasingly vulnerable state around the world. To unfold the many dimensions of agrarian distress, I employ a methodology for cross-cultural inquiry that seeks to align historical record, aesthetic representation, political economy, and cultural psychology with a lively sense of our local and global goals in studies of societies other than our own.

Indeed, this methodology grew out of my desire to come to terms with a key but often silenced issue in cultural studies—the tension between "insiders" and "outsiders." Often, indigenous scholars merely tolerate the pronouncements of exterior critics, while those coming from afar may imagine themselves in a situation of superior objectivity. Regardless of how often ethnographic theories of participant observation and reflexive viewing are invoked, these academic skirmishes continue to express a complicated and visceral desire for ownership, for authority, and for belonging. Neither casting aspersions nor enacting a bogus beneficence appears to be a satisfactory response when theoretical debate comes down to cases.

In the approach that I suggest, the issue of an absolute accuracy, of once and for all getting it right, of having precisely an insider's experiential knowledge of a given terrain, is temporarily bracketed. I propose that outsiderness be construed not so much as ignorance or uncertainty but rather as a specific, productive social negativity. By this line of reasoning, intimately knowing another culture is only one part of the job of pursuing cultural studies and is usefully complemented by the possibilities for agency inherent in the discovery—between and across boundaries—of previously unseen or inaccessible platforms, of the conjunction of marginality and the accidental, of mutually constructed, chorally articulated interspaces. Because outsiders doing cultural studies face the task of moving toward a profound, albeit always necessarily provisional, identification with more than one social scene and with distinctive but shared worldwide struggles against hegemonic structures, my aim is not only to advance a position in the ongoing debate about subject/object relations in the production of social knowledge. I want also to understand how inside and outside relations are inflected in what in the early 1990s came to be called the New World Order.

That said, some of the key questions preoccupying scholars at this period—what kind of subjectivity pertains to intercultural explorations? where precisely is the space of disengagement or "elsewhere" that so many critics have posited?—point toward the need for methodological test cases. I contend that both popular theoretical protocols and the reigning area studies paradigm controlling many of our investigations will benefit from increased procedural attention to studying the region, to the implicit, constructed filiation of regions that underlies global marketing strategies, and to the several material ways in which linked regions in the new world economy have quietly, historically woven and maintained their own provisional interspaces. Some of this intertwining—but by no means all of it—comes about in film and literature. By drawing together the voices of a given region and allowing comparison with another space's structurally significant life situation, aesthetic artifacts help outsiders to interpret the terms of their exteriority, create ideological bridges, and set into play the resonances constituting mutual awareness. It is through hybrid artifacts and arenas, as well as via the dialectical narratives of history, that the practice proposed in this volume operates. In the remainder of this introductory chapter, I map the theoretical foundations of my work. I address the evolving concept of the region in the global economy, the attention of contemporary cultural studies to spaces between regions, the usefulness of Gilles Deleuze's notion of the assemblage for understanding these spaces-between, Kenneth Frampton's pertinent theory of critical regionalism, and Theodor Adorno's equally applicable concept of negative dialectic. Taken together, these eclectic sources yield a deeply interdependent, seven-point framework for the method of cultural study that this book advances.

Thinking Globally, Marketing Regionally

By the late twentieth century, the region had come to map a semiotic field in which local, traditional identity could be recuperated as well as erased by newly imagined ways of living. One way to inspect the often tenuous equilibrium of old and new is to follow the interpretive paths blazed by business administrators. This is because at the level of global marketing, regions rather than nations have increasingly formed the target base. The region has become a flexible global administrative unit as individual spaces both self-define and are cross-affiliated not only according to production-type (agrarian, industrial, corporate, or postindustrial) but also according to marketing possibilities. Consider that after the 1992 passage of the Single European Act, the legislation designed to bind Europe into a unified trading bloc, Freddie Heineken, former head of the Dutch brewing corporation, published a pamphlet in which he proposed a "solution to what Stalin termed 'The Problem of the Nationalities'": "Heineken said that the existing national borders in Europe were largely irrelevant and the new Europe should instead be divided into 75 regions with an average population of 10 million each, all linked together in a federation. . . . The Republic of Ireland would unite with Northern Ireland, while Britain would be split in 10. . . . In redrawing the map of Europe, the brewer drew on his experience at Heineken where the marketing department, for example, treats Germany not as a single unit but as a series of distinct beer-drinking and wine-drinking units" ("Heineken Offers"). For Heineken, the expanded sociopolitical base of the European Union (EU) bodes not only an end to nationalism but also the consolidating hegemony of a corporate geography committed to refining its marketing logic.[1]

Hence the power of regional interests unfolds in tandem not only with contemporary geopolitical changes but also with transnational marketing strategies. As the issues complicating world regionalism become more pressing, we want to be clear about how to define regions, who defines them, what the political status of different regions will be, whether their continued emergence constitutes a step forward or an historical regression toward the violence of nationalism. We want to cultivate awareness that in an era when pervasive capital penetration appears to curtail several levels of individual and group agency, multinational businesses actually benefit from people's absorption in regional diversity, constructed as it is in terms of local heritage, lifestyle, values, and tastes. That very preoccupation with the traditional and immediate tends to preclude our taking seriously the international corporate logic that helps to produce exploitative symmetries across subnational areas.

One of the most forceful exponents of such symmetries is *Harvard Business Review* regular Theodore Levitt. In a 1983 article entitled "The Globalization of Markets," Levitt presents "a world with homogenized demand" as already a reality: although this assertion may still feel counterintuitive to some readers, especially those committed to cultural diversity, Levitt asserts that "at this stage in the evolution of globalization," there is a demonstrable universal desire for "world-standardized products," as long as they are reasonably priced and quality-controlled. But—and this is the interesting twist—Levitt insists that marketing success based on homogenized desires nonetheless "requires a search for sales opportunities in similar segments across the globe in order to achieve the economies of scale necessary to compete." This marketing logic emerges precisely from a cross-cultural perspective on contemporary life. As Levitt crucially states, "a market segment in one country is seldom unique; it has close cousins everywhere precisely because technology has homogenized the globe. Even small local segments have their global equivalents everywhere and become subject to global competition, especially on price." Levitt advocates in the strongest possible terms the virtues of enabling small indigenous companies to recognize that they have parallel markets elsewhere in the world and that the first effort—not so much of expansion but simply of self-preservation—must be to locate them. That is to say, in order to survive, the local company must become a global player, alert to the fact that "distant competitors will enter the now-sheltered markets . . . with goods produced more cheaply under scale-efficient conditions. Global competition spells the end of domestic territoriality, *no matter how diminutive the territory may be*" (Levitt, "Globalization" 94; my emphasis). In this scenario, in which cousin regions are sites that are homologous from the viewpoint of global capital, the corporate entity assumes a profoundly primary social agency.[2] What is most significant here for a methodology of cross-cultural studies is his insistence on a market-modulated structure of regional difference and corporate continuity. Although distinctions among market segments exist, from the viewpoint of the world marketer there is no singular segment market, no unique space. Rather, every region on the globe can be reimagined to homologous ends.

Read alongside the *Harvard Business Review*, many cultural theories paradoxically echo Levitt's admonition to compare, although in a different ideological key. Stuart Hall, for instance, recovering the early cultural studies work of the Birmingham program and its precursors, defines the field not as "simply pluralist" but as having "some will to connect" (Grossberg, Nelson, and Treichler 278). John Fiske, exploring "the culture of everyday life," particularly in regard to the relations between "dominant and subordinated habituses," works to "increase the travel between" these sites, thus supporting and strengthening existing linkages (Grossberg, Nelson, and Treichler 164). In fact, he wants to develop "a two-way traffic" between "different ways of experiencing social conditions and their different ways of knowing, different ways of thinking, different ways of producing culture," all toward the goal of "social change" (167). By the same token, Jennifer Daryl Slack and Laurie Anne Whitt interrogate an ecological reality of "interdependence" and "intrinsic relations" to map an ethics of cultural inquiry (Grossberg, Nelson, and Treichler 585). Similarly, Graeme Turner calls for the ongoing and lively realization that "where we live" must be retained as a chief object of inquiry, one that must not accede to the imperative to "speak [only] globally—thereby minimizing . . . differences." We must, Turner affirms, "acknowledge that even theory has to have some historical location, specific contexts within which it works to particular ends." Hence, he calls for increased comparative cultural study in order to see if inherited British models (again, he is thinking of the Birmingham Centre) "'work' for the margins as well as the centers'" (Grossberg, Nelson, and Treichler 649, 650). Completing my highly selective list (in that it is controlled by the cultural studies anthology edited by Lawrence Grossberg,

Cary Nelson, and Paula Treichler, which dominated the early 1990s market), Donna Haraway's "The Promises of Monsters: A Regenerative Politics for Inappropriate/d Others" seeks a discursive instrument for viewing the artifactual world in order to produce "effects of connection, of embodiment, and of responsibility for an imagined elsewhere." Haraway's elaborate project, which takes her into specific intersections among immunology studies, biomedical advertising, environmentalism, scientific discourse, and speculative fiction, is itself mediated through the subject position defined by Trinh Minh-ha's notion of the "inappropriate/d other," one who stands "in critical, deconstructive relationality, in a diffracting rather than reflecting (ratio)nality—as the means of making potent connection that exceeds domination" (Grossberg, Nelson, and Treichler 295, 299).

All of these writers, from business professors to literature scholars, indirectly but inevitably map dimensions of Immanuel Wallerstein's world system theory. Wallerstein has argued that even a self-sufficient local society now stands entirely open to hegemonic corporate invasions and is absorbed into a global analysis produced in terms of European historical change: industrial revolution, urbanization, colonialism, the migration of populations (Wallerstein 62). Much to the point of the present work, José Saldívar urges a literary critical attention to Wallerstein, accessing both local and global explanations of economic forces in order to understand the social dynamics shaping regional writing. Saldívar reminds his reader, "What distinguishes world system theory from other economic theories of development is the way it sees underdevelopment . . . as a direct result of contact with capitalism. In so doing, it understands dependency in terms of a global capitalist system where different modes of production define the degrees of dependency" (Saldívar xii). It is precisely this dependency that literary artifacts, cinematic ventures, and material histories respond to in cultural study. In fact, in much of the debate over development programs, world system theory rolls over into calls for "delinking"—Samir Amin's term for the remapping of the so-called third world around its own indigenous centers—and regrouping strategies at every level of socioeconomic organization and expression.

To address real or potential changes in definitions of national and subnational space and place, and to think as deeply and strategically about regionalism as do international financial forces, cultural analysts are beginning to create nontraditional histories, or what Gilles Deleuze and Félix Guattari call "nomadologies." I see a great deal of this work occupying the zone mapped by Heineken, Levitt, and Wallerstein—in the location of structurally cognate target-regions and the study of their portion within international power-brokerage. It stands to reason that if Region A actively seeks to think of its identity in terms of its likely marketing twins as well as those communities around the planet with which it shares a particular lifestyle and value-set, both outsiderness and priviness are complexly redefined in the process. On both sides of the equation, viewers would attend particularly to the role of economic-historical events in producing perceived symmetries and to the transplanting of seemingly local issues from one place to another through migrating populations. In many instances, they could discern and begin to compose together a unified story of socioeconomic exchange and of aesthetic production. They could also hope to decide for themselves how to respond to the political and economic linkages that increasingly write all of our dreams and desires.

The Aesthetics of Interspace

The kind of connective practice encouraged in this book rests in part on recognizing global processes and in part on assigning value to the transformative kinetics of aesthetic perception and cross-regional discourse. Art historian E. Paolozzi indicates the realm of thought I am after here: "There is a special sort of cognitive experience where a person can look at, and associate, disparate things at the same time. At once, each with each. It becomes almost a description of the creative act—to juggle with these things" (Paolozzi n.p.). Or, to look at this process from an architectural perspective, we might talk about the "forced symmetries" of a building, for example, where a design is made to fit an imposed grid rather than fulfill a strictly functional requirement or where a redundant form calls forth some explanation. Architects can view forced symmetry with approval when it sets up rhythms and patterns necessary to the detailed language of an entire building and its dialogue with neighborhood, natural setting, and skyline. In the case of cultural studies, forcing connections and probing similarities that appear accidental can become a creative, functional investigative tool.

Putting pressure on what looks like a gratuitous design may in fact generate useful information and reveal meaningful patterns in the registers of history, economics, sociology, literary criticism, and aesthetic evolution.

The phenomena of both forced and found symmetries populate the arena of Homi Bhabha's "third space," of Guillermo Gómez-Peña's borderwork, of Amitava Kumar's "locutions," of Wilson Harris's "middle passage," of Fred Moten's counter-totalitarian improvisations of the ensemble. In contemporary theory, there are ample indications that the idea of such cross-referenced and consciously produced ground has captured a register in the academic imagination. It finds an analogue in the syncretisms and synchronicities that have been a staple of New Age consciousness. The zone collectively being yearned for is also called the space-between, interbeing, dialogism, difference, nomadic space, intertextuality, hybridity, the assemblage. It is framed as "the field of cultural production" (Bourdieu and Wacquant 69), where unexpected and unmapped things can occur. This tract finds itself the desired object of deep knowledge and thick description; it stands as both center and periphery—a consciously articulated layer of meaning that exists exactly in the struggle to connect not only one distant region with another but also cold reality with transcendent dreaming, uncharted possibility with emerging meanings. It is the site to which an intersubjective spatialization of desire has been assigned, a Winnicottian ludic agora of transition.

To ground this discourse, we might turn to critics working within postcolonial hermeneutics. These writers often argue that the layering of indigenous and historical experience into previously colonized spaces renders those arenas thick with possibilities for manipulating absence and presence toward the end of producing thresholds from one zone to another, particularly from the industrially reified back to the nurturing and traditional. Despite the problematic nature of the foregoing polarities, in his essay "Fossil and Psyche" Caribbean writer Wilson Harris defends the role of art in opening the way into alternative space with its own dialogic potential for heterogeneous communication-as-community. For Harris, this parallax enables vision beyond the willed blindness of colonialism; it extends the resistance potential of certain fetishized sites such as Northern Ireland, Jamaica, India, or South Africa into places that have long been dominated by an imperialist capitalist economic agenda. As Harris has it: "this 'nameless dimension' may lie in the bearing synchronicity has upon the creation of certain kinds of imagery in certain orders of fiction; the stress of imagery in such orders of the imagination is not only one that taxes the individual artist in undermining monolithic convention but steeps him or her in a-causal (rather than cause-and-effect) links between sovereign poles of experience that begin, in degrees, to yield their mechanical sovereignties and become potent parts of an unfathomable whole which activates a ceaseless quest for community in transformed range or depth" ("Fossil" 81).

Like literary and theoretical works, individual regions encompass multilayers that host indigenous meanings, imported materials, and varieties of interconnection. In regional terms, what Deleuze and Guattari call "smooth space" or nomadic space exists amidst a "striated" or bureaucratized zone's processes of deterritorialization and reterritorialization.[3] When we detect the seams between and among these semiotic registers in literature we assume that we have located signs of the postmodern, or we sum up these laminations under the heading of magic realism. The important thing is that the restless yearning of one social space for another tends to expose the layering and thresholding of cultures. The existence of a dialogue with other regions outside our own may thus provide a foothold for our collective entrance into the future.

In some cases, then, the space-between sought by many theorists is already extant, however tentatively, in cross-regional writing and in heterogeneous, spontaneous constructions of place. This volume explores several such sites in different registers: poetic, narrative, cinematic, architectural, monastic, agrarian, administrative. In those cobbled-together zones of connection, we find strikingly parallel narrative and filmic representations; we find collective experience and multinational speculation that both spans and connects regional interests. My claim is that cultural studies can make its findings and foci more precise and socially useful by attending to the many kinds of attachment representationally and materially fostered in these co-constructed, nascent dimensions. The political economy in which they have arisen and the psychohistorical formations to which they have given life also ask to become part of our developing vocabulary of "elsewhere" and "in between." Even simply attending to existing sites of spontaneous creolization (engineered neither from above nor through institutional agenda) can tutor us in useful viewing practices and methods of inquiry.

The relational inflection of my inquiry and my initial attention to corporate practice will no doubt prompt a reader to anticipate a strongly Marxist interpretive process. To an economics-based inquiry, I add the question, what kind of macropsychology might pertain to the transregional mirroring I propose? Lacanian theorists might say that we all bear a wound or lack that seems to assure us of a fulsome elsewhere that we may seek in a homologous homeland. The nomadic analyses that make up *Critical Regionalism and Cultural Studies* draw not only on Deleuze and Guattari but also on Jacques Lacan, particularly on his vocabulary of imaginary, symbolic, and real horizons—terms that I deploy in ways specific to the micro-macro project of this book. Much as Slavoj Zizek aligns the Marxist dialectic with a Lacanian terrain, so this volume seeks to understand the desiring mechanisms within discrete social formations in terms of the economic and aesthetic productivity of global mirror-staging. I am preoccupied here with the semantics of collective behavior and political economy at recurrent moments of cross-regional identification.

At the same time, well aware of the contradictions that exist between a Lacanian and a Deleuzoguattarian analysis, I am also interested in Deleuze's model of desire founded not in lack but in abundance. In the constellation of things that make up a given scenario and in the intricate co-modeling of plenitudes, what Deleuze and Parnet label "interbeing," "co-functioning," or "in-betweenness" is achieved. Deleuze would have us attend to desire as a threshold or bridge. In fact, Deleuze and Guattari famously praise Anglo-American literature for its ability to "move between things, establish a logic of the AND" (Deleuze and Guattari 25). In that rhizomes link differing sign-regimes, cross-regionalism grounds itself in rhizomic alliance—a sort of parataxis between regions—as well as in other forms of affiliation.

In *Dialogues* Deleuze articulates this theory of in-betweenness in discourse, arguing that "the minimum real unit is not the word, the idea, the concept or the signifier, but the *assemblage*. It is always an assemblage which produces utterances. . . . The utterance is the product of an assemblage—which is always collective, which brings into play within us and outside us populations, multiplicities, territories, becomings, affects, events" (Deleuze and Parnet, *Dialogues* 51).

It must be said that it is the world itself which lays the two traps of distance and identification for us. There are many neurotics and lunatics in the world who do not let go of us until they have managed to reduce us to their state, pass us their poison, hysterics, narcissists, their contagion is insidious. There are many doctors and scholars who offer us a sanitized scientific observation, who are also true lunatics, paranoiacs. One must resist both of the traps, the one which offers us the mirror of contamination and identifications, and the one which points out to us the observation of the understanding. We can only struggle among assemblages. (Deleuze and Parnet, *Dialogues* 52–53)

As always in Deleuze, the various elements in the connection preexist in one another, just as in cross-regional comparisons we may expect that the "assemblages" both producing and produced will unfurl the terms of a mutual immanence that has been preplanted by historical and economic processes. A central component of the critical regionalism put forward in this book is thus the assemblage, construed along the lines introduced by Deleuze and Guattari in *A Thousand Plateaus*. Imbedded there in a complex language of strata and planes,[4] the assemblage emerges in terms of its dynamic relationality and its aggressive way of organizing historical details and intersocial connections: "An assemblage . . . is necessary for the relation between two strata to come about. And an assemblage is necessary for organisms to be caught within and permeated by a social field that utilizes them: Must not the Amazons amputate a breast to adapt the organic stratum to a warlike technological stratum, as though at the behest of a fearsome woman-bow-steppe assemblage? Assemblages are necessary for states of force and regimes of signs to intertwine their relations. Assemblages are necessary in order for the unity of composition enveloped in a stratum, the relations between a given stratum and the others, and the relation between these strata and the plane of consistency to be organized rather than random" (Deleuze and Guattari 71).

For the purposes of this book, I allow the assemblage to designate a construction composed variously of elements from regions that history has twinned. I see the assemblage occupying a continuum that includes additive bricolage, inventive code-breaking, and other forms of amalgamation and reconstitution. It is a level of organization in which human beings conjoin with the extrahuman, with history, with the flows of productive desire as well as what we might call constitutive lack.

By studying a variety of existing assemblages in mutually constituted, interregional spaces, we can discover materials and tools for a critical regionalist method of cultural inquiry that can hope to participate actively in social change without falling prey to recidivist longings or the induced paralysis of an ever-consolidating market economy. The connections between regions are nomadic rather than rooted and as such increasingly visible in their protostriation by capital. As a challenge to the idea of the nation, nomadism insists upon its subnational space. In effect, the region might be viewed as a potential smooth space sometimes occupied by virtual nomads. Being inassimilable, these state-resisting, nomadic elements cross borders, keep moving, and maintain a different organization, sense of repetition, and embodiment of time. Hence, Deleuze and Guattari argue that assemblages (even though they are "basically territorial") paradoxically "operate in zones where milieus become decoded." Divided by heterogeneous "lines of deterritorialization," the assemblage comes full circle, again and again, toward the nomadic (503–5). In the resulting endless series of becomings-other we can detect "asymptotic lines of causality" (Massumi 153) mapping alternative axes of social movement and change. Where the assemblage holds provisional sway, there is a perceptible elsewhere that is neither utopianly totalizing nor a mere negation of existing structures.

For the purposes of this cross-regional study, I am especially interested in the intersection of a familial imaginary and a corporate level of administration that, in its assumption of the phallic privilege on a global level, also presents to us as a virtual symbolic composed by international financial institutions (IFIs). This volume, then, poses cross-cultural assemblages as "found art" that can be used to cast light first on one region and then on its provisional other. It uses assemblages to emphasize the mediation of information and identity at every point. It uses assemblages to highlight the range of implicated experience in cultural inquiry, from individual identity to IFIs.

Kenneth Frampton and Critical Regionalism

. . . look shining at
New styles of architecture; a change of heart.
W. H. Auden

But what can be claimed for a transregional cultural studies practice beyond the excavation and impromptu production of assemblages? As the central Anglo-American theorist of critical regionalism, architect Kenneth Frampton provides some indirect suggestions, framed initially toward the assembling of aesthetically satisfying buildings. Frampton explains,

> As I see it, Critical Regionalism[5] tries, through its emphasis on "place reaction," to wage a cultural guerilla war against the ubiquitous, space-endlessness of the consumerist Megalopolis. In this struggle it addresses itself to bounded domains rather than free-standing objects. At the same [time] it tries to preserve and develop the *liberative* lie of the modern movement, above all perhaps, the way in which modern architecture, at its best, achieved a new and more liberated, harmonious relationship with nature, including our own intrinsic nature. This was functionalism at its best. I am thinking of the line extending from Wright's *organicism* to Neutra's *biorealism*, including Aalto. (Irace 6)

What Frampton opposes is what Charles Jencks describes about the architect's situation today: "With the triumph of consumer society in the West and bureaucratic State Capitalism in the East, our unfortunate modern architect was left without much uplifting social content to symbolise." The solution? For Jencks, "There's nothing much the architect can do about this except protest as a citizen, and design dissenting buildings that express the complex situation. He can communicate the values which are missing and ironically criticise the ones he dislikes. But to do that he must make use of the language of the local culture, otherwise his message falls on deaf ears, or is distorted to fit this local language" (Jencks 37).

Frampton frames his solution differently. Hence, when asked in 1985 by Fulvio Irace to note the theorists who had influenced him, Frampton cited "the Marxist criticism stemming from the 'school' of Manfredo Tafuri in Venice," the Frankfurt School, Habermas, Heidegger, Ricoeur, Gadamer, and Arendt. His sympathies are not at all with the popular line of work pursued by Jenck or Leon Krier; revisionism and revival of past styles, "collage-pastiche" and antimodernism, the "cynical populism of Robert Venturi" all fall short of the mark for Frampton, who aims for a critique of the totalizing agenda of Enlightenment-linked modernism (Irace 6). In fact, in an interview in the Italian architecture journal *Domus*, Frampton claimed his place in the generation of modernist architects who critique the utopian concept of progress. No longer certain of their role in actively creating the future, this generation either turned back to historical and popular traditions—these architects gave birth to postmodernism—or attempted to reconsider modernism's legacy in the current era. The Habermasian concern with neomodernism, then, provides a helpful framework for critical regionalism as Frampton pursues it. Frampton defines his stance against that of both the International Style and vernacular populism. Rather than focus on a revival of the local, he seeks "a critical local culture of architecture . . . in express opposition to the domination of hegemonic power." This architecture "resists being totally absorbed by the global imperatives of production and consumption"—and readers of Levitt would add "marketing." Against "universal consumerism," the critical regionalist building aligns itself with autarchic thought. In practical terms, what does Frampton recommend to the builders of the physical world of today and tomorrow? He suggests the use of craft practices in tandem with "rationalised production." He aims for some form of local building evaluation that goes beyond "economic criteria," and he emphasizes "modest" scales of investment (as opposed to megalopolitical architecture) that will "permit idiosyncratic forms of disjunction" (Frampton, "Luogo" 18). Frampton advocates the design of interzone buildings that will allow their users a vision of, paradoxically, a *built* smooth space in which journey equilibrates dwelling (Bognar 15).

Frampton's "architecture of resistance" is fertile with possibilities for a critical-regionalist analytic practice of cultural studies. He customarily cites five nodes that the practitioner must address. First, he draws attention to Heidegger's Greek-inspired formulation of a boundary as "that from which something begins its presencing." Against the "universal," the "privatised," and the "placeless" construction, Frampton calls for new conceptions of localized dimensionality in constant dialogue with the imperatives of international architecture (Frampton, "Luogo" 19). Second, Frampton draws attention to "typology" in tension with "topography," posing universalism against "rootedness." Whereas typology considers both "gridded, rational matrices, capable of admitting a wide range of institutional programmes" and "the real and/or mythic history of a particular place," topography "is unequivocally site specific." Given the transformative role of architecture in relationship to specific places, the application of "'productive' criteria . . . such as the ruthless flattening out of the contours in a typical American suburban subdivision," can only be detrimental to local culture. The kind of rootedness Frampton aspires to is not that of the Deleuzian state but rather a form of place-specificity that might signify among nomads (Frampton, "Luogo" 20).

Third, Frampton employs an "architectonic/scenographic" distinction to argue that a construction "should display in an appropriate way the manner in which the artifice interacts with nature, not only in terms of resisting gravity, but also in terms of its durability with regard to the erosive agencies of climate and time." He adds that "one should be able to identify the architectonic element itself or, alternatively, the revetement or facing by which it is represented or by which it represents itself." Scenography is "essentially representational in nature" (Frampton, "Luogo" 20, 22). Frampton objects to the postmodernist emphasis on the flatly representational rather than also the dimensional and architectonic structure.

Fourth, we are asked to consider an opposition of nature and artifice. "Nature is not only the topography and the site itself," Frampton maintains, "but also climate and light to which architecture is ultimately responsive to a far greater degree than any other art." "Universal civilization" and its technology try to eliminate "exactly those features which would otherwise modulate the outer membrane of a given fabric in respect of a particular place and a given culture." Frampton is concerned, among other things, with "the provision of natural light in relation to diurnal and seasonal change, as the antithetical, universal example of the totally closed, climatically controlled, art gallery" (Frampton, "Luogo" 22). Natural light equates with the possibility of experiencing art and the built world as changing entities, with the possibility of having experiences at all: "hermetically sealed, air-conditioned structures are incapable of responding to subtle and favorable variations in the outside climate. Once again, built-form is deprived of its *inherently* mediatory capacity."

Finally, Frampton focuses attention on the visual/tactile dimension of experiencing architecture. Materials, textures, acoustics and similar sensory elements must be considered as well as what a building looks like. In contrast to the Renaissance emphasis on perspective, Frampton insists on a more broadly biological response to the built environment (Frampton, "Luogo" 22). In this search for a tactile presence that can resist "the all too felicitous symbiosis linking visual stimuli to information rather than experience," Frampton coordinates with Deleuze and Guattari, who associate smooth space with the "intensities" of sound and tactility as opposed to the primarily visual information characteristic of striated regimes (Deleuze and Guattari 479). Movement beyond visuality favors what I have called the resonances between comparable regions and encourages attention to the interstitial and peripheral antihegemonic architecture favored by Frampton. He clearly wants architecture to provide alternative experiences to the ongoing discourses of capitalist multinationalism. Seeking a more somatically compelling and socially responsible architecture, Frampton desires an architectonics that allows space for both built and unbuilt, culture and nature, public and private dimensions. He advocates multisensory use-value; full exercise of perceptual faculties toward form, texture, kinesis, taste, smell; and the creation of encounters that resound strongly but obliquely with the interactive experience of an individual with her local habitat.

To Frampton's criteria I would want to connect the "kernel-desire"— the nonsymbolized but real, insistently returning element that interrupts the symbolic—to which Lacan and Zizek direct us. This remote, unsignified, and ineffable pressure from the real would be, in Frampton's hands, a phenomenological celebration of embodiment and of constructed cultural forms emergent from both seen and intangible spaces. Obviously, many forces overdetermine the structures that Frampton idealizes—economic, political, aesthetic, visionary, psychocultural. The beauty of his system is precisely that he helps us to focus on a logic of making that is variously open to Marxism, psychoanalysis, nomadism, and administration, all at the same time. As Botone Bognar has it, "critical regionalism consistently remains *open* to and selectively accepts elements and ideas from sources other than its own" (Bognar 15).

And in fact, as this introduction indicates, critical regionalism is compatible with insights from a variety of thinkers and schools: from Zizek to

Chomsky, from Haraway to Jameson, from Adorno to Lacan. I would defend this multiplicity on methodological grounds. In the service of the constructive vision that Frampton puts forward and in the service of an evolving, pressure-sensitive cultural studies, this volume tests complementary elements from various schools against the heretofore underinterpreted history of paired regions. The resulting assemblages continue to rotate new facets into the angles of vision accessed by both insiders and outsiders.

Not surprisingly, some theorists have taken issue with Frampton's suggestions. Of these diverging scholars, Linda Krause presents Frampton's ideas in particularly instructive ways: "Critical regionalism rests on the seemingly innocent assumption that for a given region there are appropriate architectural forms. These 'place forms' will resist the universalising tendencies of modernism, it is assumed, as well as the banal and superficial in postmodernism" (Krause 29). Whatever Krause's agenda in this critique, it is clear that she has construed Frampton's evocative prose in too-literal terms. She directly counters Frampton's caveat by claiming that he favors, say, tectonic *over* scenographic—while Frampton clearly opts for a complex, heterogeneous dialectic among any and all forces relevant to the mise-en-scène of architectural design and construction. Hence, Krause finds Frampton naively deficient in his theoretical acuity, resistant to the deconstructive facilitation of indeterminacy and multiple interpretations, favoring instead an "unmediated experience of architecture" (Krause 30). But Frampton's critical regionalism precludes neither a deconstructivist/poststructuralist theoretical sophistication nor the discriminating use of principles like that of undecidability; in fact, Frampton's attention to interpenetrating, complex, highly articulated spaces serves to dimensionalize vintage Derridean logic and to interrogate that logic as it rebounds against other historical and theoretical contingencies.

In addition, Krause objects to Frampton's demands for an ethical aesthetics (Krause 30); I would agree that I am not aware of his directly defining ways in which architecture can become permanently or even temporarily antithetical to the hegemonic culture, though if he were to do so, his interventions would risk being totalizing rather than improvisational. What I do find is a great deal of provocative potential in Frampton's region-specific analysis—and I agree with Desmond Bell that this critique can be enormously useful in the pursuit of a more sensitive, environmentally attentive, dialectical, historically challenging, hegemony-resistant cultural studies.

Above all, critical regionalism refers less to a specific kind of building than it does to the resistances that architecture can offer to a totalizing environment. Those resistances to homogenization must be linked aggressively to an imperative for collective structural change in the fundamental economic horizon. In "Some Reflections on Postmodernism and Architecture," a reprise and extension of his earlier work, Frampton affirms, "My interest in that which I was to perceive as sporadic, marginal, regionally-based pockets of resistance in the field of architectural culture arose out of the recognition of the power of Anglo-American hegemony in the field of so-called postmodern architecture" (Frampton, "Some Reflections" 75).

As a practice, a critical-regionalist cultural studies has great potential for producing a unified but highly adaptable analysis of international flows of capital and resistance to the negative effects of those flows at the local-regional level, toward the end of a more heterogeneous and tolerant future. Critical regionalism marks less a space-and-place opposition than one that allows for understanding places seeking some form of relation beyond that woven by capital. In fact, the key to a critical regionalist methodology for cultural studies is the relationality of regionalism. This approach will always adopt at least a bifocal viewpoint to establish provisional parallels and to separate local mores from practices and administrations that exist worldwide. It is thus a way of addressing the migrancy and loss of foundations that characterizes the postcolonial, the diasporic, the uncanny connections of Here and There.

Against Administered Culture

As a cultural studies practice, critical regionalism includes not only the concept of the assemblage and multivalent architectonics but also the hallmark negativity of Theodor Adorno, whose writing shares space congenially though somewhat contradictorily with Frampton, Deleuze and Guattari, and Lacan. Indeed, Adorno's framing of a negative dialectic insistently deprivileges any given viewpoint while affirming both inside and outside perspectives. In the terms of this project, we might say that intimately knowing another culture has to be complemented by recognizing the possibilities for agency inherent in the discovery—between and across boundaries—of previously unseen or inaccessible platforms, of the conjunction of marginality and the accidental, of mutually constructed spaces of "play," of articulation, of interbeing, and of negatively deployed projections. Critically engaging with the suggestions presented here allows the outsider to use the self as a way station between home and elsewhere, both sites not only deferred, not only lost, but also curiously reclaimed as the structures of social life in one world (like a kernel of the real in the symbolic) uncannily show up internationally, intersubjectively, and empoweringly. As outsiders doing cultural studies, we face the task of moving toward a profound, albeit always necessarily provisional, identification with more than one social scene and with shared but distinctive worldwide struggles against hegemonic structures. The cultural studies methodology that I envision holds onto the concepts of forced symmetry, creative connection, critical regional construction, and even coincidence—and factors them into Adorno's negative dialectic, for which outsiderly controversion provides the crucial, energizing torque. The work of the cultural critic is to imagine constructions-between while coming to understand how the materials for those assemblages had been immanent in historical processes. All of this inquiry takes place within a profound conviction that modern societal experience has been deeply regulated by capital in ways that have penetrated individuals at the level of the drives, making each of us a seminomadic compromise between the logic of political economy and that of psychoanalysis.

As Adorno's most devoted contemporary exponent, Fredric Jameson finds in the *Negative Dialectics* a proposal that we "think another side, an outside, an external face of the concept . . . we must vigilantly remember and reckon that other face into our sense of the concept while remaining within it in the old way and continuing to use and think it." Jameson ties this way of thinking to Lacan's notion of the unconscious, forever "out there," forever elusive. He concludes, "What needs to be invented, therefore—is a new kind of stereoscopic thinking in which the concept continues to be thought philosophically and cashed at face value, while in some other part of the mind a very different kind of intellectual climate reigns, a cruder and more sociological set of terms and categories, in which the form of that concept is noted and registered in shorthand and in which the existence of the financial and banking system thereby presupposed is somehow reckoned in"

(Jameson, *Late Marxism* 25, 28). This negativity, we might say, occupies all that we desire, and it is the energy of this negativity that we can draw on to rotate us toward mutual articulation in a critical regionalist cultural studies.

If administered culture sustains itself partly through our unawareness of strategically induced or strategically exploited cross-regional connections—stifling a creative will to linkmaking—it is through the stereosensory method of Adorno and Frampton that we can seek potentially less policed channels of impression and knowledge. When we really take in the idea that Adorno wanted to render contemporary culture radically indigestible—to keep us attentive to the lived conditions of our social experience both inside and out—and when we add to that perception a visceral registering of the intricate regulation of information-flow in our world, we understand that cultural studies must actively and at every point refer itself to the conception of negative dialectic. Adorno provides a framework within which cross-cultural, interdisciplinary, and subnational readings necessarily find a home.

In particular, I am interested in Adorno's desire (one that he shares with postcolonial scholars) to see not only from the perspective of existing triumphalist histories but also from the angle of vision that has been rendered subject, the position sought in a Deleuzoguattarian nomadology:

> If Benjamin said that history had hitherto been written from the standpoint of the victor, and needed to be written from that of the vanquished, we might add that knowledge must indeed present the fatally rectilinear succession of victory and defeat, but should also address itself to those things which were not embraced by this dynamic, which fell by the wayside—what might be called the waste products and blind spots that have escaped the dialectic. It is the nature of the defeated to appear, in their impotence, irrelevant, eccentric, derisory. What transcends the ruling society is not only the potentiality it develops but also all that which did not fit properly into the laws of historical movement. Theory must needs deal with cross-grained, opaque, unassimilated material, which as such admittedly has from the start an anachronistic quality, but is not wholly obsolete since it has outwitted the historical dynamic. (Adorno, *Minima* 151)

Adorno's concern with the "blind spots" and "waste products" is critical to the unfolding methodology of motivated comparison that this book traces. Both forms of Adornan excess cohabitate with the inappropriated, the creatively mistaken, and those assemblages that are extended and between. Forced symmetries yield not only grounds for positivist comparison but also a conceptual auto-critique that can serve to generate what has been called (by Stephen D. Krasner) "dynamic instability" across cultural regimes.

In that Adorno sought material resistances to hegemonic society, resistances that at the same time could bear witness, under analysis, to totalizing deployments of power, he emphasizes the endless disparities that keep subject and object from achieving identity. He was interested in the "force field" between these epistemological poles—what I pose in this study as the zone of oscillating perspectives between interior and exterior. Insofar as the negative dialectic continually seeks out nonidentity, contradiction, and concrete particulars as objects of analysis, Leon Bailey helpfully explains, "Through the continual demonstration of non-identical relations between concept and object, appearance and essence, universal and particular, individual and society, Adorno sought to open up new realms of experience and reflection foreclosed by identity-thinking" (Bailey 11).

Looking toward these cleared bridges, Adorno, obviously thinking of Hegel, tells us that the "objective goal" of negative dialectic is "to break out of the context from within." What troubles Adorno about Hegel is, in part, the totalizing inclusiveness of his program. How could Hegel's lockstep dialectical system be evaded or escaped? In his worldview, there is no elsewhere, only an endless process of sublation into versions of the absolute. "But," Adorno adds, "if our thought, fully aware of what it is doing, gropes beyond itself—if in otherness it recognizes something which is downright incommensurable with it, but which it thinks anyway," then, he reasons, varieties of estrangement, newly available aporiae, and useful incompatibilities emerge, lexias within a rhizomic cultural hypertext, extant not to lead us beyond contradictions to some Grand Truth but rather again and again to undo our perception that either side of the equation holds (there is a way out, there is no way out). Using the terms of the system itself, Adorno would have the dialectic detonate the "coercive character of logic" (Adorno, *Negative* 405, 406) and embrace the pragmatics of seeming accident within design.

So it is that in *Minima Moralia* Adorno often composes the following kind of paradox, one that deftly shifts viewing position with destablizing, dazzling rapidity: "Psycho-analysis prides itself on restoring the capacity for pleasure, which is impaired by neurotic illness. As if the mere concept of a capacity for pleasure did not suffice gravely to devalue such a thing, if it exists. As if a happiness gained through speculation on happiness were not the opposite, a further encroachment of institutionally planned behaviour-patterns on the ever-diminishing sphere of experience." The client "thus made happy" exchanges reason for the claims of advertising and the com-modified lifestyle. Exploring in ever more tortuous and ever more logically challenging ways the experience of reification, Adorno insists that "in an exchange society" (Adorno, *Minima* 38, 39) the subject is predefined as an object. Along the way, Adorno himself supplies a possible working defini-tion of critical regionalism: "Dialectical mediation is . . . a process of reso-lution of the concrete in itself. . . . The morality of thought lies in a proce-dure that is neither entrenched nor detached, neither blind nor empty, neither atomistic nor consequential. . . . Nothing less is asked of the thinker today than that he should be at every moment both within things and out-side them" (Adorno, *Minima* 74–75). And, Jameson adds, "Everything there-fore turns on whether we can imagine such a radically different, alternative way of thinking or philosophizing, let alone ourselves practice it" (Jameson, *Late Marxism* 25).

As Jameson states it, Adorno's writing conveys "the will to link together in a single figure two incommensurable realities, two independent codes or systems of signs, two heterogeneous and asymmetrical terms," whether he attends to traditional metaphysics or "the data of individual experience and the vaster forms of institutional society." Adorno's aim, Jameson speculates, is to offer, however briefly, "a glimpse of a unified world, of a universe in which discontinuous realities are nonetheless somehow implicated with each other and intertwined, no matter how remote they may at first have seemed" (Jameson, *Late Marxism* 6, 8). He wants to provide for the reader an experi-ence of the imbricated intricacy of social life, the patterned endlessness of meanings generated from the constant rubbing against one another of ob-jects, forms, ideas, and experiences, while also allowing the reader a partly argued, partly intuited, partly self-constructed vision of how global culture works and the relentlessness with which we must pursue our understanding of it through structured comparison of lifestyles, regions, attitudes, ideo-fragments, and transregional occlusions.

In fact, Jameson would have it that Adorno's premise of a single, over-riding, unavoidable institutionalization of western culture stands as the ul-timate persuader that we can indeed compare what seem to be incompat-ible apples and oranges without losing logical coherence (Jameson, *Late Marxism* 52–53). So it is that the challenge of discovering symmetries of any kind amidst poststructuralist undecidabilities, deconstructive differences, and postmodern ahegemonies is not registered as such by the negative dia-lectician, for whom the implicit grid of global control may be traced in rather unpromising places, even while the critic remains highly aware of the disjunctions that proliferate endlessly in our concerted efforts to estab-lish analytic order (Jameson, *Late Marxism* 56–59). By these means, by trac-ing linkages in an ever-ordering world, we hope to look at ourselves with the eyes of the other and to enter into the space where the uncanny side of the composite self—a sort of n-degree subjective space caught in negativ-ity—can be detected, however indirectly, much as a critical regionalist build-ing expresses, literally, the Heideggerian presencing of coconstructed "place-form" (Frampton, "Some Reflections" 83).

There is an episode of *Star Trek: The Next Generation* in which a teen-ager named Jeremiah Rossa turns up and is computer-identified as the son of Conor and Moira Rossa, killed in a Telarian raid. As a baby, Jeremiah was taken by the Telarians and raised as one of them. Jeremiah is thus hu-man but Telarian-identified. His own cross-culturalism creates conflict and suffering for the youth. His futuristic story reminds me that cultural stud-ies, while honoring specificities of ethnicity, race, geography, and national-ity, must also come to terms with the economic and cultural symmetries that make far-flung regions of the world cloistrally similar. So it is that the outsiderly critic may try on a number of roles, willingly become voyeur, dramatist, autobiographer, character, writer, parasite. In this way, our so-cial constructions of others' realities need not grossly or thoughtlessly fall prey either to sentiment or to abstraction, to overvaluing either historical detail or interpretive intuition. We can begin to engineer a methodology for richer engagement that is compatible with both psychoanalytic prin-ciples and global economic agendas. Attending to the terms of our own disinformational relationship with our scholarly selves, we can approach the seductive ideological regimes attempting to control our ability to draw conclusions about the world we live in. For this task, we would do well not only to imagine what kind of dwelling would accommodate Jeremiah Rossa but also to consider who owns it, what it would feel like to live there.

This book not only sets up a pairing of rural regions that have been "aware" of one another for some time but also uses the resulting discursive and actual assemblages to propel the inquiry into a negative-dialectical register. Where Region A and Region B come together, we encounter serendipity, migrating populations, and rather precise information about the global political economy. We can use these synchronic patterns of the past to chart future designs in ways that transcend, short-circuit, or otherwise stand tangential to the top-down administrative protocols of a market economy.

Some Elements of a Critical Regionalism for Cross-cultural Studies

In the chapters that follow, the issues listed below repeatedly surface to define critical regionalism both in terms of a methodology and in terms of lived subnational experience. Together they map a provisional framework for this project. Here, I itemize these issues in the form of injunctions or nonlinear steps toward a motivated, comparative cultural studies.

- Pursue a negative dialectic that addresses cross-regional specificity on the basis of pairings, twinnings, and their often uncanny textual apparati.
- Imagine a comparative history/sociology that is both structural and interpretive.
- Scrutinize utopian visions of the future that enter into dialogue with real local conditions.
- Study the location and interpretation of assemblages and spaces-between in a variety of organizational arenas and at a variety of organizational levels.
- Consider controls on regional fiscal environments worldwide, in the form of regional delinking and relinking, the return of profits to local and regional communities, and a worldwide cap on corporate size and profits.
- Map a psychology that reaches into political economic contexts to posit both family-level and corporate-administrative axes of desire.
- Celebrate alternative narratives, disseminate alternative modes of *jouissance*, perform alternative organizations of socioeconomic life.

U<small>TOPIAN</small> M<small>IGRATIONS</small>

Agricultural Assemblages

The ethics of psychoanalysis implies a . . . cosmopolitanism of a new sort that, cutting across governments, economies, and markets, might work for a mankind whose solidarity is founded on the consciousness of its unconscious—desiring, destructive, fearful, empty, impossible.

JULIA KRISTEVA

For the purposes of this inquiry, the regions chosen as my privileged examples are rural Ireland and the American Midwest. For the sake of a scale and demography roughly comparable with the Irish island, the part of the Midwest that supplies most of my illustrations is the state of Iowa—the heart of the heartland. For the past century and a half, this pair of spaces has been intimately linked through direct migration, shared agrarian values, and the influence of increasingly global trade arrangements. Both of my targeted regions have long been emblems of rural life: perpetually stereotyped, routinely exploited, subject to persistent population loss and faced with symmetrical environmental threats. To address the bases of comparison, it is worth considering Peadar Kirby's similar framing of Irish issues with Latin American ones (Kirby 7–9) and his conviction of the profound, instructive similarities between those two areas. Kirby's work abundantly demonstrates the point argued by Saldívar, that cultural studies must fill in the jigsaw puzzle created by rationalization in order to discern an explanatory design larger than the parts of which it is composed. My choice of focal regions is not intended to suggest that we could not benefit as much or more from coscrutinizing Bangladesh and Baltimore, or from triangulating Donegal and Senegal. Rather, the homology palpated in this book draws on an overt filiation of farming areas peripheral to world-metropolitan power centers. As such, I draw on a similar angle of vision on and from the viewpoint of consumer culture and global capitalism to nurture a bifocalism that unearths and also creates mutual significance.

In the largely factual first half of this chapter, I set the historical and aesthetic stage for a study of cross-regional assemblages specific to my chosen spaces. I do so realizing that much of this information may be new or at least eventually subjected to novel arrangements when judged from the perspective of an Irish audience accustomed either to studies of population loss from their island or to celebratory accounts of Irish-American life and lore. Interrogating power relations mutually effective among Irish and mid-American psychologies, politics, and economies, this use of parallel regions facilitates and instructs in the process of generating information in a negative dialectical fashion. I draw on structural, causal energies to reinforce this assemblage, both isomorphic and historical, of Ireland and the Midwest. From this comparative cultural study of rural, subnational America and regional Europe, I explore the regionalization of theory and the theorizing of regionalism, deployed in mutual awareness and in opposition to relentless worldwide homogenization.

MIGRATORY LINKAGE

> *One thing that we have never had in Iowa is a famine.*
> LOREN HORTON

The fundamental affinity between rural Ireland and the American Midwest grows from a legacy of oppression. From an American viewpoint, large populations of Irish and German Catholics struggling to escape starvation and abuse migrated throughout the 1800s and particularly near the middle of that century to and beyond the Mississippi valley—what would become the watershed "heartland" of the United States. From the Irish angle of vision, that emigration has for almost two hundred years been a key causal event in Irish history, influencing economy, demography, sociology, marriage patterns, class structures, politics, and interpersonal attitudes. Famine victims leaving Ireland, especially in the late 1840s, said farewell to a society both negligently and iniquitously destroyed, and they remade themselves on an outrageously fertile soil pliant to a newly evolving regional identity. The constitutive links between the American Midwest and Ireland may be symbolized in the coincidence of Iowa's 1996 sesquicentennial celebration of statehood and Ireland's 150th commemoration of the famine.

A generation after the famine, the Irish population was the second largest in Iowa, standing at over 40,000 in 1870. Interestingly enough, at this time the Iowa Board of Immigration decided to encourage increased migration from Germany, Holland, and Scandinavia, so that by the census of 1940, in all ninety-nine Iowa counties German, Swedish, Norwegian, Danish, and Dutch populations predominated (*Iowa* iii).[1] But various small-town centenary books provide ample evidence that, whether or not Irish immigrants were desired, they found their way to Iowa's cheap lands and open prairie. Out of that history of massive demographic shift emerged a motivated similarity recognizable from several disciplinary and topical angles. It is beyond the scope of this project to detail all of the relevant bases for comparison, but there are many compelling symmetries, from the challenge to farmers posed by bogs and fens to sociological organization, from economic roles within trade blocs to agribusiness consolidation, from groundwater pollution by agricultural chemical runoff to the strategic rural siting of incineration facilities. And those likenesses—both latent and overdetermined—continue to exercise force even 150 years after the fact.

When I address the similarities and differences pertaining to Irish outmigration, I want to trace not so much a state-apparatus history and not so much subaltern history as the diverse instances of assemblage created between 1850 and 1990. To inflect the case toward psychocultural terms, I want to understand how and why Ireland returns as a symptom of Iowa, and vice versa, because of the complex and often traceable processes of mirroring, misrecognition, transference, and repression of the real historically established between and currently functioning in the two regions.

As a researcher might expect, there exists a large and ever-expanding famine literature, a good part of it specifically dealing with the movement from Ireland to the Mississippi valley. For example, in *A Farewell to Famine*, Jim Rees, a historian from Arklow, relates the story of Father Thomas Hore, parish priest of Killaveny and Annacurra, County Wicklow, who determined to escape the aftermath of crop failure on his island by removing his entire parish—1,200 inhabitants, most of them small farmers—to America. Originally aiming to settle in Arkansas, the group arrived to discover that their contact in Little Rock had died, leaving them unprovided for in the New World. Many of those who survived the trip and a bout with fever cast their fate permanently in St. Louis. Others eventually made their way to a Texas colony already settled by Wexford Irish men and women. Meanwhile, Father Hore, in touch with an order of Irish monks in the newly established Melleray Abbey in Dubuque, Iowa, purchased in excess of 2,100 acres of land for his settlement. By the spring of 1851 (the same year that England held its Great Exhibition), eighteen families—nearly a hundred people— were still willing to journey north with their priest. Father Hore returned to Ireland in 1857, first having deeded excess real estate to the Dubuque monks, land later sold to area farmers when plans for a second Iowa monastery, this time in Wexford, were deemed unnecessary. What stand out in Rees's narrative are both the haphazardness introduced even into carefully charted emigration plans and the search for a visual and environmental fit by the several constituencies seeking homes: the terrain had to feel like rural Ireland to attract Irish settlers.

Another fascinating aspect of Rees's book is an appendix that lists the emigrants who traveled with Father Hore. Rees discovered the name and age of each parishioner, the ship on which she or he sailed to America, and the town in which he or she settled. Presented in the restrained format of a catalog, these migrants are oddly silenced even while being made newly recognizable. Reading Rees reminds me that I am always moved and saddened when I pause to examine one of the many graveyards of the European-born that are scattered throughout the Midwest's hillsides and farmlands. Often a single stone in the midst of a cornfield not only testifies to a migrant's early death on the desolate prairies but also indicates the resiting or removal of long-gone dwellings built by those first European farmers trying to replicate their homeland. Cemeteries throughout eastern Iowa promote sobering reflection on likely reactions by migrants to the temperature extremes, the fertile and rolling but wild landscape, and the disorientingly empty socius that confronted newcomers to the Midwest from the 1830s onwards. The pathos that attends these witnesses to economic necessity is perhaps highest at the cemetery outside of Melleray Abbey itself. There we find listed as places of birth not only Wexford but also the following Irish counties: Dublin, Waterford, Limerick, Down, Galway, Kilkenny, Tipperary, Cork, Roscommon, Monaghan, Mayo, Clare, Cavan, Derry, Donegal, Antrim, and the anachronistic Kings and Queens. Some of those who traveled with Father Hore may well have found their way to this part of Iowa to join in that quiet resting place with people named Powers, Healy, Sullivan, McCorcoran, Callahan, Duggan, Murphy, Ryan, McGovern, McDermott, Hurley, Kinniry, Cunningham, McCarty, Walsh, Hanley, Larkin, Connolly, O'Brien, Cavanaugh, McCloskey, and Donnelly.

Similarly, near Windham, in a small graveyard overrun with bushes and gopher trails, standing alone in the midst of farm fields, lie people bearing the names of Bevins, Curry, Kerrigan, O'Riley, Flannery, Cusack, Murphy (Bridget, born in 1787 and living to the age of 102), Mungovan, Bradley, Reynolds, Maher, MacCabe, Barry, Mooney, Rodgers, Molloy, Corbett, Dempsey, Kivlighan, Mulcahy, Healy, O'Connor, O'Brien, Griffin, Donohoe, Costolo, Kinney, Rohret, Torphey, and one Patrick Finn (County Clare, parish of Killerbayh, died in 1887 at the age of eighty-five).

In nearby Holbrook at St. Michael's Church, we locate a Donohoe from Cavan, a Reynolds from Antrim, a Molloy from Meath, a Hansen from Westmeath, a McGillan from Tyrone, a Casey from Louth, a Grey from Waterford, and a host of McBrides, Kernans, Nolans, Coakleys, Cashes, Shannahans, Blacks, Furlongs, Collinses, Carneys, Noones, Fitzgibbons, Newcombs, McGuires, McCanns, McGillicuddys, Coffeys, Driscolls, Hannons, Gaffeys, Boyles, and Gallaghers from Dublin, Cavan, Carlow, Armagh, Waterford, Louth, and Wicklow. The Parnell graveyard of St. Joseph's yields names previously seen and unseen on a cemetery tour of eastern Iowa: Tiernan, Carroll, O'Brien, McGraw, Naughton, Dwyer, Costello, Browne, Curry, O'Neill, Quinn, Doyle, Sheridan, Tuomey, Hoyt, Hanson, Conkley, Murrin, Eagleton, Raher, Ward, McCune, McGurk, Dunn, Butler, Vaughan, O'Meara, Lawler, Muldoon, Burck, Hanley, McDonald, Giblin, O'Rourke, Sullivan, Daley, and Boland.

In the churchyard of St. Peter's Church in Cosgrove, we find the remains of Thomas Kelly, a native of Kings County, Ireland, who died in 1920 at the age of eighty-eight years. His wife Anna was from County Armagh, and their graves indicate the birth of many children as well as the death of an infant daughter. Apparently of a meticulous temperament, Lawrence Cusack, born in County Clare in 1825, found his way to Cosgrove and lived to the age of eighty-one years, ten months, and one day. Daniel Maher lies under a stone that announces his birth in the parish of "Nockevellew Tipperary Co. Ire." Occasionally we find the isolated intermarried German: witness one William Schneider, who died in 1895, survived by his wife, Ellen, of County Kerry.

In John Ford's film *The Searchers* (1956), a Swedish settler proclaims that someday the frontier will make a good land to live in but that it may take all of their "bones in the ground" before that happens. Tracing the history of Irish migration even to the limited area of the current state of Iowa enhances the sense that Irish bones went a long way toward domesticating the often barren wilderness into which those early settlers—not those with urban instincts but the hard-core agrarians in love with or otherwise fated to land—found their way. And the story of the Irish in Iowa is just one of many tales about settling the vast middle of the country: Minnesota, Michigan, Illinois, Indiana, Wisconsin, Nebraska, Missouri, Arkansas, Kansas, Oklahoma, North and South Dakota—not to mention the lonely Canadian peat bogs and plains. It is a tale that Irish visitors from Ireland to the Midwest often attempt to reimagine. As Gabrielle Mullarkey, a London-based Irish journalist, wrote in "Importance of Being Iowish":

> The coffin ships of the 1850s offered destitute Irish a stark choice between the perils of the old world and the pitfalls of the new. . . . The *Boston Pilot* was among several newspapers exhorting the arrivals to keep moving inland. . . . Western-faring Irish sent back tales of blightless crops in a land never darkened by the shadow of the gombeen man. . . . Some heard the call. In 1858, Martin Coonan and his family, from Kilkenny, settled in the heart of Iowa and built a cabin which became known as Coonan's Hotel, a stop-over for other pioneering souls. . . . In 1870, Coonan arranged for local lots to be surveyed, laid out an urban site complete with named streets and called his town Emmetsburg, after Robert Emmet. . . . Elsewhere in Iowa, you can visit the towns of Parnell, Cosgrove and St. Patrick—which does a roaring trade in postcards on March 17. (Mullarkey)

In 1991 Mullarkey visited the Midwest to see what the Iowa Irish are like, and she expressed her sense of sorrow over what she viewed as the overt attempt to remake Ireland from afar. She saw tremendous pathos in the fact that Irish people were forced to leave their island in order to reconstitute a sense of home, to restage their lifestyle in circumstances sometimes dramatically different, sometimes all too painfully the same.[2]

No doubt that restaging accounts for an item in the 1836 *Detroit Free Press* about a "sham fight" that took place between militia and regular soldiers in the area. The fight was enacted by the governor of what was then called "Lower Canada." His excellency ordered fifty Irish militiamen to assume the "Yankee" side while his troops (two hundred regulars) fought for England. As the *Free Press* has it, "Instead of wailing about being outnumbered four-to-one, the Irish Yankees, led by fiery John Morris, immediately charged with fixed bayonets, completely routing the regulars" and earning themselves a banquet at the governor's expense. With charming unself-consciousness, the *Des Moines Register* explains, "Dubuque . . . had become a haven for Irish Catholic immigrants and the . . . report of a victory over His Majesty's troops was as warmly welcomed by these British-hating folks as the news now, say, of the Hawkeyes beating Michigan in football" (White).

In mid-nineteenth-century newspapers, in the saga of New Melleray Abbey, and also in the memoirs and letters of many who arrived in Iowa on their way westward, we find mention of Dubuque's Bishop Matthias Loras as the conduit for midwestern Irish immigration. Bishop Loras was not alone in his endeavor to populate the Midwest with exiled Euro-Catholics; for instance, Father Jeremiah Trecy's (or Tracy's) helpful exploits also float through the histories and personal narratives that made up the *Iowa Catholic Historical Review* from its initial publication in 1930. The aim of the journal, emerging as it did in a time of international economic crisis, appears to have been a recovery of the pioneering spirit and indomitability of the European Catholics whose stories are narrated. So it is that Father Trecy occupies a prominent place in the autobiographical musings of Catherine Jones Twohig. Recording her story in 1925, Twohig begins with her father's work almost a century earlier on the Erie Canal. Catherine's father rented land during all of his early life, as many as four hundred acres in New York, where he raised cattle. But the west was calling him, and by the 1850s the family headed for the territory, stopping at Irish boardinghouses and with Irish friends along the way. At that time, she tells us, East Dubuque went by the Celtic name of Dun Lieth (meaning "Gray Fort"). On their treks toward the receding frontier, the Jones family met many other pioneering parties, encountered occasional anti-Catholic sentiment among neighbors and Know-Nothings, endured the terrible winter of 1856–57, and touched base with Irish settlers at every point. When they contacted Bishop Loras, he passed them on to Father Trecy, who found the family some land for rent in the town of Garryowen. Heading out again with a mule-pulled wagon on which her father and brother had painted the words "Going where no one lives," the Joneses were reasonably typical Irish migrants to the old new territory (Henderson 3–13).

As Mullarkey points out, during the 1840s Bishop Loras of Dubuque wrote letters to the Boston *Pilot* recommending that Irish migrants make their way west to Iowa; the newspaper itself suggested that any unemployed Irish in the eastern metropoli "walk a day and work a day, until they find a home" in the West. The concern was not only to help the Irish avoid penury in the eastern cities; Iowa needed development in transportation and agriculture ("Irish in Iowa," 43, 45), and the church played a major role in that development. In Garryowen, a town started by Irish-Catholic immigrants in the late 1830s, the ever-present Bishop Loras provided six hundred dollars to help in the building of St. Patrick's church, a task accomplished mostly by the forty-two men who made up the settlement (*St. Patrick's* 5).[3] Iowa's black soil proving excellent for growing all manner of grain and other crops as well as raising animals, the territory of Iowa gave safe haven to Irish families and enabled them to depict their world on the midwestern canvas.

Like the church, the Mississippi River had a key role to play. Near and along the Mississippi, many place-names suggest Celtic heritage: McCausland, New Bolton, Toolesboro, Montrose, Donnellson, Cotter, Nichols, Donahue, Holy Cross, Lost Nation. Across the river from Iowa is Galena, the Illinois home of Ulysses S. Grant and a town in which the first house was built by an Irish migrant, who, like his Iowa neighbors, grew to prosperity on the cargo pipeline to America's interior. The river gave ready access to visitors: over the years, many Irish patriots and public figures visited the Midwest, including Thomas F. Meagher, Mrs. Jeremiah O'Donovan

Rossa, Michael Davitt, Charles Parnell, and T. P. O'Connor. Local lore has it that the old river town of Morris was, like Dubuque, a funnel point for immigrants into the Midwest; settled Irish farmers found jobs for new arrivals coming through on their way to the Irish communities in Neola, Dyersville, Keokuk, Independence, Gilbertville, Temple Hill, Bankston, Farley, Cascade, and other towns. Marking the progress of the frontier across Iowa, Irish communities flourished in Des Moines, Newton, Casey, Red Rock, Imogene (a town whose late nineteenth-century Irish citizenry is featured in Michael Carey's portion of the collective play called *Dear Iowa*), Atlantic, and Council Bluffs. Woven into the official centennial and sesquicentennial histories of even those communities settled predominantly by Germans and Scandinavians we find prominent Irish names and treasured stories about the men and women who brought those denominations to the new heartland. Throughout the Midwest, the state historical societies' collections of manuscripts and published materials abound with information about famine victims and the sometimes glorious, sometimes disreputable accomplishments of Irish families descended from those migrants.

But of all the Iowa towns, the little settlement of Parnell has been the most elaborate in asserting its Irishness, its anxiety over continuity with the past turned to celebration. In the town's centennial year of 1985, residents composed a 708-page book bound in kelly green and ornamented with tiny gold shamrocks, tracing the facts and effects of "100 Years in Little Ireland." The abundance of detail makes compelling reading for anyone interested in the midwestern Irish experience. In the beginning, in 1885, the town of Lytle City moved lock, stock, and barrel three miles west to position itself on the new Milwaukee Railroad line. For the many families that still trace their ancestry to the defunct Lytle City or the eventually thriving Parnell, the editors of the commemorative volume offer histories that include the clan's place of origin in Ireland, the year and circumstances of emigration, the various points of settlement on the way to Iowa, political affiliation, names and circumstances of family members, and notable contributions to the life of Parnell. Township plat maps from 1886 forward name the owners of various quarter-sections—Thomas Shuell, J. H. Kelley, S. J. F. Dean, P. W. Rock, Michael Doyle, the Flannagan Bros., and Sarah Garrity are among that number—and the 1984 plat map still shows a preponderance of Irish names. Vintage advertisements from T. J. Carney's "The

Fair Store," Carroll & Coen's "Headquarters for Ranges and Heaters," Hannah Daley's "City Restaurant," and M. Dwyer's "Implements" depict the commercial side of Parnell's Irish narrative. Sections on neighborhood organizations, resident pastors (many born in Ireland), the state-funded school system (run by the Sisters of Humility from 1901 until the state disallowed sectarian instruction in the 1930s), athletic events, musical concerts, high school classes, veterans' records, and the many pairs of twins born in the town display in affectionate detail the history of this community.

One brief family history may be taken as exemplary: Edward Carney was born in County Galway in 1820, his wife Margaret in Wicklow (Black Ditch parish); they married in Ireland and then emigrated to Iowa, finding their way to the farming territory of Holbrook and Parnell. Four sons and two daughters were reared on their farm. John Carney, the second son who was born in 1855, married Mary O'Toole of Muscatine, Iowa, and fathered ten children; he died in 1934 shortly after his wife's death. One of their boys "tended the farm thereafter." Two fuzzy photographs depict John and Mary Carney with eight of their children, as well as the parents with their own son John in his World War I uniform, together with a chum of John's who wears a large white bandage over his battle-torn lower face. The house behind them has bare wooden planks; beside it is the delimbed stump of an old tree to which a saddled horse is tied. Six more pages of the volume outline the lives of the Carneys' offspring.

Elsewhere, the browser meets notables such as Jimmy Kelly, the "first in the area to shuck 100 bushels of corn in one day" (*Parnell Centennial* 464). There are also numerous biographies that somewhat defensively describe what is put forward as a standard scenario: a migrant arrives in Iowa with limited means, quickly achieves the ownership of 160 acres or more of prime prairie, and enthusiastically embraces civic responsibilities. We also find many Irish place-names in various states of corruption (similar to the nonstandard spelling on some tombstones)—such as the hailing of Bridget Meager from County Kel Kenna, Ireland (*Parnell Centennial* 446). From these records we can glean information about education and language skills, the rigors and pleasures of pioneer life, the economic vicissitudes of American farming, the local circulation of European folklore, the upwards and sometimes downwards changes in fortune that attended the move to the

Scene Near Parnell, Iowa

Undated vintage 1-cent postcard addressed to Miss Winnie Kelley, RR #1, Parnell, Iowa: "Dear Winnie I believe you had better try & come up Friday afternoon. From Bella."

Midwest, and what is at once the remarkable coherence of this Irish community's self-identification and the dense network of hyphenated Irish relations that has unfolded from Parnell not only within the immediate area but across the nation and around the world.

That said, it must be noted that when the Irishman first came to America, communities were worried over his alleged profligacies. Early twentieth-century Irish socialist Robert Lynd helps us to understand the etiology of this fear. Before the 1881 Irish Land Act, it was a matter of course for land agents to raise rent when an Irish farmer seemed to be prospering on the lands that he did not own but had had the foolish temerity to improve. Hence, as a matter of preemptive self-defense, the Irish farmer had acquired the aspect of laziness, his plot the look of desuetude. As Lynd explains, it was not "Irish blood" but "Irish conditions" that had created the overall unkemptness and inefficiencies of the Irish farmer's life and the life on the land (Lynd 14). So it is no surprise that in the Parnell commemoration book, there is a wry record of the earliest years in Lytle City, where intoxication and brawling were regular though regretted occurrences (*Parnell*

Centennial 13–14). But once installed in the more prosperous Midwest, these migrants immediately shifted into high-geared efficiency and farm improvement. Tracing the emigrant from Ireland, where she was downtrodden and reduced, through the various stages of westward movement that characterized the restless search for better, more improvable land highlights the role of material conditions in composing supposed national traits. When discriminatory practices and their consequences were escaped, so too were the negative features so often taken to be the indelible signs of the Irish national character.

Long-term effects of Irish migration go beyond character expression and even well past phenomena such as the political machinery in Chicago or the Irish fests celebrated annually in the Twin Cities, St. Louis, and Kansas City. The prosperity of Irish farmers echoes even now in the stories of greatest midwestern success; Allan G. Bogue says that the most "spectacular of the prairie landlords" was the Irish William Scully, founder of a family still present in Illinois, Kansas, and Nebraska. Scully owned over a quarter-million acres in the midwestern states, much of which he bought up when farms were foreclosed during hard times in the 1870s (*From Prairie* 57–58). Putting wealth and achievement aside for a moment, it would seem that European migration patterns contributed to regional relations that emerge now as diffusely shared attitudes roughly coordinated with settlement patterns.[4] For example, one might turn to the consumerist regional maps of the United States that began to proliferate in the popular news of the 1990s. In a review of Michael J. Weiss's *Latitudes and Attitudes: An Atlas of American Tastes, Trends, Politics and Passions*, for instance, we find the Midwest charted according to seven market types based on buying trends, political alignments, and television viewing preferences (Nusbaum). Interestingly, the main areas of Weiss's attitudinal map substantially echo Glenda Riley's map of the five zones of Iowa settlement: the gradual movement westward from the 1830s into the 1870s divides Iowa most overtly into a "Log Cabin Frontier" and a "Sod House Frontier" (Riley 33), each of which aligned with a different European population mix. Many aspects of midwestern American life have been overdetermined by these migration waves. Indeed, today, among the estimated 44 million Irish Americans in the U.S.—a total of 18 percent of the U.S. population and the second largest ethnic group in the States—we find a substantial 21.3 percent of Iowa's population claiming this descent (at least, so reported the *Irish Voice* newspaper in 1993). The arrival of the Irish in the new world was by no means the end of the story from the perspective of a regional cultural studies. Hybrid Americans and their territory-specific attitudes form only the most obvious kind of cultural assemblage.

Dislocated Discourses

> In the discount drugstores of Iowa, you can buy some of the world's corniest postcards. One of the more ghastly downhome types has the words "BUSHEL OF PORK" superimposed on a close-up photograph of two clean, pink piglets wearing shiny blue ribbons and peering semi-blindly out of a bushel basket, their flat, oversized noses wetly drawing the eye. On the back, the card says jauntily, "All Dressed Up and No Place to Go!" What an Iowa postcard, I thought, until I read the fine print and discovered that it was "PRINTED IN IRELAND."

Edward Said observes that "we can read ourselves against another people's pattern, but since it is not ours . . . we emerge as its effects, its errata, its counternarratives. Whenever we try to narrate ourselves, we appear as dislocations in *their* discourse" (Said 140). Much of the mutual invention of the Midwest and Ireland takes place today at the International Writers Program at the University of Iowa. The Writers' Workshop actually composes a metatext of "writing" that has implications for many publications and styles worldwide; it is a sort of clearinghouse for world writerliness in the academic tradition and in this sense a significant factor in the ideological work done by poetry and fiction around the globe. As workshop historian Steven Wilbers suggests, the workshop experiment is based in regionalism and in the middleness of the Midwest as an alternative to or space-between the hegemonic writing factories on both American coasts. In producing its own alternativity, the workshop has also altered the texts of spaces far removed from Iowa City. So it is that at this midwestern turning point of the moving world, we find spinoffs of pattern and idea that etymologically align and resonate with work in Ireland, that draw the world into the same template for a moment before the rotation shifts the design and makes some other relationship visible, destroys one continuity and produces elsewhere equally meaningful patterns of significance.

A great many Irish writers have commented on or responded to the Midwest in their writing. Between 1967 and the present, Irish visitors have included John Banville, Peter Fallon, Sebastian Barry, Eavan Boland, Kevin Casey, Harry Clifton, Kevin Kiely, Thomas McCarthy, Martin Roper, and Tomás Murphy. Poems like Boland's "Love" and "Ghost Stories" are set in Iowa City: "Dark falls on this Midwestern town / where we once lived when myths collided"—"Our American Hallowe'en was years ago. We wore / anoraks and gloves / and stood outside to watch the moon above Iowa." In turn, Irish-American poet Kathy Calloway's "Love in the Western World" tells a story of Ulster family solidarity as her people moved through the Midwest; "Carrie Usher's Journal" beautifully evokes the process of pioneering, complete with "cattle / belly-deep in prairie grass, / a Cedar River settlement, Misquakee playmates." The child in the poem veers between wagon-trail wildness and the sanctity of a "vision in a yellow clearing," to make the setting the site of an interpenetration, a bridge between cultural situations and subjectivities. Writers' Workshop graduate Sally Stepanek's "Sonnet for Everybody" says, "39 miles NW of Dublin, / at the / end of a river. There remains the / young girl at the well, who asks to be clothed, who asks for the/ correct time, who heard the shooting / in the distance, who remembers a star. / . . . She is not the river, nor the source / of wells, / she is afraid to stop the / weaving, to answer Iowa who calls / out of the blue, asking for maps."

Another workshop-based response to Ireland, William Murray's *Michael Joe*, has become a central text for Irish graphic realism. Written in the 1940s, *Michael Joe* depicts life in a small Irish town. Murray, a Clare man, has lived in Iowa City for more than thirty-five years, teaching in the workshop and in the English department at the University of Iowa. Another Murray novel, *A Long Way from Home*, responds to the dual perspective of an Irishman in the American Midwest. In *Long Way*, Murray describes the identity crisis of a middle-aged English professor torn between the breakdown of his marriage in the States and his long-term contention with his native land. When he returns to Ireland to make peace with his family there, the subtext of American mores routinely surfaces to keep the protagonist at a distance from what used to seem immediate.

> In the backyard, the cowcabins gleam, freshly whitewashed. Down the yard, the red-domed hayshed where I had once almost made love. "No hay yet," I say.

"I'll start to fill it from the meadows tomorrow. Never fear," Tom says. Have I criticized his farming methods? He leads the way in a back door to what had once been Father's shop. Now a dairy. Milking machines, milk cans, buckets neatly arranged. All gleaming. The old order changeth. Even here. On the shop counter, open ledgers. I read. Molly, Bossy, Kate, Bridget . . . records of milk yields, butterfat content. On the walls, photographs of cows. No bulls? "How many cows do you keep?" I ask. "Twenty cows. Cattle, too." Not a lot by Iowa standards. Big by his. "Father kept five, if I remember rightly," I say. (Murray, *Long Way* 7–8)

Murray views his writing, including the more recent *Irish Fictions*, as composed against the grain of his Irishness.[5] The tension between heartlands—the lateral movement back and forth—forces both symmetries and differences in Murray's writing.

Similarly striking—and my prime example of this small but significant genre of cross-regional writing—is a dislocational poem by Irish poet Paul Durcan. His acclaimed volume *Daddy, Daddy* includes a complex piece entitled "Loosestrife in Ballyferriter: to Brian Friel on his sixtieth birthday." I quote the text in full here because it has become a reference point for the integration of economic history and interpretive psychoanalysis that I want to appropriate for critical regionalist cultural studies. The poem reaches from the apparent loss of the family imaginary toward a vision of macro-historical cycles.

I

Dear Master—Homesick for Athens
In this summer of rain, I prayed to the Mother
Of God but she did not appear to answer
And the Loosestrife in Ballyferriter near broke my heart.

II

But then I came to the Gallarus Oratory.
Its small black doorspace was a Mount of Venus.
Within the womb of that miniature iconostasis
What I saw was a haven white as salt.

III

An Trá Bhán, an Trá Bhán,

Cá bhfuil m'athair, cá bhfuil mo mháthair?
An Trá Bhán, an Trá Bhán,
Cá bhfuil m'athair, cá bhfuil mo mháthair?

IV

I stood in a delivery ward outside the Gallarus Oratory,
Surprised by coachload after coachload of tourists
From Celtic, from Medieval, from Modern times,
Expiring, only to be given birth to, in that small black doorspace.

V

The embryonic majority were from the Heel of Italy.
There were French, Swedish, German, Dutch.
There were siblings also from North America
To whom Ireland is an odyssey odder than Iowa.

VI

('Iowa'—she keened from behind a drystone wall—
'Iowa—I don't want to have to go to Iowa.
Iowa doesn't want me and I don't want Iowa.
Why must I forsake Ireland for Iowa?')

VII

There was a traffic snarl-up at the Gallarus Oratory,
All of the newly born vying to find parking space
In a gauntlet of fuchsia. In the small black doorspace
I gave vent to my grief for my foreign mother.

VIII

What is the nature of Loosestrife in Ballyferriter?
What class of a massacre occurred on the Great Blasket?
Who burned the islanders out of their island homes?
Was it the Irish who burned us out of our island homes?

IX

What we did not know as we scurried out over the waves
In the rain-laden sunlight to feed our eyes on the corpse of the Blasket
Was that we were being observed from a small black doorspace
By a small old man darker than his own doorspace.

X

Only the small old man living alone in his own doorspace,
Counting us swooping in and out of the corpse of the Blasket
In the showdown, saluted me and he whistled in the cosmos,
His eyes peering out of the sheep's carcass of his skull,

XI

His larynx thinned by the white sand of his eyes:
'It was the Irish who burned us out of our island homes,'
And his smile was moist so that it stuck on the breeze:
'It was the Irish who burned us out of our island homes.'

XII

An Trá Bhán, an Trá Bhán,
Cá bhfuil m'athair, cá bhfuil mo mháthair?
An Trá Bhán, an Trá Bhán,
Cá bhfuil m'athair, cá bhfuil mo mháthair?

XIII

Dear Master—Homesick for Athens
In this summer of rain, my closest grief
Lies in Tyrone dust. There is no man
Who would not murder his brother. Joy of all who grieve.

XIV

There is no God—only his Mother;
There is no God—only his Mother and;
There is no God—only his Mother and Loosestrife;
There is no God—only his Mother and Loosestrife in Ballyferriter.

When I first read this poem, I was at once riveted, disconcerted, and delighted by the mention of Iowa. I read the poem three times in a sort of
reverie of invocation. I noted with satisfaction the glancing eye of the old
man, both deep-insider and self-constituted observer, and the persistent
tourists gazing endlessly at the Blaskets. Recognizing the initial stanza's reference to Friel's play *Translations* ("Homesick for Athens"), I assumed that
the sense of equally endless birthing drew power from the play's presenta-
tion of mid-nineteenth-century Gaelic culture as possessing, at the very

Close-up of the Gallarus Oratory, 1992. Photo by John Herr.

least, the intellectual sophistication of the Greek and Roman world. Friel's portrayal of English speakers as insular, as insisting that all geographical space be translated imperially into English space through anglicizing place-names, contrasts with Friel's picture of the hedge schoolmaster and his pupils' linguistic fluidity, as it does with Durcan's own Estyn Evans-inspired (and startlingly Leopold Bloomian) suggestion that "Irish" is an aggregate term designating different people at different times and in different places. Those living on the Blaskets and similar islands had routinely seen mainlanders as invading their worlds; Durcan's speaker identifies with the small-islander as well as with the main-islander in oscillating perspective; he is the man peering from the black doorway as well as the mother keening from behind the wall. In Durcan's poem, the repeated stanza in Irish, itself composed of subtle repetition, mourns, "The White Strand, the White Strand, where is my father? where is my mother?" Assuming all the roles (mother, father, and newborn child), the poet also takes his place at the Gallarus Oratory. A site of prayer and solitary monastic withdrawal, this breastlike stone hut is readily pictured as a mound of Venus; its pubic protuberance gently encloses the poet and the old man. The mound's threshold might be compared to St. Patrick's Purgatory at Lough Derg; there medieval pilgrims sought to pass between worlds as today's penitents hope to do. The poem bristles with virtual gateways.

I talked with Paul Durcan in February of 1992. On that day the *Irish Times* had printed a picture of Brian Friel accepting the Man of Europe award. Durcan savored Friel's success; he told me that he regards Friel as the only person writing in Ireland today who is truly a "maestro." Although when he wrote "Loosestrife in Ballyferriter" he was thinking of Friel's work in general, he said that he had seen *Philadelphia, Here I Come*—perhaps the premier Irish emigration play—when he was a young man, and he had been profoundly moved by it. He had read many times the passage ending Friel's *Faith Healer* because the healer's final statement "says everything that . . . can be said about what it is to *be* an artist."

> And although I knew that nothing was going to happen, nothing at all, I walked across the yard towards them. And as I walked I became possessed of a strange and trembling intimation: that the whole corporeal world—the cobbles, the trees, the sky, those four malign implements— somehow they had shed their physical reality and had become mere

The Gallarus Oratory in its landscape, 1992. Photo by John Herr.

imaginings, and that in all existence there was only myself and the wedding guests. And that intimation in turn gave way to a stronger sense: that even we had ceased to be physical and existed only in spirit, only in the need we had for each other. And as I moved across that yard towards them and offered myself to them, then for the first time I had a simple and genuine sense of home-coming. Then for the first time there was no atrophying terror; and the maddening questions were silent. At long last I was renouncing chance. (Friel 44)

Because Durcan's poem celebrates Friel's work I began to view the piece not as a lament but even more as a tangibly constructed place—a siting of possibility composed of white strand, an eventful past, and a present abundant in loosestrife. In any event, Durcan suggested that I go to Ballyferriter.

Following the poet's suggestion, my family and I visited the Dingle Peninsula in early 1992 to trace the sites in Durcan's poem. As we moved along the coast from Dingle Town to Ballyferriter, it became ever more clear to me that far from pointing to a single viewing situation, Durcan was insisting on a multiple perspective—a heterogeneity of roles, persons, and onlookers. From that diffused subjectivity, Durcan's speaker asks us to consider the vista of the white strand across the bay. About the "Trá Bhán" stanza, Durcan had said that when you look from the mainland over to the Blaskets on a clear day, there is a white strand "shining over at you." It could be Greece, he said, it's so white. The poet added that this is "a holy place for the Blasket Islands."

Having just returned to the Republic from the north, and this after two weeks of severe violence in Belfast and Tyrone, I still retained in my mind's eye a retinal image of camouflage-clad British soldiers, of khaki Saracens with squinting windows. These phantom images began to make themselves visible while we were rounding a bend on the road to Ballyferriter, on the main road in Waterville, and on the way back to Dublin, on the Ennis Road in Limerick. At this time, the news was preoccupied with the alleged discovery of an IRA arms cache in County Kerry as well as with renewed charges of a shoot-to-kill policy being carried out by British soldiers against nationalist paramilitaries. These notional soldiers, these virtual Saracens placed themselves eerily before my eyes: I found these violent ghosts deeply disturbing and thought about Durcan's poetic invocation of invaders from ages past and present. But I discovered that violence has long been part and parcel of this storied space.

Near the rural town of Ballyferriter is Dún án Óir, a fort that in 1580 was attacked by "a band of Italians, Spanish, English, and Irish . . . backed by papal funds and rallying to support Catholic Ireland against Protestant England." Against that force, the Irish, putatively numbering among them Edmund Spenser, won the day (Doran, Greenwood, and Hawkins 269). Early twentieth-century writer Stephen Gwynn adds that "at Fort del Oro, near Smerwick, two Spanish expeditions landed in Elizabeth's reign. The second, of eight hundred men, entrenched itself there; but Lord Grey came down, breached the defences; the garrison surrendered at discretion and were all put to the sword—Walter Raleigh being in charge of this butchery" (Gwynn 190).

It was presumably to abjure such ways of the world that the Gallarus oratory was erected. Located close to Ballyferriter and dating from the twelfth century or before (Harbison, Potterton, and Sheehy 67–68), the oratory is a sophisticated version of the small, externally rounded, stone "beehive" huts on the Skelligs—regional architecture of the Middle Ages. Irish architectural historian Maurice Craig comments on the primitive character of the several hundred early Christian churches of disputed date scattered around the islands of Ireland. He notes that one "line of development" in this architectural style operated totally without wood, using instead corbelling techniques of stone construction (Craig 27). In virtually all of the guidebooks and architectural studies that picture the Gallarus Oratory, we find the same picture of this building, a close right frontal shot that cuts it off from the landscape and emphasizes its hutness. What no one I have read mentions about this structure is how moving it is, how lovingly molded into a gently curving roof. There are no jagged edges but rather a smoothed outline that fits a palm's curve. Have the stones weathered to such smoothness? They seem to indicate more craftsmanship and actual sculpting than nearby exposed stonework. To me, the oratory is both retreat and environmental sculpture. The construction of that space, so womblike and loving, would have been a meditative act, stone chipped, sanded, fitted together in a pattern reflecting the puzzle pieces of a universe deemed divine in origin.

Once inside the building, I saw that portals to the outside offer details that utterly elude the usual handbooks. For example, at the back is a small deep window, an aperture that widens as it cuts through rock to trap the light and possibly to disperse fire smoke. Standing inside, I traced the axis that runs on the long spine of the roof from window to door to ocean vista, and that draws the eye toward the stunning, sedative exterior. Was there ever a door on the oratory to keep out the winter wind, I wondered. The inside of the entrance has a lintel. Each stone on either side of the passage has a hole in it, so there may have been a rod or pin that held a wooden door, its other edge stopped by the dirt floor. This structure, which may be described either as all roof or all walls, which signifies eight centuries of weathered artistry, and which for Durcan stands imaginatively counter to the golden fort, provides inspiration for the poet as a conduit between and among worlds.

The oratory has attracted other writers, too, including Seamus Heaney. "In Gallarus Oratory" describes a dual sense of monastic community and isolation as well as the overwhelming weight of the construction, a "core of old dark walled up with stone / A yard thick." This piece sports a classic Heaney ending, which moves from the "black weight" of the monks' "breathing" to a splendor-in-the-grass climax in which the sea is "a censer, and the grass a flame." Heaney is adept at taking us back into history and its psychophysical imprints, while Durcan throws us into less satisfactorily aesthetic images, into the contradictions of looking from the temporal/spatial outside as well as from the inside, and from the interstices between, rather than from a reclaimed, centered, historicized, and wholly indigenous viewpoint.

In Durcan's poem, we find a coincidence of contraries that supports the oscillation of viewpoint he proposes and enacts: joy/grief, foreigners/natives, outsider/insider, ancient/modern, Father Time (his sandwhite eyes running through his hourglass throat)/Mother Space (womb, Mount of Venus). The Mater Space is also what we can contact of the divine ("There is no God—only his Mother"); she is Mother Ireland and Maeve, an older goddess ceaselessly giving birth through the Gallarus delivery ward to Celtic, Medieval, and Modern eras. Birth, reincarnation, and emigration all figure as modes of invasion or, worse, of tourism. In this position, place runs the risk of becoming space—totally given over to an indifference that might well find Iowa and Ireland not only similarly structured but also flatly The Same. Paradoxically, what keeps the regions separate is also what joins them,

View from inside the
Gallarus Oratory, 1992.
Photo by Gary Peter
Ellingson.

the undecidable, deconstructive register-between that pulls to itself exile, displacement, resistance, loose strife, the transitional oratory. That birth-canal threshold from monastic tradition integrates a cultural imaginary reaching from Ireland to Iowa with a vertical, spiritual economy.

Reading Durcan's poem further reminds us that economically forced emigration was no picnic. Iowa stands not only as the sound of keening but also as a sort of nightmare imaginary, a negative space to Ireland's solid, drystone reality and classical culture. This bad dream might as well be named Loose-Strife-as-Iowa; the fact that loosestrife may designate a number of related flowering plants, yellow or purple, does not undermine the force of the implied abstraction. I read that term as a meandering but pressingly present set of contradictions and struggles tied to the processes of birthing and dying as well as to the unresolved question of Irishness and the Iowishness that results from migrating populations. The "nature of Loose-strife in Ballyferriter" is the same as the nature of Irishness in that transitional space—up for grabs, unbounded. The spaces among worlds produced by the poem's provisional thresholds force us to look from a position incorporating many Irish perspectives. Seeing the oratory, I suddenly was aware that in Durcan's poem "Iowa" becomes tangible not only as a destination but also as a *word*. And this word disrupts and channels the poet's storytelling. When I called Durcan, I asked him about his use of the state's name. He observed mildly, "It's like a lot of works of art. It's just that in the process of composition the right word comes at the right time," and in this case the word was "Iowa." He added, fervently, that as an artist, a writer, he felt that his meaning was no more correct than what any given reader brings to a work: the reader's interpretation is "absolutely valid" and constitutes one-half of the aesthetic reality. I recalled that the old man in the doorway struck me as one with Yeats's gay, glittering-eyed hermits who survey indifferently the world's turmoil. In the midst of such complex identifications, the poet states that the Mother of God "did not appear." And yet the Mother exists, and the sign of her presence is that set of unstable oppositions and unbounded paradoxes that the work explores, including an ultimate spatial tension between two places that coincidentally, homonymically, begin with "I."

On the day that I first stood looking out at the White Strand in question, the water was far too wind-peaked for small boats to cross over from Dún Chaoin to the Blaskets. Two days earlier news had been in the paper that substantial development would take place in Dún Chaoin; the government, using European Community (EC) regional development funding, had decided to install a Blasket Island "interpretative centre" there. The published design showed a long building in the valley facing the Blaskets, accompanied by a large parking lot for cars and tour buses. The people of the Dingle Peninsula had vigorously protested this building; they had marched on Dublin—after a full day's drive across rural roads—to let the Taoiseach know firsthand their opposition to the spending of European infrastructural funds in this manner and on one of the few remaining stretches of relatively virgin coastline in Europe.

We watched, alone and with dismay, as two ochre bulldozers dug grooves in the earth near the Dún Chaoin dock site; we surmised that they were installing power lines to support the more disruptive work to come. It seemed reasonable to assume that we were seeing this portion of Dingle in its natural state for the last time, having been drawn to the scene just as it was being refigured, while Paul Durcan's poem pointed the way from Gallarus to yet another Irish holy place that was effectively ceasing to exist. When the Great Blasket Visitor Centre opened in April of 1994, the *Irish Times* reporter Dick Hogan praised it, saying that it "may be just the beginning of a revival of national and international interest in the western island" and its "traditional way of life that was finally abandoned in the 1950s." A restored historic village is planned for the island itself. No mention was made of local distress over the Irish state's planned influx of visitors (the forty-seven-acre site has parking for more than one hundred cars and six tour buses) to this fragile part of the island, even though the article is illustrated with a telling photograph of the smiling, shirt-and-tied manager of the center sitting next to a grim, ghansied Sean Pheats Tom Ó Cearna, "one of the few remaining islanders" now living on the mainland (Hogan, "Another Time"). From my own visit I am left with an impression of the overwhelming sense of loss in "Loosestrife in Ballyferriter" that resonates in the speaker's lack of mother, father, and country, and echoes in a poem by Liam O Muirthile.

In "Sa Daingean," the record of a place becoming a space, O Muirthile writes, "An afternoon in Dingle, / For one split second I forget where I am from— / Surrounded by polished foreigners who stroll about / Precision-dressed for rain." He notes their multi-European origins, their bus day-tripping through the countryside, and he watches them until he is prompted to "suddenly recall / The hand that wrote in tar on the Dunquin harbour wall / *Rith síos má tá ceamara agat.*" The Irish translation reads, "Run down here if you have a camera." In the same ironic spirit, the poet acknowledges that at this edge of the island, among the beehive huts, he can no longer escape the tourist horde: "there's nowhere else to go."

TWO

Transmuting Geographies

*We are now asked . . . to think another side, an outside, an external face
of the concept which, like that of the moon, can never be directly visible or
accessible to us: but we must vigilantly remember and reckon that other
face into our sense of the concept while remaining within it in the old way
and continuing to use and think it.*

FREDRIC JAMESON

At its simplest level, Adorno's negative dialectic suggests that the way to
deal with a confining story, a situation of perceived lack, an instance of
historical catastrophe, is both to discover and to invent alternatives. Perhaps the representative father and mother mourned by Durcan can be structurally reinvented within different circumstances, both discursive and spatial. That is the premise for the first assemblage constructed in this chapter,
one that confronts the pain of migration with a history that spans religion,
agriculture, two countries, and the defense of a communal lifestyle. The
challenge of nation with nomadism installs an interzone from which we
can learn a cross-regional architectonics of the spirit.

MOUNT MELLERAY AND NEW MELLERAY

Among the earliest Irish emigrants to the American Midwest were the
Cistercians of Mount Melleray, County Waterford. Both in Europe and in
the United States, the Melleray monks have a fascinating history, which

sweeps up political and economic hardships, the perils of frontier life, and the aesthetic challenges of merging different landscapes with Cistercian architectural traditions.

According to *The History of Mount Melleray Abbey* (1952) imprimatured in Waterford, the Irish Abbey was established in 1833, seven centuries after the first Cistercian abbey, reaching out from France, was founded in Ireland (Moloney 3). During the outlawing of Catholicism in Ireland that began in 1644 and extended into the early nineteenth century, the Cistercians were not represented on the island, but many Irish monks joined their Celtic brethren during that period at the Abbey of Melleray in Brittany. In 1832, when suitable property was found in the Knockmealdown mountains and donated to the order, hundreds of local residents volunteered to help the monks fence in their land, and in turn, throughout the famine years of 1845 to 1849, the monks supplied four hundred to seven hundred people a day with food (Hoffman 25).

The early role of the Cistercians in Ireland comes forward as an architectural intervention in Roger Stalley's brilliant *The Cistercian Monasteries of Ireland: An Account of the History, Art and Architecture of the White Monks in Ireland from 1142 to 1540*. Before the first Cistercians arrived in Ireland in the 1140s, the Irish church as a whole followed a non-European organization based not on "episcopal government" but on the division of Ireland into clans or *tuatha*. Each monastery had a distinctive mode of living and identified more with its tribal environment than with an overarching hierarchy. Corresponding to the system of government that tolerated "over a hundred kings and sub-kings," Irish religious life at the end of the eleventh century was in the hands of "about two hundred monasteries" (Stalley 10–11). Indigenous monastic life made use of decentered oratories like that at Gallarus. At the same time, decadence in varying degrees, a casual style of living both within and outside the monastic confines, actual fortification of the abbeys, and the incursion of powerful laybrothers complicated the spiritual geography of Ireland as encountered by the Cistercians in the twelfth century.

Cisterican architectural style had a complexity at odds with the home-grown monastic tradition, relying on imposing, unified structures centered on a basilica. There was resistance among Irish monks to the ascetic Cistercian life. And it was difficult for natives to separate the encroachment of Anglo-Norman political power from that of Cistercian expansion (Stalley 9, 15, 18). In both the twelfth and the sixteenth centuries, the Cistercians were charged with "gluttony and licentiousness" of their own. Animosity, competition, and contradiction thus marked the entry of the Cistercians into Irish life and their continued power both in Ireland and throughout the continent.

While contributing to a social ideology of centralization, the Cistercians also responded to the Irish preference for decentering. Stalley notes, "Attempts to summarise the 'Irishness' of Irish Cistercian art are bound to be misleading, for the complexities of Irish society, both religious and secular, produced an overall picture that was far from uniform. It was inevitable that cultural and racial tensions within the monastic body would assume visual expression in architecture" (Stalley 236). Hence, although the Cistercian influence can be isolated, especially during the first century of the order's presence in Ireland, especially in terms of the introduction to Ireland of European Romanesque and Gothic architecture, Irish monastic buildings, metalwork, and sculpture all display a marked heterogeneity. What Stalley's groundbreaking work indicates is the creation of a new, extracontinental, post-Gallarus monastic spatiality in Ireland—a critical regionalist architecture invested in capturing and enhancing stages of becoming.

Interestingly enough, this composite zone also reaches toward the American Midwest in a number of ways, perhaps most generally as an allusion in James Joyce's widely read story, "The Dead," where Melleray appears as a shadowy place of penance. Melleray is associated with Freddy Malins, the incorrigible alcoholic who introduces his own brand of tension at the dinner party while Gabriel Conroy and his aunts entertain the assembled company.

All the gentlemen, except Gabriel, ate some of the pudding out of compliment to Aunt Julia. As Gabriel never ate sweets the celery had been left for him. Freddy Malins also took a stalk of celery and ate it with his pudding. He had been told that celery was a capital thing for the blood and he was just then under doctor's care. Mrs Malins, who had been silent all through the supper, said that her son was going down to

Mount Melleray in a week or so. The table then spoke of Mount Melleray, how bracing the air was down there, how hospitable the monks were and how they never asked for a penny-piece from their guests.

—And do you mean to say, asked Mr Browne incredulously, that a chap can go down there and put up there as if it were a hotel and live on the fat of the land and then come away without paying a farthing?

—O, most people give some donation to the monastery when they leave, said Mary Jane.

—I wish we had an institution like that in our Church, said Mr Browne candidly.

He was astonished to hear that the monks never spoke, got up at two in the morning and slept in their coffins. He asked what they did it for.

—That's the rule of the order, said Aunt Kate firmly.

—Yes, but why? asked Mr Browne.

Aunt Kate repeated that it was the rule, that was all. Mr Browne still seemed not to understand. Freddy Malins explained to him, as best he could, that the monks were trying to make up for the sins committed by all the sinners in the outside world. The explanation was not very clear for Mr Browne grinned and said:

—I like that idea very much but wouldn't a comfortable spring bed do them as well as a coffin?

—The coffin, said Mary Jane, is to remind them of their last end.

As the subject had grown lugubrious it was buried in a silence of the table during which Mrs Malins could be heard saying to her neighbour in an indistinct undertone:

—They are very good men, the monks, very pious men. (Joyce 201–2)

The passage works both by absence and by presence, by correlation and contrast. Having carved the goose, Gabriel eats and waits for the moment of his speech. Freddy's volubility exerts tacit pressure on Gabriel's silence. Throughout the story, Freddy and Gabriel stand in opposition as drunken fool and solid man, but that contrast underlies their roles as mutual foils, even twins in some sort of negative register. Gabriel, it seems, has never been able to sustain deep emotions; Freddy obviously has a tumultuous inner life and as a result retreats to alcoholic buffering. Gabriel is tied to his aunts' apron strings, while Freddy's domination by his mother has held him in adolescent limbo. Freddy is heading for Melleray and its encoffined monks, while Gabriel's end, as far as we know, is in the darkened confinement of the room at the Gresham, which he shares not only with Gretta but also with the ghost of Michael Furey. The Melleray experience that will engulf the delinquent Freddy Malins also absorbs the fading vision of the good archangel in Gabriel Conroy. Melleray gives emblematic access to a sacred space in danger of being obviated by a cultural atmosphere of anomie and reification, even at the Misses Morkans' self-consciously traditional Christmas celebration.

That said, it is useful to ask to what extent the diners' view of Mount Melleray can be verified historically. Throughout the twentieth century, travel writers have provided varied portraits of Cistercian life on the mountain, almost all involving a contrast between expectations about monastic life and the startling realities of Mount Melleray. For example, Lynn Doyle went there in 1935: "I was shown through the monastery by a pleasant courteous gentleman in a monk's robe. I felt a certain embarrassment as he came towards me, then we fell into natural easy chat. He showed me the cloisters, the refectory, plain to bareness, where he and his brethren ate their simple meals in a silence broken only by the voice of the monk appointed to read. He showed me the dormitory, bare also and austere, where the monks took their few hours of sleep. . . . In the dormitory there is no distinction of persons. Abbot, Prior, and monks, there is a similar little cubicle for each. They sleep in their robes, and will be buried in them." Doyle adds that "a warm sense of our common humanity" rapidly replaced the "veil of false romance" that had occluded his view of the monks before his visit (Doyle 41, 40).

Similarly, in a pamphlet called *Cistercians of the Strict Observance*, under the heading of "Cistercian Austerities," we find reference to behaviors mentioned by Freddy Malins: "In the popular mind, the austerity of the Cistercian Order is usually misunderstood and often grossly exaggerated. . . . It is perhaps a hopeless task to try to trace the origin of some of these unusual ideas concerning our life. It may be, however, that some arose from a remarkable similarity between our Order and another which went out of existence in about the 16th century: The Brothers of Death. These had a Rule and a religious Habit somewhat similar to ours; and, among them, were found many of the strange practices attributed to our Order. There would be no point in our treating of these ridiculous notions here, since, to do so would contribute only to their diffusion." Of those matters that he does discuss, the writer says, "Perhaps the most appalling of the Cistercian observances is that of perpetual silence." As Aunt Kate knew, silence is a rule rather than a vow; it helps the monastic to seek "silence of the heart." But there are occasions for which and persons for whom speech is appropriate, and at any time the monks can use a limited language of manual signing. The writer acknowledges that Cistercians wake up for their day's labors at two A.M. and even earlier on Sundays and feast days. He adds that they go to sleep at seven P.M. in the winter and an hour later in the summer; they sleep on a "hard" bed "fully dressed, except for . . . shoes and socks" (Abbey of Our Lady of New Melleray 41, 43). They do not eat meat, fish, or eggs, and they exclude milk during Lent and at other times.

It is interesting that the word *appall* appears more than once in records about the Cistercians. Doyle notes that as he left the monastery, he no longer felt uncomfortable—"appalled"—by their "silence" or their "austerity." He continues, "when I said good-bye to that monk in the name of a brother I did it with sincerity. To me he was no longer a mystery, a thing to gaze at in vulgar astonishment. He was a man like myself . . . [who] gazed on man's folly when it flowed to his doors—as it sometimes did—with pity and understanding; felt the comedy and tragedy of it." He adds, "I saw . . . that a holy man may be a good judge of cattle and perhaps even of horses; that much may be done by work in silence; and that the Legislature of the Free State might with great advantage be transferred to the Knockmealdown Mountains" (Doyle 41, 42).

A dozen years after Doyle's visit and shortly after World War II, a travel writer named Charles Graves found his way to New Melleray and also used the word. He describes how he drove to Cappoquin and then up into the mountains: "The road twisted and turned like a wounded snake . . . up hill and down dale until finally we drove through a green archway of beeches to Mount St. Melleray" (Graves 91). He tells us that the laybrothers dressed in "brown cowls" and might wear beards, while the Fathers wore white and eschewed facial hair. Graves briefly sketches the history of the monastery, including Father Vincent O'Ryan's first trip to the Cappoquin area where the new monastery had yet to be constructed. One Sir Richard Keane had donated the land to the community, and the Prior accepted it, having been told directly by Keane that the neighboring people and the land would be enriched by the monastery's presence. "On his arrival Father Vincent was quite appalled by the scene. No wonder the local people called it scrahan, the coarse land. It lay on the southern slopes of the Knockmealdowns, rough and uneven, covered with heather, gorse, rushes, and patches of genuine bog land. There was not a tree, nor a fence, nor a shelter of any kind, except for a dilapidated gamekeeper's lodge." By the time that Graves saw the monastery, however, there were exceptional buildings, "herds of pedigree cattle," and hundreds of acres being farmed with "first-class" equipment (Graves 93, 92, 94).

Graves confirms the belief of those gathered in "The Dead" that "anybody can come and stay for a month at a time without paying a penny." Returning us to Freddy Malins, he adds, "The Guest House, by the by, specializes in curing dipsomaniacs. It is claimed that some of the worst cases are returned home within a matter of days, all traces of alcohol having left them. The cure itself is not revealed, but from what Brother Adrian told me it is more spiritual than medical. One presumes, therefore, that most of the patients are Catholics." Graves reports that another curious visitor, H. V. Morton, in his travel book *In Search of Ireland*, had given a graphic account of a night in the Guest House "where he heard the most terrible cries and hysterical laughter from the dipsomaniacs taking the treatment."

In 1948 there were 154 monks living in utterly communal fashion at Mount Melleray; many had diabetes. In Graves's estimation, "the lot of a Trappist is a very hard one and several of the monks I saw had, strangely enough, exactly the same expression as the Battle of Britain pilots suffering from flying stress in 1940 and 1941. . . . I was tremendously impressed by the expressions of these monks who have vowed themselves to a living death. Even the Guest Brothers who are continually in contact with the outside world . . . have extraordinary eyes. They look straight at you, and their faces have been washed of all the major human emotions like anxiety, envy, fear, surprise, physical love, depression, malice, frustration, and ambition" (Graves 93–95).

Rather than sleep in their coffins, however, the Cistercians are buried without coffins, a practice that had in fact been foregone in Ireland for a time prior to 1848, when regular canonical visitation was begun by the abbots of La Grande Trappe and Melleray in France (Hoffman 24). The reason for this deviation from standard practice may well have something to do with the shocking shortage of coffins at the time of the famine in rural Ireland. Then women often begged on the streets not for food money but for cash to inter their children according to custom: Irish tradition deplored placing a body directly in the ground. It was only when the system of burial was overrun with starved corpses that the infamous hinged coffin, which allowed multiple use, came into being. Meanwhile, the ships that took emigrants not to America but to the ocean floor were coffin ships. The text of famine deprivation and death resonates loudly amidst the plenty of the Misses Morkans' dinner and provides a context for Gabriel's abstention from sweets.

One hundred years before Graves's visit and in the midst of the famine, the Irish monastery decided to open a daughter house in America. At that time, Bishop Loras bought the Cistercians five hundred acres of "prairie and woodland about twelve miles south-west of his episcopal city" (Moloney 41). Father James O'Connor notes that there were one hundred "hungry monks" at Mount Melleray then, and it was decided to send some brothers "so as not to see them dying of starvation" ("Mystery" 5). So it is that sixteen Irish monks set out for what would become New Melleray. As Brother Kieran Mullaney wrote in his journal of that plague year, the Cistercians departed from Liverpool on 18 September 1849, and arrived in New Orleans on November 6. The next day they headed up the Mississippi for St. Louis, enjoying the "beautiful villas, the sugar plantations with the poor slaves as busy as bees, the orchards of oranges weaving in the odoriferous tropical breezes of southern Louisiana." In quick succession, twenty-six persons of the four hundred on board died of cholera, more than half of them monks from Mount Melleray. By November 26, the righteous remnant arrived in Dubuque, just as a classic Iowa winter set in (O'Connor, *Monastery Seasons*, 12 June 1978).

Brother Mullaney wrote a history of the community's experiences during that first of the New Melleray monks' midwestern experiences. He tells us that on the second day in Dubuque they saw the site for the monastery, "which when contrasted with the home we left in Ireland was a sad affair. The country, at least some miles out from town, had a desolate appearance, hilly, rugged and bare, snow-covered and chilly, with but very few people,

Dubuque, Iowa, 1846. Undated 1-cent postcard.

as its wild uncultivated appearance indicated." He talks of the "frozen breeze" at night and of the locals having dug into the earth to escape the oppressive wind (*Monastery Seasons*, Winter 1974). Speaking of that first winter, the newsletter adds that "the prospects must have been almost as bleak as Skellig Michael. . . . A cold icy wind was probably sweeping across the frozen prairies and thru the dark virgin forests as the monks first looked at the land where they were to live out their few years and be buried" (*Monastery Seasons*, Winter 1974).

More members were sent from Ireland; by 1856 the estate included 1,800 acres; and in 1862, New Melleray also became an abbey, by 1952 numbering its membership at 140, with a daughter house in Missouri (Moloney 42). Father O'Connor, a late twentieth-century member of the Cistercian order in Iowa and a sort of communal folk historian for New Melleray, lingers in one of his essays over the American prairie. He tells us that one of the original brethren had written, with the true voice of an Iowa farmer, "The wild uncultivated prairies . . . presented a delightful appearance, one vast weaving sheet of green grass with no cattle to eat it." Certainly for an Irish person, the lack of cattle on such prime grazing land would be startling, even affronting—a matter to rectify immediately. The prairies presented a saga of glacial activity, treeless terrain, cornucopian soil, and an ecosystem as fascinating as that of the Burren. Like the woman keening in

Durcan's poem, the Melleray monks came to Iowa out of sheer necessity and with heavy hearts, but over time the material culture of the monastery, umbilically connected to its Knockmealdown home, embodied a union of regions, Irish and Iowan. The two establishments chart a reintegration of identity out of penitential isolation, dislocation, and diasporic suffering.

Hence, when Iowa's monastery church was rebuilt and consecrated in 1976, there was a continuing architectural connection between the two Mellerays. Father O'Connor notes, "In addition to a stone from 12th century Holy Cross monastery in Ireland,[1] a similar memento dating back to the 6th century was also incorporated into New Melleray's new church. Through the instrumentality of Brother Conrad Carey, a stone was procured from the ruins of an abbey built near Ballyvourney, County Cork, during the era of St. Benedict," all to celebrate the possibility of a "golden age of Irish monasticism . . . in America." The heterogeneous tapestry of Cistercian design continued to cast out threads in new spaces.

But there is also another aspect to Irish missionary monasticism. Given the triumphalist cast of accounts of New Melleray and its predecessor, it may be useful to turn from an Irish viewpoint to one that strives to be both specific and alien. This maneuver occurs explicitly in Gretchen Fitzgerald's *Repulsing Racism*. Fitzgerald describes herself as "a black woman born in India with a mixed Portuguese, British and Indian culture, who has chosen to spend my adult life in Ireland" (Fitzgerald 21). Growing up in Goa, she was educated by Irish nuns. She came to understand the conceptual and material slippage by which missionaries became agents of "development," and she resented the scenario that makes outsiders patronizing toward her people. Fitzgerald recaps the well-known history of British colonizing of the Irish and the concomitant figuring of the Irish as a lower order of humanity. But when they moved to other countries, she argues, "the Irish . . . quickly realised that they could benefit from the situation of institutionalised white superiority," often becoming strongly racist in their activities in the United States, Australia, South Africa, and India.

Complicating this scenario, Fitzgerald argues, "Ireland's missionary tradition has meant that Irish people have played their part in reinforcing and continuing the effects of colonialism. . . . While Irish missionaries have brought many positive things to the inhabitants of previously colonised countries, there is little doubt that the Christian churches, by introducing

New Melleray Abbey. Undated 1-cent postcard. The physical plant of New Melleray Abbey has been altered and refurbished over the years.

what they believed to be a superior code of beliefs, values, educational system, language and lifestyle, created an elitist and divisive structure within communities visited by missionary groups" (Fitzgerald 7–8). The sacred/vertical space at the heart of the Irish rural experience was, at the very least, used to colonize the new world for the church through a continuous re-articulation of boundaries and centers.

An unusually caucasian American state, even Iowa offers us bits and pieces of information that suggest the church's complicity with racial and ethnic rivalries marking nineteenth- and twentieth-century Iowish culture: we might argue that in Iowa racism developed in part without color differences as clues. German and Irish immigrants assumed rivalry as part of their ethnic origins and racialized one another on that basis. At the same time, the mid-nineteenth-century anti-Catholic bias of middle America also demonized and ostracized many of Irish descent. All of this material history is relevant to Joyce's portrayal of Freddy Malins. As inebriated as he is, Freddy hotly defends the voice of a black singer performing in Dublin—against those at the table who would refuse first place at a *feis ceoil* to a person of color.

Freddy's compulsive chattering also provides a foil for the long-term failures of communications between Gabriel and Gretta, Gabriel and the rest of Irish society. Like Stephen Dedalus, Gabriel actually fears the people of rural Ireland from whom Gretta has sprung. He both envies and refuses their passion, the fervor of Michael Furey and his kind. Additonally, he views the population in the west of Ireland as racially inferior, undereducated and backward. If Gabriel's "journey westward" indeed marks a mystical accession of some sort and a spiritual, symbolic unification of Ireland within "The Dead," Gabriel markedly discovers his way in terms of the silence, celibacy, and memento mori that mark what we might call the jouissance particular to the Cistercian monastic life. Gabriel's intuitive tendency to seek out such monastic forms of bliss becomes clear in Joyce's narrative: Gabriel yearns to be alone in the snow instead of surrounded by family and merrymakers; he eats in silence; he prefers celery to pudding. While trying to conform to the existing continental-metropolitan version of culture, Gabriel discovers his desire veering always toward the contrived, chastening lack that makes up monastic spiritual abundance and that produces the monkish aura of calm, even of semi-shell-shocked detachment. Within and beyond Joyce's story, in the cultural register mapped by its semiotic grasp, Melleray is an icon for an Irish monasticism, an Irish social order that reaches from Gallarus all the way to the Mississippi. It is also a part of the small-scale farm economy that dominated nineteenth-century rural culture both in Ireland and in the American Midwest. The family farm imaginary rests on the assumption that being forced to migrate does not alter the possibilities for actualization: what was lost during the famine can be restaged elsewhere.

In Durcan's poem, the poet pleads for a mother and father who have disappeared in a peripheral site of endless human reincarnation; in doing so, the speaker defines his own sense that something is missing in his life, and the poem, while celebrating both the inspiring art of Brian Friel and the monastic life of the past, discovers itself caught up in multilayers of mourning. The collection in which the piece appears, *Daddy, Daddy*, meditates on the gap between a parent and his child—a circuit court judge and a sometimes schizophrenic son—a gap of violence and disapproval bridged by the poet's love and sealed by the father's death. In a way, Brian Friel is for the poet a good father countering Daddy's black moods. At the same time, the father has always been defunct in an Ireland still haunted by stories of eviction and emigration. When the monks of Mount Melleray took vows of silence and self-denial, they transmuted into rigorous discipline their self-heightened perception of something lacking at the heart of human experience. Joyce's narrative turns that lack into a secular plenitude existing in negative dialectic to Cistercian mores as well as into a covert racism and a refusal of rural tradition by an increasingly reified urban sensibility. The assemblage that I have been impelled to construct as a monastic stratum endlessly reinstalls indigenous resistance to centralizing, regulating forces.

ENTER THE DEPARTMENT OF AGRICULTURE

The public record of New Melleray Abbey is a quarterly newsletter called *Monastic Seasons*. Often, it includes humorous stories of experiences in Iowa or recollections of the past culled from the writings of long-deceased members. The spring 1987 issue discusses nearby towns with Irish roots dating back to the 1840s, including ones that obviously translated the Irish townland system to midwestern space: Filmore ("big cliff" in Irish), Ballyclough ("a town built in a rocky area"), Garnavillo ("an oak tree surrounded by shrubs"), Tipton (Tipperary Town). Hence, the hills around New Melleray were known by the early settlers as the Connacht hills. The names given to monastery fields are Calf, Church, Woods, Quarry, Dairy, Willows. They are also McCann, McAndrews, Quinn, O'Hagen, Dodds, St. James, Murphy, Graces, Fischers, Meyers, Willards. In spring of 1990, the publication notes the town of Garryowen's 150th anniversary, the hailing of the original residents from County Cork and County Limerick, and the saying of mass in Irish to commemorate the anniversary.

By far the most absorbing topic that the newsletter discusses is the process of farming in Iowa. There is overwhelming evidence of the monks' sincere endeavor to run their farm effectively and economically in spite of the endless challenges of drought, hail, freezing cold, strong winds, thunderstorms, and other climatic extravagances offered by a country where, to put it mildly, little effect is gained from the Gulf Stream that washes and moderates all of Ireland. The 1991 schedule, which notes seed planted and dates of planting, accompanies a map of the abbey grounds in which 1,129 acres were devoted to corn, 599 acres to beans, and 62 acres set aside in clover. Cattle and equipment share pride of place. As early as 1877, English land agent James Lonsdale Broderick reported that on a visit to the Iowa abbey, whose farms were at that time split between 2,900 acres in Dubuque and a property in Council Bluffs, he was shown "a very fine thoroughbred shorthorn bull that had taken several prizes." Broderick and the brothers talked cattle at length; finding one cow "too wide across the hips," Broderick explained "that the fashion in that respect had altered of late in England." He also viewed at New Melleray "any quantity of hogs," "about 300 sheep," and a "splendid barn" with ingenious haying fixtures (Horton 160). By the spring of 1973 there was reference to a "souped-up John Deere combine" owned by the Abbey. Two years later we read that "Melleray Emulous Master 444, alias Big Doc, a 15-month-old black angus bull, won the Summer Champion award at both the Iowa and Missouri State Fairs."

Other issues of *Monastery Seasons* mention the growing challenges of modernization—such things as the reduction by 50 percent of use of nitrogen fertilizer to protect the groundwater from agricultural chemical runoff, always a problem in the Midwest (spring 1991). For instance, Robert James Waller tells of a 1990s article called "Scores of Rural Iowans Drinking Tainted Water," which "summarized the results of a research project conducted by the Iowa Department of Natural Resources and the University of Iowa's Center for Health Effects of Environmental Contamination. Wells were tested in all of Iowa's ninety-nine counties, and the results showed, 'More than 94,000 rural Iowans drink water that contains one or more pesticides, most commonly atrazine, and 130,000 rural residents consume water from wells that contain high concentrations of nitrates.' . . . according to that report, 'Nitrate contamination has been linked to cancer, birth defects, and blue-baby syndrome.'" Ironically, Waller comments, "All of this is enough to drive one in search of monastic solace in the high mountain country of Asia" (Waller 138).

By the same token, the spring 1983 newsletter explicitly ties the Irish-midwestern retreat to an outside world that includes aggressive mechanisms for agricultural subsidies and control. "Along with three-fourths of the eligible Iowa grain farmers, the monastery has signed up in the U.S. Government's 1983 payment-in-kind (PIK) program. In an effort to reduce costly surpluses and lift the agricultural economy from its worst recession since the 1930s, the U.S. is inducing farmers to curtail production by offering grain from surplus stores in return for idling farm acreage." Five years later, in autumn 1988, the summer's drought in the Midwest takes center stage in the newsletter as in every other aspect of life in the beleaguered state. And the following autumn's newsletter, in regard to the harvest of soybeans and corn, notes a reprieve from the two-year drought. In short, crop reports are what the monks of New Melleray contemplate along with the liturgy—bushels per acre expected yield versus actual harvest, the relationship between last year's crop and this one, U.S. Department of Agriculture statements about the depletion of subsoil moisture, and the position of Iowa in relation to the other portions of the agricultural United States.

There is also the occasional glimpse into a life of austerity and self-discipline shared by monks and family farmers alike. Father O'Connor emphasizes in his writings the cyclic history of New Melleray, a monastery that has prospered on occasion but also yielded to various decimating forces—poverty, lack of the faithful, death. Even at the moment of his writing the following words in 1977, during a relatively easy period in Iowa, Father O'Connor notes, "It is 102 degrees and one sticks to the furniture, and where are we going to get the rain to pull the corn through the next boiling month?" (*Monastery Seasons*, September 1977). This is a common enough complaint among farm folk on the prairies. Similarly, the winter 1975 issue wears the headline "1974 Abbey Harvest on the Lean Side" and explains that the Midwest saw spring rainstorms, a summer drought, and early frosts. This combination kept the soybean and corn crops from achieving their usual levels.

The monks, of course, display more of an affinity for lack than other farmers: "For the first time since World War II, the country was experiencing what it was to be less than invincible, to be deprived of things, to have to sacrifice and suffer a bit, and endure. It is perhaps the beginning of a return to a more simple life, a less wasteful life, a more genuine and human life, a life lived more in harmony with nature" (Winter 1974). But however one slices the pie, monastic communities—and farm culture as a whole in an increasingly reified, interlinked econometric world-system—open questions about agriculture, self-subsistence, global political economy, and the role, if you will, of dialectically intersecting symbolic orders. The monastic approach to bad weather or oil shortages or global economic recession provides an excellent pathway to a critical cross-regionalism and paves the way toward other space-spanning assemblages.

A NORTHERN IRELAND OF THE MIND

Use a wide-angle lens and keep the horizon low.

IRISH FILMMAKER JOHN DAVIS'S RESPONSE TO THE QUESTION OF
HOW HE GOT IRELAND TO LOOK LIKE THE AMERICAN MIDWEST.

In 1987, a midwestern architecture student produced a meditative design for a futuristic Irish parliament building, the aim of which was specifically to enter into the erstwhile Northern Ireland conflict with a rectifying, healing assemblage—interventionist but also marked by indigenous materials. Pursuing a nomadic rather than a history-"verified" text, Mark Haukos pointedly aligns and celebrates elements of jewelry design, weapon construction, the state apparatus, and a projective "beyond" in his elevations and descriptions of New Ireland's parliament.

Haukos, at the time of writing an architect with the Bernard Tschumi group in New York, became fascinated by Irish culture and its troubled politics. His thesis draws both on an outsider's perspective and on the design repertoire of Irish jewelry, metalwork, poetry, and history. In his working notebook from the late 1980s, Haukos quotes liberally not only from Breton, Tzara, Mr. X, and Corbusier but also from Irish-American historian Alan J. Ward, Irish poet Brendan Kennelly, Francis Canavan, and Yeats. Haukos writes, "This thesis assumes the reunion of Northern Ireland with the Republic of Ireland. It does so on the premise that a revolution of social attitudes and their reflection in politics, not civil war, will be the ultimate assurance of peaceful reunion. . . . The challenge of this thesis is to create an architectural expression and a capital complex for a new era of Irish society and politics in the year 2000." Speaking in terms of Christopher Alexander's pattern language, Haukos writes, "The language of bird, fish, snake, island and metallic machine combine with archetype forms, producing an expressionistic architecture with mysterious overtones." Specifically committed to a historical perspective, he sites the new parliamentary complex on the grounds of the existing Stormont, which for the purposes of a fictive space-

Front gate of Stormont, Parliament Building. Illustration from informational booklet printed by W. & G. Baird Ltd., 1985. Courtesy of Her Majesty's Stationery Office.

clearing, he imagines as having become "a public ruin" after a bombing incident. Drawing on elements of castle and museum, his design thus reaches toward a future in which "yet another complex is imposed," when "remnants of my design will remain as monument and ruin." Hence, the "complexity of layering continues."

A few words on the selected Stormont site may be in order. After the Government of Ireland Act (1920), Northern Ireland had its own legislative and administrative powers but at first no permanent site for the government. The Presbyterian Assembly's College in Belfast was used temporarily; various estates close to Belfast city were considered; then Stormont Castle, on a two-hundred-acre demesne, was purchased by Westminster for the price of £20,000. The site itself, outside the city limits, had to be partly deforested and made accessible by new roads. The combined parliamentary and administrative building was completed in 1932. During the world war, Stormont was painted in dark camouflage, and the nearby roads were resurfaced with "bitumen, clinker and cinders" (*Parliament* 4–8). After postwar reclamation, the building housed the Northern Ireland parliament until 1972 when the administration reverted to Westminster.

Aerial view of Stormont, Parliament Building. Illustration from informational booklet printed by W. & G. Baird Ltd., 1985. Courtesy of Her Majesty's Stationery Office.

The Northern Ireland Parliament Building stands on an elevated site at Stormont, about 5 miles from the centre of Belfast. The main approach to the building is by a broad processional avenue three-quarters of a mile long and rising some 180 feet, planted on 300 acres. At the top of the avenue, a staircase of granite steps 90 feet wide leads up to the building itself, 365 feet long, 164 feet wide and 70 feet high, rising to 92 feet at the centre of the main facade.

It was designed by Mr (later Sir) Arnold Thornely, FRIBA, of Liverpool in the Greek Classical tradition, with an exterior facing of Portland stone above a plinth of local granite from the Mountains of Mourne. From the top of the building Britannia and her guardian lions look out over the south-eastern suburbs of Belfast and Castlereagh, while on the pediment below her a group of statuary represents Ulster presenting the golden flame of loyalty to Britain and the Commonwealth. Immediately over the main entrance is the Royal Coat of Arms. In general, however, the building relies for its effect more on its sense of proportion than on any external embellishment. (*Parliament* 3)

It is into this centralized, deeply administrative, colonial history that Haukos inserts his design.

Haukos imagines his plan entering the field of conflict, debate, and negotiation that marked the early 1990s. Referring to chaos theory, Haukos agrees with James Gleick and Norman Packard that information is generated by systems that create new links, new connections, new information. His notion of "free architecture," which lends itself to dialectic and which is intended to stimulate the production of fresh information through debate, rests on a design process that makes use of "ambiguity, a complexity of accumulated information, random sketching, and most importantly an intuitive leap, a chaotically driven process to generate a new architectural expression." In Haukos's plan, the old government signifies an "Absolute View," while an aspirational social democratic pluralism produces the "Serial View." He provides a standard classical style portal with parallel lengths

The Senate Chamber of Stormont, Parliament Building. Illustration from informational booklet printed by W. & G. Baird Ltd., 1985. Courtesy of Her Majesty's Stationery Office.

behind for the ruins of the old capital. Then he maps the "planned remnants" added to this assemblage: THE DRIVE, PLATFORMS, SHIELD, and INNER CHAMBERS. Hence we find an "absolute view"—the perspective of the old government—and weaving through it the "serial view" of a pluralist present. "The first response to the site was to break the symmetrical Beaux Art plan [note the symmetrical, columnar Stormont ruins] with the serial drive (DEVICE) and to warp the axis to create a complexity of views off into the landscape. Always a view through. Beyond."

Using the pattern language approach, Haukos isolates specific building elements: wall, jaw, shield, platform, fish, coilsnake, pyramid, obelisk, and panther. The house itself is thus a panther hood superimposed on a coiled snake chamber on a platform island. There is also a fish chamber within a pyramid on another platform island, a public shield with an oppositional "jaw" (home of the opposition party's chambers), an insistently aggressive, open mouthing of floors that both facilitates interior design and delimits spatial authority. The wall allows parliament a measure of privacy while also presenting a barrier punctuated by numerous, nonhierarchized points of entry for public forums, debates, and display—all signifying the "dichotomous necessity of government to be both removed from society yet responsible to society." The enclosed sector of the building is modeled from a Celtic brooch, which opens into the elements of embrace, shield, and puncture. The formal shielding actually constitutes the concavity of embrasure, while the "wall becomes fragmented segments caught between public areas." Haukos intuitively composes the building with both a monumental public identity and overt vulnerabilities and privacies. He uses different colors to mark contained spaces, public forum spaces, controlling party spaces, remnants of previous structures, and iconic elements of design in order to map a complex spatial play. This ludic design builds into parliamentary modalities the possibilities of new information-processing and information-generation for the future.

Surrounded by both wild and formal gardens, the parliament building insists on its role as mediator and generator, as it does on the viewer's position in front of the building and deep within its interior. Given the fish-eye perspectivalism of the drawings, the work creates its own sense of threshold space. These drawings (with their "utopics of outsiderliness") thus have

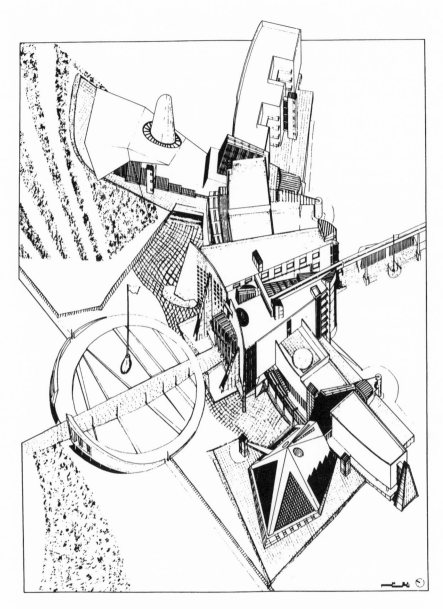

Plan for a new Irish parliament building. Drawing by Mark A. Haukos.

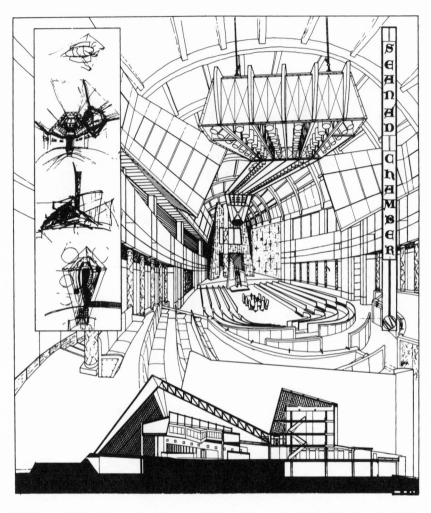

The Seanad Chamber in plan for a new Irish parliament building. Drawing by Mark A. Haukos.

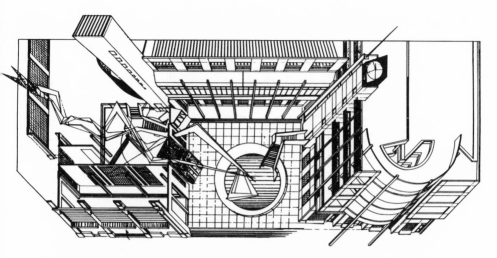

Plan for a new Irish parliament building. Drawing by Mark A. Haukos

an Adornan "surplus" that encourages critique of Irish spaces and designs in their present as well as historical forms. Further, the use of a Celtic brooch in the heart of the parliamentary chambers takes on marvelous tactile resonances when we turn to Irish folklore. According to tradition, at Navan Fort near the town of Armagh, Queen Macha used a brooch to draw a circle-map of the structure to be built there. Both territorial and mobile, Macha's brooch designates status and power. Recirculating for a contemporary viewer the meanings associated with the world-famous Tara Brooch, the Haukos design also draws on the National Museum's display of existing artifacts, including the Ardagh Chalice, which urges viewers to conflate religion with ornamentation. Does the cultural coding that has accumulated around these objects innoculate them against the infectious diseases of capitalism, thereby rendering them still pure and virtuous objects for architectural expansion? There is no way to position Haukos's design on the side of any particular and rigidly held right or wrong; as an aesthetic object and pure projection into an imaginative, utopian future, the design remains charmingly successful in exploiting the ornamental ethos for purposes that hope to transcend the commercial and regulative. His multiple design references do not create a claustrophobic semantic closure but insistently question one form with another toward creating new constellations of promenade and of meaning. They stand open to interplay with a variety of environmental and cultural elements.

In *A Thousand Plateaus*, speaking of the relation of desire and assembling, Deleuze and Guattari argue that "jewelry has undergone so many secondary adaptations that we no longer have a clear understanding of what it is. But something lights up in our mind when we are told that metalworking was the 'barbarian,' or nomad, art par excellence, and when we see these masterpieces of minor art. These fibulas, these gold or silver plaques, these pieces of jewelry, are attached to small movable objects; they are not only easy to transport, but pertain to the object only as object in motion. These plaques constitute traits of expression of pure speed, carried on objects that are themselves mobile and moving." In fact, this discussion is part of the Deleuzoguattarian consideration of the nomadic war machine, and they argue that jeweled designs have to do ultimately with nomadic weaponry: "Jewels are the affects corresponding to weapons, that are swept up in the same speed vector" (Deleuze and Guattari 401). The state apparatus insists on an ethos of sedentary work, of definitive tools, while the nomadic elements conflate signs and tools into a single affective assemblage that we read as jewelry. Dialectically, Haukos appropriates nomadic art for housing a complex, in-flux state apparatus.

In fact, in an imaginary space suspended between inside and outside, Haukos poises an assemblage for an assembly, negotiated, dialectical, unfolding, with rich concrete particularity that defies the administrations of society, whether nationalist, unionist, socialist, or other. At the boundaries between interior and exterior, of course, liminal expansion joints typically require play. This important structural feature finds expression and energy in the mind of the observer, whose job it is to introduce "play" or nomadic dimensionality-in-assemblage toward the end of reconfiguring both culture and administrative policy. By way of an instructive comparison, Tschumi's architectural drawings take place within an equally and even more complex theoretical matrix. Tschumi views drawn constructions as "operations" that "have their own internallogic—they are not aimlessly pluralistic" but cannot be explained in terms of closed systems and a fixed notion of order. Rather, his buildings push against the very concept of limits, insisting on their undecidable relation to and situation of being affected by what is putatively outside. With one eye on Derridean deconstruction, Tschumi emphasizes that there is always an "old fabric" undergoing dismantling in order to get at alternative concepts of structure. His drawings are thus "constituted by traces of another construction." According to Anthony Vidler, Tschumi also nods in the direction of Roland Barthes, choosing to create texts rather than works. In this sense, his buildings are not meant to be constructed and then consumed as is but are rather subject to demonstration, structural interdisciplinarity, and jouissance. Drawing on a formulation by David Carroll, Vidler calls Tschumi's work "para-architecture," meaning that it is located both "alongside of" and "beyond," constructed as neither nostalgic nor avant-garde (Tschumi 13, 15, 17–19). I believe that it is within the imaginary terrain of Tschumi's drawings that Haukos's design for an Irish parliament may be located, in all of its agile symbolizing of ongoing transformation. From Tschumi's ludic, deconstructive assembling and akin to Frampton's architecture of social critique, Haukos engineers structural change as an expressed yearning, administrative as well as migrant, vertical as well as lateral.

This concept of a new model of "functional" architecture resonates extraordinarily well with a 1976 proposal placed before the European Community by artist Joseph Beuys and writer Caroline Tisdall. They put forward a plan for a Free International University for Creativity and Interdisciplinary Research, a campus that they wanted to locate in Dublin. Clearly influenced by the deschooling movement that joined Ivan Illich to MIT, the Bauhaus, the Birmingham Centre for the Study of Contemporary Culture, and a host of alternative programs, Beuys and Tisdall proposed a think tank to combat the overspecialization they felt was at the heart of a failed "creative democracy" in Europe (Beuys). I would say that their multipoint booklet supplies a virtual text for the Haukos design. Like Frampton, they eschewed the increasing isolation and abstraction of every aspect of contemporary life. The work that they envisaged sought to energize the EC from the perspective of Ireland's peculiarly receptive marginality. In that mid-1970s time of global economic crisis, Beuys and Tisdall advanced this plan of a decentralized, dialogic unit that could take creative advantage of Ireland's so-called underdevelopment—its apparent relative freedom, at that time, from bureaucracy. On an Adornan note, the two supported an engineered, communal escape from administered culture, a structure intent on its own dissolution and replacement. They wanted to question everything from ecopollution to voting practices, from violence to futurism, from aesthetics to multinational combines, from comparative models of inquiry to spiritual growth. They applauded Ireland's "resistance to standardisation" as something Europe would do well to emulate (Beuys). With Heinrich Böll and Mary Robinson, Brian Friel and Ivor Browne, Ronald Laing and Nina Sutton among the many prominent figures on board, they sought immediate funding and temporary quarters in Robert Emmet's Milltown house, which they planned to let from the Marist Fathers before moving into the Royal Hospital at Kilmainham. They praised Dublin for its initial enthusiasm: "The interdisciplinary nature of the Free University was grasped immediately, and has found support, cooperation and willingness to participate among a wide range of professions and from people of different backgrounds to an extent quite unprecedented elsewhere" (Beuys). Although this plan was never implemented, the program's vision remains enormously seductive—a provisional map of the elsewhere sought by so many cultural analysts even today. As Zizek would have it, the elsewhere is a fantasmatic unit, a kernel of the real (in this case, composed partly of IFIs) that always returns, is always repressed, gets passed back and forth without ever fully surfacing in the complex cultural transactions between paired, mirror-staging regions. Adventurous critical regionalist architecture is one way of responding to various silenced narratives and ineffable objects of desire. It is a way of thinking of the people-claimed region as a mediation between thresholds and elsewheres yet to be mapped.

In her study of Jean Baudrillard, Sharon Willis maintains that the need now is "not to re-establish 'perspective,' but to theorize and inhabit a mobile, shifting analytical perspective—a series of positions that always temporarily fix or install a relation and a reference, out of which analysis emerges" (Willis 66). Over the past eight hundred years, many have glimpsed this mobile interzone, from the builders of the Gallarus Oratory to Paul Durcan, from Cistercian architects to Mark Haukos, from migrating famine victims to Kenneth Frampton. In Ireland, that assembled space-between has long been called the fifth province, an imaginary property owned by all the children of the nation, Protestant and Catholic, Orange and Green, rich and poor, male and female. In Iowa, a close approximation might be the concept of the five seasons: in calling itself "the city of five seasons," Cedar Rapids emphasizes an idealized midwestern sense of time as space, in which an imaginary and projected diversity is the key element in a virtuous, inherently rural lifestyle. I would want to claim the space-between as a particular rhizomic connection between the fifth province and the five seasons, a touchstone for the critical regionalist methodology I propose.

Recycling the Heartland

Assemblages are passional, they are compositions of desire. Desire has nothing to do with a natural or spontaneous determination; there is no desire but assembling, assembled, desire. The rationality, the efficiency, of an assemblage does not exist without the passions the assemblage brings into play, without the desire that constitute it as much as it constitutes them.
DELEUZE AND GUATTARI

For a critical regionalist architectural design to exert a positive impact on a community, the building has to be supported by a flexible economic infrastructure with congenial social aims, a particular configuration that draws on a comparative paradigm to mandate a dialectical relation of, say, a family farm and an administrative symbolic. The intersection of artifacts with governance and a market economy can produce useful or harmful effects on the world's heartlands, depending on the nature of existing rural policies, especially those having to do with individual ownership, corporate farming, value-added processing, food safety, watershed management, environmental responsibility, and overall land stewardship. Regardless of what may be built on the land or in its name within the metropolis, the territory itself has to be divided among more rather than fewer owners if working populations are to benefit communally from any sort of aesthetic-political-critical intervention.

Complicating this need—immeasurably influencing the force of a critical regionalist social aesthetic—is a recurrent cycle of agrarian economic collapse during which land that has been previously distributed or made available to a low-income population is recovered by large-scale landlords and lending institutions. Linking rural Ireland and the American Midwest within a single analysis enables a startlingly clear view of this agricycle made up of an individual family's settlement on available land, eventual loss of ownership or tenancy, migration to new frontiers, the reinstalling of economic aspiration within the family unit, the recovery of fiscal viability by the individual farmer, and a reasonably rapid decline into a new cycle of dispossession and despair. The profits generated by this transregional machinery rarely if ever remain in the local community to sustain an infrastructure capable of surviving through natural or induced disasters in the farming economy. Although it is beyond the scope of my argument to pursue in minute detail this reorganization of ownership, it is necessary to be emphatic about this historical cyclicality, both in Europe and in the Americas. From the perspective of a critical regionalist comparative methodology, the most poignant aspect of that history is the familial linkage that allows us to posit one generation of Irish peasants leaving the land of famine and eviction for an America of plenty, their children's initial success on the land, and their later offsprings' decline into the throes of dispossession during dust bowl crisis and depression—the same cycle recurring on the way to the 1980s crash in midwestern land values.

Hence it is not enough, for example, to observe similarities between victims of the Great Famine and those dispossessed during the Great Depression. What must be brought consistently into the foreground is the fact that these unfortunate farmers are in fact the same people, divided only by a few generations; the dust bowl Okies descended from famine migrants moved ever westward by agricultural crisis and the subsequent reclaiming by larger ownership of their tenure on any land whatsoever.

Along the way, of course, the railroads were built, canals were created, the land was cleared, and production soared to meet old demands and create new ones; a thriving market economy established itself in the wake of migrating farmers both then and now. And such tokens of ease and progress readily capture a culture's consciousness. The emotional economy that results from agrimarket boom and bust creates utopian projections that are themselves complex representational assemblages profoundly underwriting social history, ethnography, and the expression of these contradictions in provincial self-representation. Sometimes, projecting the heartland has been the only mass psychic defense possible against the market's endless recovery of profits. This chapter begins to examine such representational assemblages and their contexts of both economic and psychological crisis across paired regions.

A HEARTLAND ARCHETYPE

David Anderson has argued that the paradigmatic literary rendering of the midwestern experience is *Adventures of Huckleberry Finn* (1884).[1] Poised on the western edge of the Mississippi River at St. Petersburg (Hannibal), Missouri, Huck travels to the edge of Illinois and back, rides down the Mississippi toward the south and returns—eventually following the American historical path westward when he leaves the comforts of Aunt Sally's and decides to "light out for the Territory." While residing in Aunt Sally's house, Huck finds himself pursued by the baroque metropolitan civilization represented alternately by Miss Watson's nagging persnicketiness and Tom Sawyer's romantic fantasies. Outside the St. Petersburg confines, he faces both the pleasures of living on the edge of civilization and the recurrent brutality of his alcoholic, incorrigibly abusive father. Will Huck choose settled townlife or the nomadic frontier? He resolves these opposing claims by heading westward, sweeping around or through—the ambiguity is calculated—the geopolitical space encompassing much of the contemporary American heartland, some of it in the zone created by 1787 ordinance as the Old Northwest Territory and some of it in the Louisiana Purchase of 1803.

There is something eerily representative about Huck's movements and emotions. Consider that when he wonders if Pap has returned to town and spent Huck's found-fortune, which the Judge has invested, Jim reveals that Huck's errant progenitor has been dead for quite a while. It is knowing his father's death—rather than the mere fact of having monetary security— that allows Huck to move further into the heartland toward the utopian dream of an uncomplicated, fully satisfying life beyond the sometimes magnetic pull of town-culture. The image of the dead father that occurs here, as it does in "Loosestrife in Ballyferriter" and in many of the rural representations that I generically chain together in this book, forms the subject of chapters 5 and 6. At this point, I want merely to note the emancipatory power of Pap's demise and to recall that like many of the migrants who passed into and beyond the Midwest during the nineteenth century, Huck traveled frequently and finally beyond tracking in his quest for something better than the life he had already experienced in either town or countryside.

If we assume that around the year 1880 Pap Finn was approximately the fifty-odd years old that Huck says he is, we can imagine that Pap's birth in the 1830s brought the infant Finn into the arms of a family of recent or soon-to-be Irish immigrants.[2] Not that Pap speaks with an Irish accent or says anything to link him to an Irish or even European background, but he fits unmistakably into a demographic and stereotypical picture that not only echoes in Huck's own planned expedition to the Territory but also recalls the circumstances feeding the settlement of the American frontier. An animating dream of utopian self-determination, an experience of harsh social conditions in both the town and the countryside of the North American continent, a performance of drunken deviltry to express the relentless battering by circumstance, the displacing of a cruel but accustomed paternal order by business mechanisms that guarantee a 6 percent income but threaten to smother the investor—these are the elements of a complicated cycle of boom and bust that describes the intimately linked historical and economic role of the heartland and of Ireland in Huck's time. An adequate history, a socially useful cultural studies, requires a vision not only of Huck as town boy, not only of Huck as feral child, not only of Huck as frontiersperson, but also of Huck's complex relation to investment capitalism and the desire for personal autonomy. Again and again we encounter a symbolic order seemingly split between a tangibly human patriarchy and an authoritarian market.

The Geopolitics of the Midwest

In *The Midwest and the Nation*, Andrew Cayton and Peter Onuf discuss the hopeful pioneer's conflict in this way: while many migrants sought to recreate in the heartland their abandoned European lifestyles, they were also the vehicle of the international market economy and its patterns of extension (30–31). Hence, the pull between local self-determination and a growth ideology imploded again and again in western history, and even today we have collectively done little to resolve or even address this contradiction. Cayton and Onuf help us to see that the Old Northwest, while becoming a world-class agricultural center, uneasily juggled an atomistic pluralism with a profound commitment to the market economy, or what we might see as a local utopianism with an international axis of desire.

The psychoeconomic pull and counterpull were often expressed in terms of cultural values. By the 1850s, nativists were anxious to restrict immigration into the United States, feeling that the fundamental values of an evolving America—hard work, family, community, piety, temperance—were coming under attack. Under the putative influence of Protestant-identified mores but more realistically caught up within the production needs of the transcontinental railroad system, a full-fledged market economy had emerged midcountry. Farmers who were in tune with this economy viewed themselves as natives following from east to west a receding frontier somehow synonymous with capitalist acumen and virtuous behavior. In strong contrast to the eighteenth-century migration of Ulster Protestants to Canada and America, the nineteenth-century influx of Irish Catholics engendered alarm in the hearts of those who increasingly saw themselves as the salt of the American soil. Cayton and Onuf document the process by which the early nineteenth-century, Midwest-associated commercial classes not only religiously pursued self-improvement schemes but also strove to indoctrinate in-migrating Irish and German Catholics whose lifestyles were perceived as deviating from commercially favorable behavior (58). Education, temperance, and religion became tough fields for the contestation of traditions, beliefs, individual prosperity, and group ideals.

The resulting debates hardened into the class-based interests of American political life; as Daniel Walker Howe confirms, Whigs/Republicans prized bourgeois social homogeneity while Democrats made themselves more available to the diversity of lifestyles embraced by, among other groups, Irish-Catholic immigrants (Cayton and Onuf 77). At midcentury, the alignment of wealth and labor that supported the growth of the Democratic Party on the East Coast gave way to a vast Republicanism united in its embrace of the market economy, its self-proclaimed dedication to the Protestant work ethic, its interweaving of middle-class morality and bourgeois aspiration, and its suspicion of foreigners. Party competition signaled the

"County Antrim Girls." From Robert Lynd, *Home Life in Ireland,* 1909.

binding into American politics of positions on family values, faith in the
banking system, and the market. What Cayton and Onuf help us to appre-
ciate is how fully the American Midwest became identified with middle-
class belief structures and thus with the Republican party that in fact achieved
self-definition at first by attacking immigrant groups for their putative moral
and economic deviance. Overall, the political tug-of-war in the nineteenth
century involved a history of class demarcation, ethnic slurring, nativist
Know-Nothingism, and refusal of American heterogeneity (Cayton and
Onuf 85, 87).

By the end of the century, however, "many midwesterners no longer
sought identity and meaning in the celebration of progress, or in wars against
alternative cultures, or in the excise of their own characters. Rather, midwestern culture expressed itself in the making of myth, imagining a frontier
era in which people—middle-class, midwestern people—had once been the
powerful progenitors of a new civilization." This imaginary complex rendered the small-farm lifestyle and its chosen values increasingly irrelevant
to the consolidation empowered by international capital. It is this regional

myth—constructed after the fact—that we now reanimate every time we speak of the heartland; its nostalgic ideology flourished only because the Midwest's much advertised utopia of abundant land and endless opportunity for family farmers had already been undermined by market pressures to recover and consolidate capital, land, and identity (Cayton and Onuf 121–23). With the closing of the frontier in 1890, agrarian paradisal desires were relocated firmly in an imagined past.

It is important to note, however, that only twenty years before the frontier's ending, the Iowa Board of Immigration had printed sixty-five thousand copies of a pamphlet called *Iowa: The Home for Immigrants, Being a Treatise on the Resources of Iowa, and Giving Useful Information with Regard to the State, for the Benefit of Immigrants and Others* (1870). These brochures were printed in English, German, Dutch, Swedish, and Danish. Land grant railroad companies interested in seeing their holdings developed by potential freighters of farm products shipped the pamphlets to the East gratis. In fact, in 1870 not only Iowa but also the states of Minnesota, Kansas, Nebraska, and Wisconsin were "especially active . . . in the promotion of foreign immigrants" (*Iowa* i–ii, iv). The idealized portrayals of the region make inspiring reading. For instance, described as "the richest and loveliest portion of the North American continent," Iowa is presented as "remarkably uniform" and possessed of "a perfect system of drainage" (*Iowa* 9, 14). A prospective pioneer toiling on his rocky or boggy plot could read about rich soil, ample rivers, well-stocked lakes, and the constant improvements of canals and railroads to complement the fertile prairie grasslands covering nine-tenths of Iowa's surface. Stone, marble, and gypsum could be mined in abundance. Peat, lead, and other metals were evident. More than this, what would be music to the ears of a famine-phobic European farmer was the statement that Iowa had "never failed at the return of harvest to give her people bread," and corn could be grown "with less than half the labor usually required on the worn-out soils,[3] or among the stones and stumps, with which the Eastern farmer has to contend" (*Iowa* 28, 29). Whether a farmer sought to grow Irish potatoes or to raise livestock, Iowa provided auspicious terrain. Further, given the availability of railroads across the state, "The farmer of southern Iowa, with judicious management, can hardly fail to become independent from the profits on his hogs and corn; while the

farmer of the northern portion of the State is equally fortunate in his superior advantages for raising wheat and cattle." Climatologically sound, envi-
ably gorgeous, Iowa offered inexpensive, railroad-owned grant lands for
sale—from five to fifteen dollars per acre in lots of forty acres or more, with
ten years' credit available at 6 percent interest (*Iowa* 32, 48).

These paradisal pamphlets—following in the path of earlier utopian book-
lets such as Albert M. Lea's *Notes on the Wisconsin Territory* (1836), *Galland's
Iowa Emigrant* (1840), and Major John B. Newhall's *Sketches of Iowa or the
Emigrant's Guide* (1841)—outlined in considerable detail the means by which
individuals could acquire their own land. As the Burlington and Missouri
River Railroad claimed, "All will readily see that these several methods of
disposing of these lands adapt themselves to the circumstances of all—to
men of limited means, as well as those who have the ready cash. Availing
himself of the advantages of the *long credit* terms, the poor man may secure
a home, and long before the expiration of the ten years, pay for it, after
having supported his family and improved his farm. He gets really a loan of
so much money-value, for which the land itself is security" (*Iowa* 48). The
plan offered by the Des Moines Valley Railroad prompted this commentary: "It has often been demonstrated in Iowa that the first crop of wheat, at
$1.00 per bushel, will pay for the land at $10 per acre, as well as for breaking and fencing." Meanwhile, government lands were available outright
for a cash fee of between $1.25 and $2.50 per acre to legitimate homestead-
ers, up to a maximum of half the standard quarter section, eighty acres
(*Iowa* 56, 58).

How were the migration and initial planting to be accomplished? The
Iowa Board advised that if a farmer moved to the region around April, he
could build a home suitable for the summer in two or three days and then
turn to planting an initial crop of sod corn: "the corn is planted by dropping it in the furrows after the plow, or by cutting into the sod with an axe
or hatchet, dropping the seed into the crevice and covering it by stepping
upon it. It requires no further attention until it is harvested" (*Iowa* 69–70).
Even given the advantages of planting in a virgin soil thick with vegetable
mold within the context of an insect environment not yet distorted by mono-
crop technology, this planting program sounds idealized, if only in its
neglect of meteorology. In concert with this utopian mise-en-scène, the

The Richest Crop in the World.
Iowa Leads, Others Follow.

It's been said, there's a spirit found here like no other place on earth. A spirit that knows no boundaries. No limits. A spirit that knows no end to what a person can do. To other Americans, people from here "come from good stock." Raised from generation to generation with honest values. A firm handshake. A willingness to help. And a work ethic that never knows when to quit. The Heartland. It's where people from the Dakotas, Minnesota, Iowa and Wisconsin call home. And so do we.

There Are No Boundaries.

We're Metropolitan Federal. The Heartland's bank. Since 1926, we've been helping generations of families in the Heartland get started. Today, we're one of the strongest and most secure savings banks in the country with more than $4.5 billion in assets. You'll find Metropolitan Federal offices in nearly 110 communities. From Williston to West Des Moines. And we're growing. Because in the Heartland, there's a spirit found here like no other place on earth. A spirit that knows no boundaries.

The Heartland's Bank

METROPOLITAN
FEDERAL BANK

(above) Iowa's utopian self-image finds expression in this 1-cent postcard bearing a 1908 postmark from Shambaugh, Iowa. The reality behind the image may be detected in the message on this vintage postcard: "Miss Edna Kime. Well I was glad to hear from you but verry sorry to hear you was not feeling good. I expect Joe thinks if you could of got holt of them lines when Vera's team run off you would of stoped them. Awating an answer respectively F.C."

(below) Advertisement for Metropolitan Federal Bank, *Des Moines Sunday Register,* 22 September 1991, 6A. Note the use of an ear of corn as a margin. Courtesy of First Bank System for Metropolitan Federal Bank, Minneapolis.

"golden opportunity" for young people to become "wealthy, influential, and independent farmers" was strongly and repeatedly stated. And the pamphlet drafters were entirely conscious of the contrast with consolidated Euro-landholdings. England is presented as being owned by "less than *one six hundredth* of the population"—a compelling opposition to the Midwest's much touted equal opportunity for all: "We now have in the United States an aggregate of over *five and a half millions* of land owners, not less than *four millions* of whom are agricultural freeholders. . . . In no other country in the world have so large a proportion of the citizens an absolute interest in the soil, and indeed, history furnishes no parallel. This distribution of the landed proprietorships of the nation places in the hands of a free people the complete control of their own political and social destiny" (*Iowa* 69, 68). These promises move well beyond claims for life, liberty, and the pursuit of happiness; they virtually guarantee economic success to those willing and able to take on the most primitive farming operation. As John Murray suggests, this was "the garden of the world."

The concept of utopia, like the idea of the five seasons, the fifth province, or the heartland, is a peculiarly unstratified term. It does not factor into its cultural calculations unanticipated climatic challenges, uneven development, or striations in access to social power along lines of nationality, gender, race, and class. But as Cayton and Onuf persuasively document, by the turn of the twentieth century, the values that European migration had been thought to endanger had already receded into an idealized past; the writers who made up early twentieth-century regionalism collectively produced a postmortem on that heartland culture, and already puzzled over the apparent slipping away from simpler and more wholesome times. Nostalgia for the frontier and its largely agrarian fundamentalism expressed itself both in repeated lament for what had been squandered and in satire over the contemporary mores that had arisen in a mature market economy. Somehow the machinery of the Protestant capitalist enterprise had not only assimilated alternative communities, German, Irish, and otherwise, into the larger and more homogeneous system of American customs but had also begun to promote a reconsolidation of wealth in the United States, ironically and immediately following the largest land giveaway in human history.

One of the first and best explicators of the midwestern experience was Hamlin Garland, whose memories of farm life were constructed in two perceptual modes, one purely nostalgic and Wordsworthian, the other partially but deeply brutalized. As unable to reconcile these image-sets as American history has been, Garland voiced them in alternating rhythms. For all of his efforts to combine the two terms into a single logic, Garland's most intimate writing gives us beautiful moments and disastrous ones in shocking alternation, a quintessentially healthy prairie-world populated by starving wraiths, a farmyard full of vindictive mega-insects through which merry children caper toward magical, Mississippi valley cornfields.

His first book, *Main Travelled Roads*, has a grim air of naturalistic detail that created an uproar among western op-ed writers and critics, many of whom angrily rejected his depictions: as he notes, "Statistics were employed to show that pianos and Brussels carpets adorned almost every Iowa farmhouse." Garland was erroneously attacked as a mean-spirited East Coast writer. "True," Garland notes of this early 1890s period, "corn was only eleven cents per bushel at that time, and the number of alien farm-renters was increasing. True, all the bright boys and girls were leaving the farm," but these things were interpreted as "signs of prosperity and not of decay"; the move to town was thought by outsiders to signal not disenchantment but merely the success of farmers grown wealthy from the soil (Garland, *Main* 415, 416).

In *A Son of the Middle Border* (1914), while he narrates the story of his life and his family's pioneer farming, Garland never loses sight of the West's dwindling supply of unclaimed land, along with urban bankers' ever-tightening grasp on the American dream of individual ownership. However beautiful the rugged landscape, he saw more and more clearly the loneliness of life on the plains, the ever-greater difficulty of purchasing land from speculators once government giveaways were used up: "I now perceived that these plowmen, these wives and daughters had been pushed out into these lonely ugly shacks by the force of landlordism behind. These plodding Swedes and Danes, these thrifty Germans, these hairy Russians had all fled from the feudalism of their native lands and were here because they had no share in the soil from which they sprung, and because in the settled communities of the eastern states, the speculative demand for land had hindered them from acquiring even a leasing right to the surface of the earth" (Garland, *Son* 368).

At that time, the laboring life on the family farm in America had yet to be depicted by one of its own, and Garland was encouraged by sympathetic editors to go forward. To this end, he reimaged the agrarian experience as a kind of "warfare," a "sordid monotony" punctuated by pain, despair, failure, dirt, mechanical routine, and early death. These realities did not negate the "tinkle of the bobolink's fairy bells" and the "mystical sheen" of the undulating prairie (Garland, *Son* 371, 375, 365); rather, both ends of the rural-experiential spectrum took shape as ancient contradictions made increasingly visible across North America's enormous canvas as the Old World intersected with the New. The glories of nature did not dispel the struggle of farm life as it had been constituted on the middle border; instead, those splendors clouded an outsider's ability to perceive agrarian suffering as such, to listen to rural complaint as anything more than what often seemed to be the eternal, worldwide lamenting of farmers.

Garland was determined to educate the nonfarming sector about the extreme hardships endured in the countryside. In *A Son of the Middle Border*, Garland describes both good and bad times in early settlements in Wisconsin, Iowa, and the Dakotas. A trip to California with his family enables him to work the pioneer/settlement story to its teleology, to display for his readers often trial-ridden moments in Montana, Arizona, and the far West. Finally, leaving his birth family, Garland moved to Boston and New York, following the trail of culture and literary success, until the Columbian Exposition brought him back to that most middle of midwestern cities, Chicago. Throughout the compelling narrative of his looped peregrinations, Garland describes not only the treacheries and drudgeries of farm life but also the values, beauties, and expectations that have always generated massive westward migration.

Garland cannily identifies the precise ideological claims that sent his father ever forward in search of better lands, bigger farms, and a profitable or just break-even lifestyle. For instance, the ideal of service on the part of young and old prevails in the Garlands' lives (Garland, *Son* 31); loyalty to family, even as the distances among kin become ever larger, motors their collective history; even so, pride in fiscal accomplishment and ineradicable shame over economic failure push people toward the sunset and drive wedges between individuals and their birth communities. In Garland's work, the belief prevails that the common person can and should achieve ownership of the land; resentment of the hard life created in part by monied interests at the expense of farmers is voiced only in collective protest situations, never by the lone individual critic, least of all by the pioneer women whose rugged lives Garland himself draws the line at describing in graphic fullness; above all, the "Golden West" (Garland, *Son* 463) is regarded as more important and always brighter than current circumstances east of the middle border. Garland giftedly unfolds the contradictions in this mixed bag of received beliefs and displays for a largely urban reading public the biased view of the American adventure that they had been sold and that even those living out the agrarian contradictions clung to in the grimmest extremities. Garland records his thoughts as an adult in the 1890s: "All my schooling had been to migrate, to keep moving. 'If your crop fails, go west and try a new soil. If disagreeable neighbors surround you, sell out and move—always toward the open country. To remain quietly in your native place is a sign of weakness, of irresolution. Happiness dwells afar. Wealth and fame are to be found by journeying toward the sunset star!' Such had been the spirit, the message of all the songs and stories of my youth" (Garland, *Son* 437–38).

These contradictions find clear expression in two songs that Garland's family would sing around the fire. The first was a ballad of emigration in dialogue form, a husband complaining that Colorado land is more fertile than his current unprospering fields, his wife replying "Oh, stay on the farm and you'll suffer no loss, / For the stone that keeps rolling will gather no moss." Garland's father much preferred the second song, a stirring musical call to travel, which reasoned, "When we've wood and prairie land, / Won by our toil, / We'll reign like kings in fairy land, / Lords of the soil!"[4] Garland affirms,

> The significance of this song in the lives of the McClintocks [his mother's Scottish family] and the Garlands cannot be measured. It was the marching song of my Grandfather's generation and undoubtedly profoundly influenced my father and my uncles in all that they did. It suggested shining mountains, and grassy vales, swarming with bear and elk. It called to green savannahs and endless flowery glades. It voiced as no other song

did, the pioneer impulse throbbing deep in my father's blood. . . . Un-
questionably it was a directing force in the lives of at least three generations of my pioneering race. . . . [I]ts pictures continued to allure my
father on and on toward "the sunset regions," and its splendid faith carried him through many a dark vale of discontent. (Garland, *Son* 44, 45,
46)

So it is that when Garland's father decides to leave Iowa and pursue the
utopian dream in the Dakotas, where he eventually farmed close to a thousand acres, the son is caught up in the spell of wonderful, powerful imagery. The pictures from songs, ballads, and stories interweave with his search
for work as a teacher. Heading into "some of the new counties in western
Minnesota," he writes of an evening when he bedded down with some Iowa
farmers and their migrating families: "It seemed to me at the moment as if
all America were in the process of change, all hurrying to overtake the vanishing line of the middle border." By the next evening, after a day riding
the train west, he finds that "the talk was all of land, land! Nearly every
man I met was bound for the 'Jim River valley,' and each voice was aquiver
with hope, each eye alight with anticipation of certain success" (Garland,
Son 244).

And yet images that might have been mined from Ireland's famine literature explosively surface in Garland's writings. His depression-era volume of poems called *Iowa, O Iowa!* (1935) oscillates between nostalgic images of fun in the fields and moving portrayals of the midwestern family
farm as a site of endless, thankless toil. For example, in "A Farmer's Wife"
we find a dialectal rendition of Kavanagh-compatible abjection:

> "Born an' scrubbed, suffered an' died."
> That's all you need to say, elder.
>> Never mind sayin', "made a bride,"
> Nor when her hair got gray.
>> Jes' say, "born 'n worked t' death";
>> That fits it—save y'r breath.
>> . . . .
>> Wasn't old, nuther, forty-six—no,
> Jest got humpt an' thin an' gray,
>> Washin' an' churnin' an' sweepin,' by Joe,

F'r fourteen hours or more a day.
    Brats of sickly children every year
    To drag the life plum out o' her.

    Worked to death. Starved to death.
Died f'r lack of air an' sun—
    Dyin' f'r rest, and f'r jest a breath
O' simple praise fer what she'd done.
    An' many's the woman this very day,
    Elder, dyin' slow in that same way.

Even so, Garland sentimentally transforms the drudgery into "those sun-lit prairie lands, / Unstained of blood, possessed of peace and plenty / Untouched by greed's all desolating hands" ("Home from the Wild Meadows"), into the amusing sights of prairie chickens and wild gophers, rattlesnakes and herald cranes, frogs and whip-poor-wills, "opalescent dawns and saffron sunsets" ("Vanishing Trails"). Finding cities to be "like fungi, unhealthy" (Garland, *Crumbling* 73), Garland spoke with special favor of the Mississippi valley, and he praised Chicago chiefly because its population came from the "splendidly American" states of Indiana, Illinois, Iowa, Wisconsin, Kentucky, and Ohio—"the real America" (Garland, *Crumbling* 176). In his poem "Corn Shadows," childhood images from the country actually interfere with the speaker's adult urban pursuits: standard tropes (the prairie as ocean, the cornfield as forest) create the remembered Iowa as a space of nostalgic interlude. In the metropolis, the virtual corn's beatific presence enables a return to early days and early ways, to a "wizardry" far surpassing that of the sultry city. Hence, precisely because Garland has remained a controversial figure over the years, it is not too much to credit him with voicing the moment when the heartland was being constructed in its current formulation.

The life of Luna Kellie, secretary of the Nebraska Farmers' Alliance and publisher of the *Prairie Home* newspaper, displays the same oscillations between joy and suffering, hope and despair, that Garland expressed. Kellie's life as a frontier child and as a farm woman in Kearney County, Nebraska, is punctuated by the sort of restless aspiration that we find in the works of Garland. When she describes her recollections of childhood, Kellie reveals the openness and resilience of a young girl, but she always understatedly registers a good deal of hardship at the same time: "Well 2 years of farming bankrupted Father so we moved off the farm without even a team. Spent the hard winter of '72 and '73 in Austin where Father worked in a round-house and developed a bad cough from his old army wound. . . . [W]e spent the summer on the east bank of the Mississippi. . . . Everyone around us had the ague and expected to have it. Mother held off until fall then got the malarial Typhoid and died" (Nelson 10). Only a paragraph separates her record of these catastrophes from Kellie's analysis of her family's having been lured west by the railroad companies. Acutely analytical, she realizes that "the minute you crossed the Missouri River your fate both soul and body was in their hand. What you should eat and drink, what you should wear, everything was in their hands and they robbed us of all we produced except enough to keep body and soul together and many many times not that as too many of the early settlers filled early graves on account of being ill nourished and ill clad while the wealth they produced was being coldly calculated as paying so much per head" (Nelson 10). Kellie fully understands the emotional effects of the westward movement: youthful hope made people happy, but when time and experience had eroded this groundwork, poverty, illness, death, and disillusionment were always waiting in the wings. In fact, by the turn of the century, Luna Kellie had ceased even to write down her exposures of the midwestern agrarian life and to take part in political agitation for change. Her health had been entirely undermined by her stressful participation in the Nebraska farmers' eternally unsuccessful efforts to recover from the banks and railroads control of their lands and lives. She closes her political memoir by saying, "I feel that nothing is likely to be done to benefit the farming class in my lifetime. So I busy myself with my garden and chickens and have given up all hope of making the world any better" (Nelson 145).

History with a Vengeance

Read against the grain of utopian aspiration, a microreading of regional interaction between Ireland and the Midwest might be said to display global cycles of economic recession that from time to time systematically clear out a given heartland and that explicitly resonate in the Irish famine, in succeeding recessions throughout the United States and Europe, and in the writings that have represented these disasters. Horizontally linked by moving populations, the Midwest and Ireland also experienced symmetrical administrative pressures. The imaginary zone sustained by hopeful, deluded family farmers was cyclically interrupted by an invasive monied symbolic. The resulting mirror-staging of agrarian regions around the world has produced a wealth of writings that echo Garland and Kellie.

Certainly there are endless sources of evidence about recession years in the Midwest; one of the most eloquent is a diary published by Iowa State University Press in its extensive Iowa Heritage Series. In *Years of Struggle: The Farm Diary of Elmer G. Powers, 1931–1936*, we find weekly and sometimes daily notations on the onset of the 1930s farm crisis. Powers never actually complains; rather, he notes from the centered perspective of Old Quietdale Farm and with clear-eyed conviction the manipulation of the agricultural community by banking interests and the essential powerlessness of fellow farmers. For instance, on 10 October 1931 he writes:

> I worked in the "back forty." It is from this field that I can see the cemetery where my grand parents and other pioneers are buried. While I was putting on my husking hook I looked over the corn fields, hundreds of acres of them over the countryside, without a down row started in them yet. And I said aloud to myself, yes this corn husking is our portion for several weeks to come. Then I thot of the ruinously low price of corn and as I looked again in the direction of the cemetery and saw the white gravestones glistening in the fall afternoon sunshine, I thot of the many, many farm men and women who had worked hard and toiled early and late and who were going into earlier graves because of these circumstances over which they had no kind of control. I do not like to keep thinking of these things and occasionally writing of them, but they are hard, cruel, bitter facts, very much with us; have been with us too long now and the scars of these days are going to show on the farms of this community for years to come. And worse than that, on the souls of the farm folks almost forever. (Grant and Purcell 9)

The year 1932 found the harvest excellent but the prices worse than ever (Grant and Purcell 15). Rumors and glimpses of the farmers' "Holiday" strike circulate through Powers's records. Dust storms come and go along with all manner of challenging weather conditions and the steady passage of neighbors' lands into the hands of banks and insurance companies. And yet in the spring of 1936, he reflects on his years in farming: "I still think no other place in the world could have brot the satisfaction to us that this piece of land has. . . . [W]e love and respect every foot of the farm" (Grant and Purcell 98). Powers's effort to figure out the best ratio of production and price persisted in his diaries, but so did the increasing note of resignation that can be found in the earlier memoirs of Luna Kellie.

Unlike Powers's diary, *The WPA Guide to 1930s Iowa* does not linger over the depression; the purpose of the guide was to describe the state's natural setting, history, cities, and features for the traveler to the Midwest. But it was New Deal money that paid the writers of this book, and a part of the milieu that could not be utterly ignored was the early spring migrancy of tenant farmers across the land. In fact, the guide cites a presidential commission's report that farm tenancy was steadily on the rise during the 1930s: "In Iowa tenancy has risen steadily from 23.8 percent in 1880 to 49.6 percent in 1935," a number not including either heavily indebted owners or the "cash renters" that they sometimes turned to for fiscal stability. Describing a scene from which the writer removed the crying children and neglected, eroded lands, the guide says, "Trucks and wagons crowded with furniture rumble over the frozen roads and tired herds of cattle and sheep trudge in their wake. Load after load jolt past the farm houses, stretching out like a gypsy caravan going on to camp elsewhere for a brief time . . . hoping that the new farm will be a little better than the last one" (*WPA* 65, 67). Similarly, Bogue's classic study, *From Prairie to Corn Belt*, reports both that pioneers to Iowa and Illinois often began farming on a tenancy basis before buying their own land, and that some owners later lost their lands and had to become tenants again (13). The full-circle effect of profit reclamation could not have been more emphatic as landowning repeatedly gave way to the perils and poverty of sharecropping.

That process continued throughout the settlement of the frontier and on into the current century. The 1857 depression was succeeded by both the Civil War and the recessionary 1870s. Following the 1893 panic over gold and silver standards, the "Golden Age of Agriculture" lasted from the late 1890s through 1920, with high production after World War I eventually leading to a glutted market. Farm income fell by 50 percent; the crash of 1920 occurred. In the aftermath, the Farm Bloc was formed in Congress; still the 1920s saw not only "urban prosperity" but also "rural depression" (Sage 254, 260, 271), culminating in the hard times of 1929 to 1932. True, bank failures in 1931 led to the protests of Milo Reno and the Farmers' Holiday Association and to the salvage operations of the New Deal. Under Franklin D. Roosevelt, Iowa's own Henry Wallace was appointed Secretary of Agriculture, and the Agricultural Adjustment Act of 1933 brought on a voluntary parity system with idled acreage to increase agricultural purchasing power (Sage 299–300). But a corps of displaced and migrant farmers had been recreated in the rural heartland while the surplus value they generated was siphoned off by the metropolis. The end result of land distribution—whether through giveaway, loan, homesteading, or auction-purchase—often turned out to be foreclosure, eviction, and corporate reclamation.

Ruth Suckow, another midwestern writer, built her massive fiction *The Folks* (1934) on the breakup of families whose European sociohistories had centered on sustaining the family farm system. As delighted as she is in representing the minute dramas of town life for the family of a well-off banker, Suckow includes moments when characters return to their mostly deserted, now tenanted family farm in search of a center in a time when children have ceased to carry forward the American dream of endless progress and a brighter agrarian future, when their lives foreground the contradictions of the American class system, and when the decline in the agrarian economy once again emits signs of impending disaster.

In fact, this 1934 saga is an Iowan version of John Steinbeck's *The Grapes of Wrath*. Rolfe and Vina, renters on the Ferguson homestead, are caught up in the depression plunge that has closed one of the banks in town and that has pushed the price of hogs below the profit level. Fred Ferguson, the nominal owner of the land and newly retired executive of the town's bank, comes to realize that he has spent a lifetime discounting the complaints of farmers, that his role as businessman had blinded him to the escalating loss of farms to insurance companies, that no one in the younger generation will work the family's land, that what had seemed the steady betterment of each decade in America will not continue indefinitely. It is clear that Fred's combination of Presbyterian and Republican faiths does not equip him to deal with the Great Depression. All that Fred can naively conclude—caught between his desire to do good and his belief that moving to town was a step up for his family, caught between an economic depression that could erase his provisions for the future and a conviction that the American family represents a superior form of social organization—is that the soil itself "was here. That was good. If folks treated it right, it would never let them starve" (Suckow 720). The novel ends at nightfall in a nostalgic, sentimental tentativeness, the family saga having narrowed to a parental couple alone in bed, uncertain about their future. As in Garland's world, the middle border holds these people, the heartland keeps them just barely in place and their dreams only nominally viable.

What *The Folks* displays most poignantly is wonderment that the dream was slipping away, a feeling of betrayal over having been lied to from the inception of America as a nation. Suckow and Garland join their voices to Steinbeck's in naming the cause of debt-driven farmers and collapsed dreams: they call this diverse, unified phenomenon monopoly, speculation, the owner men. Fred Ferguson finds himself standing with his renter "in the grip of a long slow movement of change which neither of them could comprehend" (Suckow 716). Similarly, in *The Grapes of Wrath*, Tom Joad tells Ma, "I been thinkin' a hell of a lot, thinkin' about our people livin' like pigs, an' the good rich lan' layin' fallow, or maybe one fella with a million acres, while a hunderd thousan' good farmers is starvin.'" Tom wants to organize the unemployed farm laborers to protest these conditions, to demand land redistribution. John Ford's cinematic version of Steinbeck's novel, drawing as it does on his knowledge of the Irish famine (O'Toole, *Mass* 139), goes further, posing Tom as aiming to get far enough "outside" to see what's going on, to understand the causes of his family's poverty, to locate who is making money while the Joads and Wainwrights and other migrating families starve by the road. Tom and the preacher Casy (a classic nomadic Irish descendant) work toward an external force that they have not come to understand yet but that they are determined to fight. It is interesting that Garland also asserts an Irish connection at a key moment of insight; he writes of hearing a lecture in Boston by Henry George ("Beginning his campaign in California he had carried it to Ireland, where he had been twice imprisoned for speaking his mind, and now after having set Bernard Shaw and other English Fabians aflame with indignant protest, was about to run for mayor of New York City"), and writes his fictions, under George's inspiration, against what he calls "the selfish monopolistic liars of the towns" (Garland, *Crumbling* 377, 416).

While American writers struggled to understand the etiology and cycles of agrarian economic collapse, rural Ireland saw not only a bourgeoisie arise from farming interests but also the effort in the early twentieth century to break up the larger grazing farms amidst an uncertain relation of Irish nationalism to farming interests. Still, the prevailing iconography of Irish farm crisis oscillates between images of outright starvation and depictions of tenants being forcibly evicted from their humble homes. In the 1947 British film called *Captain Boycott*, for example, director Frank Launder displays the 1880s agrarian conflict in Mayo as a story of poor Irish farmers fighting off the aggression of Olympian landlords. The historical farmers' refusal to pay rent added the word *boycott* to our shared lexicon. Irish cinema scholar John Hill has discussed this film in terms of the tension between mob violence and peaceful, collective action, but for the purposes of this inquiry it is the eviction scene that assumes supreme importance, not only echoing both factual and dramatic accounts of earlier crop failures but also foreshadowing the banker-landlord versus family farmer scenario that still punctuates both American and Irish cinema.

From 1926 onwards, Ireland saw a 30 percent or more decline in the Republic's agricultural population as family farmers were forced off the land (Munck 29). A key figure in Ireland during the early phase of this reorganization was Patrick Hogan, the minister for agriculture who in fact viewed agrarian interests as the basis of Irish identity. Irish historian Joseph Lee tells us, "He pushed through the 1923 Land Act transferring the still unpurchased holdings from landlord to tenant. He pursued a vigorous, and far from universally popular, interventionist policy to improve breeding and marketing standards." He worked against the image of inferior Irish produce that had circulated during the war. Hogan envisioned an economy fueled by prosperous farmers buying a multitude of goods. He determined to help Irish farmers reduce costs of production so they could maximize profits against variable international selling prices. But, Hogan reasoned, in order to keep other countries from boycotting Irish agricultural goods, Ireland would impose no industrial tariffs. Additionally, low taxation during Hogan's tenure meant less money for the government to spend on social services and industrial development (Lee 113).

As a result, all of Hogan's efforts to be modern, competitive, and image-conscious were not enough to sustain economic growth for the new state. To understand this situation, we have to turn to the formation of the Irish Farmers' Union in 1917. Despite its name, the middle-class union was in conflict with wage laborers on the farms who supported enhanced nationalization of the land—part of a series of movements toward land reform in Ireland that alternated with the reconsolidation of fiscal interests. In fact, there was persistent conflict, ideological and otherwise, between Irish laborers (on the farm and in industry) and farmers. After the war, the laboring classes joined the Irish General Transport and Workers Union (IGTWU) and agitated for higher wages from farmers. But those same producers were being encouraged to save money, and big graziers who purchased stock from small farmers also had cost-cutting priorities. The situation transformed advantage for one constituency into disadvantage for another because Hogan "instinctively equated 'the ordinary farmer' with the 200 acre man, when only 8000 out of 382,000 holdings belonged to this category in 1930." It is these "differences of interest within agriculture" that Lee characteristically investigates, displaying the sizable gap between platform rhetoric and sociological reality, the difference between what benefited the "strong farmer" and what benefited the country as a whole (Lee 115, 116), especially the small farmers increasingly forced off their property and into migrancy.

In a formulation that would do justice to the rhetoric of a Sean O'Casey and that would surprise many American readers accustomed to regarding the Irish diaspora as a tragic necessity strictly related to the famine, Lee rebukes the Irish for being "prepared to scatter their children around the world in order to preserve their own living standards." The emigrants followed the "golden calf" around the world, according to Lee, while at home the remainder showed themselves devoted "to the primacy of the pocket in marriage arrangements calculated to the last avaricious farthing, in the milking of bovine TB eradication schemes, in the finessing of government grants, subsidies and loans, of medical certificates and insurance claims, in the scrounging for petty advantage among protected business men, in the opportunistic cynicism with which wage and salary claims, not to mention professional fees, were rapaciously pursued." Lee charges the Irish with a spirituality that "must be defined as covetousness tempered only by sloth"

(Lee 522). Such denunciation, in the tradition of ancient satirical verse and the country rhetoric of Kavanagh and Murray, plays a central role in the literature of the Irish farm.

It is during the early 1930s that in many ways the most contradictory of writings on rural Ireland appeared. In *The Irish Countryman*, Harvard anthropologist Conrad Arensberg displays a static and idealized view of the small Irish farmer. In Ireland, Arensberg claimed to have discovered an unvarying round of work on the farm presided over by a stern patriarch, what he regarded as an "organic" and healthy system of farming within a community grounded in reciprocal obligations and cooperation. Arensberg's emphasis is on tradition, ritualized inheritance rules, and balanced social structures, all fixed by the relation of the family to their land (Arensberg 61, 67, 69–71). But this was an outsider's viewpoint. In contrast, Lee cites *The Irish Countryman* as evidence that hegemonic forces were able to turn what was actually catastrophic decline into a depiction of a static, stable society "at peace with itself." This was, he claims, a "highly selective social construction of reality" (Lee 651) that held force until the 1950s and 1960s when the conflict with reality was too great to be sustained. Extending the critique of Arensberg, Donna Birdwell-Pheasant adds that his Ireland "seems to float in a timeless void, isolated from the perturbations of modern history and disconnected from any meaningful cultural linkage with Ireland's Gaelic and British past" (206).

The oft-noted ahistoricity on Arensberg's part grows from his decision to study Irish farm life precisely in order to find the idyllic stasis of communal and familial experience. In fact, even during Arensberg's fieldwork, the situation of the farm family was considerably more flexible and dynamic than his narrow window allowed him to perceive. D. F. Hannan and R. Breen agree: they believe that Arensberg witnessed a western community that was strong and self-sustaining, but they argue that the local economy and social structure were, all things considered, of fairly recent vintage, developing within an up-cycle out of the late nineteenth-century land war and the depression conditions of the 1870s. Far from being an ancient system that had proven itself amidst an often hostile and extensive history, the small family farm system in the west of Ireland as perceived by Arensberg might better be viewed as a rather brief historical interlude within larger patterns of cyclic change. Certainly by the middle of the twentieth century the western counties were in substantial decline as farming centers. In Ireland as elsewhere, small farmers were being forced out by larger producers and by processes of consolidation.

Irish media critic Desmond Bell's commentary on *The Irish Countryman* adds an additional caveat: "Since the 1930s the study of Irish cultural relation and social structure has tended to be dominated by a . . . model drawn from an imported social anthropology." He adds that anthropologists of the 1930s imagined into being a nativist paradise in the West of Ireland with a "privileged moral status" to the rest of the country (Bell, "Cultural" 89). Oscillating between an exterior viewpoint and an Irish perspective shows us the American ethnographer as Orientalist and brings into view a situation similar to the one that Cayton and Onuf discover in the American Midwest—the projection into the past of an unmediated agrarian utopia.

In the context of America's then recent stock market crash, however, the writing of Arensberg's volume is best viewed as a symbolic resolution of American rural issues, a recreation of the wiped-out heartland family farm in a distant Ireland where it could be held within a fixed, apparently timeless tradition. Arensberg thus occupies a projective space adjacent to that of *The Quiet Man*. Having shown the nightmare side of American farming in *The Grapes of Wrath*, when he turned to *The Quiet Man*, director John Ford drew on the enduring image of Ireland that Arensberg commemorated. Although Ford directed his famous film in 1952, the story on which it was based, part of a set of interwoven tales by Maurice Walsh, dates from 1935. In contrast to Ford's cinematic redaction, Walsh's story foregrounds the slow emergence of a free republic under large graziers. In fact, Walsh's stories, in which he depicts six men and four women during the Black-and-Tan war exchanging anecdotes at a hotel in southwest Ireland, depend on a crucial, politicizing framework that the film suppresses. The storytellers include one Paddy Bawn Enright, who would become Ford's Sean Thornton. According to Walsh, Enright left Kerry at age seventeen and did not return until fifteen years had passed. Enright discovers on his arrival in Ireland "that the farm of his forefathers had added its few acres to the ranch of Will Danaher of Moyvalla" (Walsh, *Quiet* 127)—as it happens, in an unscrupulous fashion. Buying another small cottage, then, Enright spends five years having his search for quiet interrupted by his role in an IRA flying column. When Enright finally marries and his wife asks him to claim her dowry, with a mixture of historical irony and calculated indifference he merely responds mildly, "The times are hard on the big ranchers" (Walsh, *Quiet* 138). Eventually he does battle with Will and wins back the love of his wife, though in far less flamboyant fashion than in Ford's version.

The much later film by Ford presents viewers with a rural paradise in which old ways remain vital, and the only sign of Will Danaher's status as large bourgeois farmer is his use of machinery. In fact, Sean returns to Ireland to restage in the future-present his mother's nostalgic recollections in America of her reportedly idyllic birthplace. Ford beguilingly includes toward the beginning of the film a voice-over of Sean's mother speaking about her family's cottage and its roses.[5] Returning to plant some rosebushes there himself, Sean finds himself chided by his wife, who takes the viewpoint of a famine descendant that people should plant food rather than flowers. Again, we see the phenomenon of a utopian image being projected onto a region that is hard-pressed to recognize itself in the imposed, idealized fiction. Even today, the island of Ireland is expected to absorb the desires and expectations of many other societies—witness the high number of German-owned vacation cottages in Donegal—in its EU-mediated status as the last unspoiled green space in Europe.

I conclude from the contrast of American and Irish perspectives in *The Quiet Man* that at some recurring historical stress points the global story of dispossession down on the family farm gives way to a mutual transatlantic invention of the heartland. When the symbolic order supported by family farm values shows signs of cracking in one's own region, it is routine to seek that desired reality in a likely cousin region. To emphasize this point with a film of *The Quiet Man*'s vintage, one need only turn to the work of Frank Capra. A Sicilian immigrant to the United States, from a large family in which many of the children died, Capra imbibed utterly the sweet "Give me your tired, your poor" message of New York harbor. He believed that the man on the street could prosper if American—heartland—values were actualized. In his classic films, including *Mr. Smith Goes to Washington* (1939) and *It's a Wonderful Life* (1946), he gave actor Jimmy Stewart the voice of the ordinary guy—not from a moral majority of privileged middle-class people but from a mass of underemployed workers striving to purchase a modest home in spite of the machinations of wealthy bankers and powerbrokers.

It is no accident that *It's a Wonderful Life* stars Donna Reed, Iowa's postwar sweetheart. In fact, although Capra filmed this movie in California, local heartland legend has it that the filming actually took place in the Midwest. If only by default and desire, then, *It's a Wonderful Life* provides an identifying text for many midwesterners. And this movie was not Capra's only tribute to the heartland's image. When he began filmmaking, he worked for the U.S. government making World War II propaganda films. One of these shorts includes a voice-over recognizing that it is hard to get an "Iowa farmboy" to see why he should fight for small nations in Europe, followed by motivating scenes of warfare and oppression. In a sense, the target eye for Capra's oeuvre remained that Iowa farmboy, who grew up in the war-film literature to be *M.A.S.H.*'s Radar O'Reilly, hailing from Ottumwa, Iowa. It is useful to remember that Radar is the fellow that New Englander Hawkeye constantly tries to enlighten in the ways of the world while appreciating in a fatherly fashion Radar's blend of savvy efficiency: only Radar reads the G.I. paperwork in detail and, while respecting its ways entirely and fully supporting them, is also willing, when the need arises, to bend the rules—always in the name of superior situation ethics—to help his friends. Radar takes his teddy bear to Korea; he lives precisely between the Asian war zone and the midwestern farm. While doctors and generals come and go, he maintains the continuity of the operation and its sense of community. And his is the gaze that Capra wanted to shape as well as to believe in. Capra and Radar's idealized world represents a permanent elsewhere that people of diverse nationalities have nomadically sought around the globe.

Heartland Values and Cyclic Recession

Even in the 1970s and 1980s, during which yet another long-term agricultural recession held sway, the American values Capra prizes resonated in Ireland's "rural fundamentalism," rooted in the idea that farmers are the source of national democracy (Commins 52), that the family and the farmer must be preserved at all costs. Discussing the late twentieth-century crisis in family farming, Marty Strange makes a case for reconciling "farm policy with its historic rural values," which he defines as "self-reliance, frugality, ingenuity, stewardship, humility, family, neighborhood, and community" (Strange 244). Comparatively speaking, the American Midwest evokes an evolving set of codes that accumulate as a coherent but contradiction-tolerant fiction of Americanness, place, and selfhood. Iowa, for example, is not only a state in the union but also a state of mind in the American consciousness—a metaphor accentuating an amorphous traditionalism deployed in the "family"; a largely unreflective patriotism; an ethic of hard work and democratic-socialist egalitarianism; community spirit of the action-oriented, "barn-raising" sort; a commitment to "basic values"; moral, spiritual, and educational fair-dealing and loyalty to one's employer; a parsimony on principle; a verbal commitment to the myth of the family farm even in a period of agribusiness takeover; an international export-ethic and aspiration to multinational prowess; a healthy local skepticism about all such claims; and the social practices surrounding American rural and small-town life, particularly those of the community potluck supper, the church social, and the county fair. Contradictions abound here without entirely disrupting. As in Ireland, the heartland denotes a mixture of peasant (land-based) and family farm values, both forms of symbolic capital complementing the ownership of land, farm equipment, beasts, and crops. Causally weaving together patriotism, the validity and viability of tradition, and the iconic family, midwesterners continue to supply the increasingly missing pieces from their own desire to imagine the community they believe themselves to be losing.

In many ways, that projection of rural, middle-American, down-home ideology has been sustained in and returned to the heartland from all over the world, partly by default. For many, the heartland remains both the quintessence of America and a retreat from America, the return from afar of a prefabricated and cherished authenticity that has close ties to a remote and sanitized Old World. As Sharon Willis notes of Jean Baudrillard and, by implication, other European observers of America, "the US becomes the screen on which the traveler projects his own images, and fantasies, which circulate right back to him. But this exhilarating feedback circuit also discloses a stubborn referentiality. It reproduces uncannily familiar figures; these are the coded figures of imperialism, reinstating the poles of same and other through which it represents itself" (Willis 64). By such lights, the heartland is less a place than a projection back and forth of nostalgia and aspiration. These terms of relatedness form an assemblage that ties twinned regions within a utopian register while leaving them still substantially vulnerable to the consolidation protocols and administration policies of IFIs.

American farmland: "Attention developers!" 1993. Photo by Cheryl Temple Herr.

So it is that the history of agricultural life in Iowa between the 1970s and the early 1990s resonates strongly with many experiences of the rural population in Ireland. Although after World War II the prairies confidently produced the groceries that the planet needed, by the late 1970s the Midwest had become much less central to the global food market, and interest rates in the United States, along with land speculation, started a market collapse (Waller 141). Prices for grains, hogs, and other products were pushed down by government intervention. With prices lowered, in order to compete adequately the small farmer had to be as efficient and conscious of cost-benefit ratios as the big farmer, and she had to buy huge machines and otherwise raise costs of farming to attempt a new kind of fast-moving, massive operation. Those who had traditionally farmed the land-grant plot found themselves tremendously pressed to work ever-larger farms, and still they could not compete with agribusiness firms planting thousands of acres. Buying combines and other equipment to assist in the upgrading and upscaling of their farms put small operators more and more in debt. In fact, it may be said that it was the illusion of land ownership—something dear to the American mythos—that ruined the family farm. Insofar as the family farmer improved his operation by borrowing to purchase more land and equipment, the banks came to own not only the tractor but also the farm itself. Thinking that they were financing purchases in order to retain their land, many farmers literally borrowed it away—just as the 1970s oil crisis began in earnest.

There is a pronounced parallel here between the relation of American banking to American farmers, and the relation of the World Bank to third-world countries. During the inflationary period of the mid-1970s, banks received interest on loans at a rate of 18 percent. When farm crop prices and land prices zoomed up, the banks notably encouraged farmers' taking loans to purchase more and more land. When the bottom fell out of the farm market and interest fell back to 12 percent and even to 8 percent, farmers were still compelled to pay back their loans at the 18 percent interest rate. This is exactly what the World Bank has historically done to third-world countries that are not allowed to renegotiate their loans when interest rates fluctuate. Rather than pay off the principal, these countries continue to fall deeper and deeper into debt despite ever-increasing payments to the World Bank.

In the Midwest, foreclosed family farms are often resold to willing corporations. Agriconglomerate corporations farm in striking contrast to the stereotypical Iowan who lovingly attended to the land owned by his father and grandfather. The family farm way of life and the original, admirable grants that built rural prosperity in America are being systematically erased. Small farms are pushed off the map when they cannot compete for the acreages that they need to prosper. The big farm gradually encircles the smaller farms, while it also takes its chemical, seed, and equipment purchases away from local businesses. As the town's suppliers fade away, the small farmer cannot maintain ready access to tractor parts, fertilizer, feed, and seed. Banks, restaurants, hardware stores, lumber yards, blacksmiths, implement stores—these local businesses become gratuitous. The life of the local community withers. As time goes by, greater numbers of farmers hold onto their land only by carrying an additional job in town. What happens to the totally dispossessed operators? Many become employees of the corporation farm. They live in town, drive a tractor part-time, feed livestock, and draw a wage from the land that they or their neighbors used to own. Or they move to other states and other ways of life.

This scenario of rural collapse is wonderfully presented in a 1988 film, produced on location in Iowa, called *Miles from Home*. Richard Gere plays Frank Roberts, whose father had run a prizewinning farm in the 1960s, a farm so successful that when Nikita Khrushchev visited the heartland, it was this model operation, the 1959 Farm of the Year, that he inspected. By the 1980s, however, the father has died, and Frank finds himself not only in charge but also immobilized by a web of mounting debt, escalating prices, unsympathetic bankers, and meager profits on beans and corn. Charged by his society with fiscal failure while the fields and granaries around his home burgeon with carefully husbanded produce, Frank does not possess an analysis that will protect him from crushing self-blame. The fact that the stored grain has already been borrowed against in order to produce the current crop—a miniversion of the debt cycle actually perpetuated by the federal government's management of agriculture—hovers invisibly over the film until the day that the local bank manager forecloses on the operation. Frank, overwhelmed by his putative failure, burns down his home, outbuildings, and corn crop rather than turn this capital over to the powers that be; escaping into the spectacular Iowa sunset, Frank trades his readily recognizable red Ford pickup for a sleek Mercedes parked in front of the local FHA. Before twenty-four hours have passed, desperation turns to mock-heroism and euphoria as locals sympathize with and protect Frank and his younger brother from capture by the police. Rapidly becoming a sort of "Thelma and Louise Go to Iowa," *Miles from Home* depicts Frank and his brother giving an angry interview to *Rolling Stone* magazine, complete with photographs, to be called "Outlaws for the 8os": Frank explains that during the previous twenty-five years, a new combine escalated in price from $6,000 to $130,000, while the federally set price of corn rose only from $1.05 to $1.25 per bushel.

In 1991, a midwestern farm student spoke to me of a "devastated rural scene—broken parishes, tradition, community, families, plus alcoholism and abuse. In Iowa, communities are small and getting smaller." Another undergraduate told me, "I would love to live in Ireland in solitude on a small farm since farms no longer are a reasonable means of living in America." Her incorrect assumption—not an unusual fiction—is that Ireland is a heartland that does not share our conditions of takeover, desuetude, and distress. Throughout all of the cyclic projections of utopian heartland and rural paradise in Europe and in America, the ongoing family farm story is, in fact, most notable for the striking uniformity of that narrative of displacement, migration, oppression, fixed prices and soaring costs, recession/depression, reorganization of ownership, and land consolidation. It does not matter whether we watch a film of Irish agrarian crisis such as *Captain Boycott* (1947) or *The Field* (1990), or a representative of the genre set in the Midwest such as *The River* (1984) or *Country* (1984). We witness in these films the same key scene of eviction and dispossession, of confrontation between the landlord or banker with a culture that spans cousin regions and is endlessly compelled to repeat the story of its losses. Such works register the effects of cyclic recession in a dispersed but rhizomic agriculture suspended between first and third worlds, IFIs and the family farm, or as Saldívar says, "totalization and emergence."

That said, I have observed, teaching in the Midwest through recurrent farm crises, that my students can often most readily connect with Irish society at the level of economic cuts, evictions, out-migration, unemployment, and the many threats to their own bright futures. They can see, along with the postmodernist and other analyses that pertain, along with the necessary political distinctions and pluralisms to be tabulated, that both Here and There, Iowa and Ireland, suffer from disastrous economic policies that do not privilege either working-class analyses or anything approaching constructive social vision. They know viscerally that similar historical patterns prevail in both societies and that a comparative regionalist approach currently holds much promise for their own penetration of the power structures that aim to keep them in place in Iowa, to keep their peers in place in Ireland.

The Political Economy of Consolidation

Nothing less is asked of the thinker today than that he should be at every moment both within things and outside them.
THEODOR ADORNO

In assembling the story of Mount Melleray and its offspring house in Iowa, chapter 2 addressed a sacred sign-regime, vertical in its orientation between God and man, as a stabilizing force and resistant energy within the lateral movements of dispossession and emigration. This chapter builds on that distinction between horizontal and top-down systems of meaning and of administration by investigating the hierarchy of IFIs that exercise control over every aspect of contemporary life from demographics to discourse. The next chapter uses both found and forced symmetries, assemblages, and homologies to chart the psychic and narrative effects on the family farm of administered culture. The current territorializing of human society by capital manifests as a displacement of a patriarchal-agrarian imaginary by a global economy that has become our symbolic horizon. The unstable alliance between sacred economy and commercial economy that the farming monks of New Melleray have been able to maintain is registered elsewhere in this inquiry as corporate takeover and a structural alteration of the heartland's traditional, communal values into a bottom-line attention to growth-oriented, value-added processing.

A cross-regional perspective encourages local populations to gain a better sense of the world-system they inhabit and of how much of that collective experience may be called an epiphenomenon of transnational capital. In fact, what is useful in reading across structurally paired regions is less disciplinary "history" than an oscillating or dialectical microreading of interaction from two mutually enlightening spaces. As the last chapter demonstrates, comparing the political economy of rural regions in Ireland and America reveals a recurrence of crisis, sliding along in alternating rhythm with an aspirational ideology. But a more comprehensive reading is also possible, both on structural grounds, as in this chapter, and on the psycho-cultural grounds explored in the final two chapters. In this final unit of this book, I pose several kinds of assemblages to explicate the existing parities in rural communities and to suggest constructions that may be able to exercise force against administrative apparati. This process is helped along considerably by the existence of professional analysts who, in variously addressing the American Midwest and rural Ireland, have put forward the material for parallel solutions to agrarian decline.

In addition to scholarly insights we can find "ordinary" Irish farm folk deploying the American heartland as a frame of reference for their local agri-economy. Two examples will have to suffice here. In the 25–30 June 1992 issue of the *Irish Democrat*, it was reported under the headline "One Third Drop in Farming Population" that "135,000 left agriculture in the state of Iowa in the USA in the past ten years. . . . The reasons given for the decline are a slow agricultural economy, expanding farm sizes and a drop in the number of farming families" (16). This pro-farmer Irish newspaper indicates an editorial effort to pursue a connection between local and international farm communities in crisis. Similarly, the following letter to the editor appeared in the *Irish Press* in 1993 (Manifold):

> A few years ago, the following letter was sent to the Department of Agriculture in Washington D.C.
>
> "Mr friend Ed Peterson, over at Wells, Iowa, received a cheque for $1,000 from the government for not raising hogs. So I want to go into the 'not raising hogs' business next year. As I see it, the hardest part of this programme will be in keeping an accurate inventory of how many hogs I haven't raised. . . . If I got one thousand dollars for not raising 50

hogs, will I get $2,000 for not raising 100 hogs? . . . Now another thing, these hogs I will not raise will not eat 100,000 bushels of corn. I understand that you also pay farmer for not raising corn or wheat. . . . Signed John Partridge."

This letter . . . was published in *The New American*, November 16, 1992.

Irish farmers might please take note. There may be something in it for them too!

> D. Manifold, Fatima,
> 15 Dalysfort Rd., Galway

As Irish farmers know, tracing the path of similar economic constraints across worldwide rural communities reveals not only interconnected cycles of agrarian boom and bust but also an ideology of capital consolidation pursued from the fifteenth century to the present. So it is that today multinationals not only set prices and sell goods but also take a strong hand in designing governmental policy for all aspects of economic life throughout the world. The endless recolonization of politically liberated third world states by transnational business insures that cash flow is always toward the same integration of power brokerage. In a sense, family farmers have become an off-the-chart example of use, abuse, exploitation, and economic dependency. These international social forces in their repetitious persistence have marked cultural experience and representation in strictly comparable ways in the two sites that I pose as cousin regions.

Lousy Fare

Historically, Britain deterred economic development and selectively exploited both resources and production in parts of the empire beyond the center. In the British Isles, where arable land has always been at a premium, numerous enclosure procedures wrested control from those who produced crops and garnered power for larger and larger graziers, mostly in the interests of mega-wool producers. The Irish economy, a victim of "dependent development" (Munck 1–2), has consistently been manipulated to satisfy the desires of absentee English landlords, English manufacturers, and Anglo-continental traders and bankers. Quite apart from nineteenth-century famine conditions, Irish farmers suffered losses on the basis of this manipulation.

Because this chain of events has echoed in the American Midwest, where European migrants have found the continuing coexistence of heartland idealism and recurrent recession, both utopian and dystopian phases of the worldwide rural economy must be understood as techniques of international capital consolidation. In fact, there have been eight inflationary cycles since 1776, three in this century, and at each stage protocols of amalgamation have swung into gear in the world's major farming regions. Iain Wallace helps us to comprehend both British enclosures and midwestern agribusiness as symptoms of the same processes; he cites Mabogunje's argument for "a 'big push' approach to agricultural development," noting among his four examples both "the British enclosure movement" and "the homesteading of the Great Plains."[1] As Wallace asserts, the world system runs by "comprehensive" change rather than "incremental" alterations (234).

One of the values of Marty Strange's agricultural advocacy is his dedication to defining the slippery category of "family farm." Emphasizing the diversity of crops, the entrepreneurial quality of owner-operation, a parity between one farm's size and that of neighboring operations, as well as the traditionally tight interconnection of running a farm and rearing a family, Strange insists that size is of less importance than such qualities as environmentally sound production (Strange 32–36). The fact that a third of U.S. food production takes place on superfarms that grow more powerful with each passing year clearly troubles Strange, because of the disjunctions between farming as a way of life and farming as a business and the contrasting values that pertain to each role. Strange is particularly concerned with the agency provided by land ownership rights from the beginning of American government. In concert with many agrianalysts, he argues that when the use-value of the land began to give way to its investment-value, the goals and behaviors of farm families began to change.

For this reason, it is instructive to turn again to the British Isles, where large-scale commercial farming may be said to have started with the enclosure movement. In England and its domains, the redefinition of commons land as private property persisted from the time of Henry VIII onward, as severe inflation and the Enclosure Acts dispossessed many peasants of lands and created a pool of unemployed, rural homeless. This disfranchisement affected a large sector of England's populace: although Elizabeth I reigned over an era of expanding trade and commerce, 80 percent of her majesty's people were still rural. Further, rises in agricultural prices from the 1760s through the early nineteenth century encouraged landowners to turn "scattered open-field holding into compact farms" and to bring "overstocked commons and unproductive wasteland into the cultivated acreage" (Mingay, quoted in Lucas 104). Between 1793 and 1815 more than two hundred private Acts of Parliament authorized the enclosure of various parishes. Between 1750 and 1850 about six million acres—25 percent of farm acreage at the time—were taken over.

Ireland's rural situation was complicated further by the enforcing of enclosure legislation by an often hostile imperial administration, by laws limiting the ownership of land by the Catholic peasantry, by the transport of farm products to England, by the recovery of subsequent profits by the empire's industrialists owing to restrictive duties on Irish products, and by an absentee landlordship that allowed the flourishing of corrupt middlemen and congested districts in the west of the island. Ronnie Munck describes the enforced migration toward the west of Ireland from 1688 onwards as well as the Land League's nineteenth-century efforts to secure "freedom of contract" for tenants. Notably, Irish nationalism and Catholic emancipation were, from the start, bound up with resistance to British capital consolidation. The crucial historical simultaneity of the Act of Union with the 1801 General Act of Enclosure "made it a great deal easier to drive squatters from village ground and marginal freeholders and copyholders from their holdings." After this, the poor could be arrested for gathering wood, killing game, and fishing on land previously accessible to them. This history of privatization stands behind the events resulting in the Great Famine and subsequent waves of emigration. In his many books, including *Farming Collapse: National Opportunity* and *A Radical's Response*, Raymond Crotty[2] argues the necessity for the Irish government to reject, even at this late date, the imposed consolidation arising from the inflationary woes of Henry VIII. He claims that "today's mass unemployment and mass emigration are the price an Irish State pays to secure the sustained advancement of that landed interest which was created by the Tudor conquest" (Crotty, *Farming Collapse* 29). Kieran Allen adds that in the postfamine period landholdings were merged, and cattle pastures replaced corn and wheat fields (Allen,

Southern Ireland 12–13). Ultimately, various acts created the new category of "peasant proprietor" and enabled a partial redistribution of land (Munck 101). But when the British government eventually supplied monies to redistribute a portion of Irish land to the Catholic population, even this transfer cost was multiply recuperated through the use of Ireland as a geopolitically captive market.

In *The Practice of the Wild*, Gary Snyder defines the European commons as "the ancient mode of both protecting and managing the wilds of the self-governing regions" (Snyder 30). Snyder emphasizes that the commons land in England was not open to unchecked use by any single member of a community. Quite the contrary, the commons concept was ruled by customs that included penalties for misappropriation. The Norman legal concept of "levancy and couchancy" prevailed: no one could graze more cattle on the common range than could be maintained in his own corral over the winter months. There was no question of exploiting the lands bordering cultivated fields or of any farmer's eventual ownership of the commons land. Nor was there the possibility that control of that land/custom assemblage could pass out of the hands of local governance. Privatization was not an issue. Snyder lyrically describes this communal place:

> Between the extremes of deep wilderness and the private plots of the farmstead lies a territory which is not suitable for crops. . . . This area, embracing both the wild and the semi-wild, is of critical importance. It is necessary for the health of the wilderness because it adds big habitat, overflow territory, and room for wildlife to fly and run. It is essential even to an agricultural village economy because its natural diversity provides the many necessities and amenities that the privately held plots cannot. It enriches the agrarian diet with game and fish. The shared land supplies firewood, poles and stone for building, clay for the kiln, herbs, dye plants, and much else, just as in a foraging economy. It is especially important as seasonal or fulltime open range for cattle, horses, goats, pigs, and sheep. (Snyder 30)

This place offered itself to a variety of personal and group assemblages and thus resisted the abstraction of private ownership at every point. Clearly, when Frampton and other architects interested in a critical regionalist aesthetic speak of space and place, they access a dormant but strongly visceral commons tradition. The importance of this kind of space to island cultures with limited resources gains weight and value when viewed from a frontier-based American mentality. The gradual enclosure of British and Irish commons land in the interests of proto-agrienterprises goes a long way toward explaining the precise ideological work done by the Midwest's utopian advertisements in drawing to the New World those who felt that the old one was either used up or off-limits. Farmers displaced by enclosures in England formed the industrial base of the changing cities of Britain and the United States. And in the Midwest, transnational agribusiness and enlarging corporate farms took the place of the Tudor conquest of Ireland.

Postwar Power Blocs

Crotty asserts that when the Irish Republic achieved its independence, rather than pursue the full liberation of the land, that new state maintained the ruling-class-biased structure that it had inherited, with "25,000 or so grazier farmers"—or 1 percent of the population having "absolute title to over 50 percent of it" (Crotty, *Farming* 5–6). The entry into the EC, Crotty argues forcefully, has only continued the cost-benefit ratio for those owners and the ever-increasing poverty of the rest of the Irish people. This cynical approach to Irish farm life was enshrined in the Free State's self-regulation; while De Valera touted the virtues of rural sanctity, the Irish government set the grounds for processes that have eventuated in the control of Irish agriculture by world trade agreements and the EC's Common Agricultural Policy (CAP).

Crotty discusses in some detail the state's agricultural incentives over the past seventy years, the disastrous effects of the overdependence of Irish agriculture on milk and beef products (akin to the earlier overdependence of the Irish tenant farmer on the ill-fated and easily grown potato), and the even more disastrous impact of EC quotas on dairy-producers since 1984 (Crotty, *Farming* 10–12). Caught in spirals of high interest rates on the outsized national debt and higher taxes to meet its outgoing payments, Ireland extends the ceding of control over its own economy to outside powers that perpetually reinscribe the Tudor conquest, the disfranchisement of ordinary people. In Crotty's narrative, the Irish government has been both manipulator and pawn for interest groups, most recently for the EC itself, which comes across in this situation as a huge multinational investment clearinghouse.

Rather than being simply a slow or nondeveloping nation, Ireland is, Crotty maintains, experiencing "retrogression or undevelopment," which it shares with "the 140 non-European countries with the same historical experience of colonisation by a European power" (Crotty, *Farming* 22–23). The Irish state's subsidizing of farmers since the 1920s has thus been a failure because it has not tackled the inherent structural consequences of long-term colonization and because the subsidies themselves have, in fact, kept acreage in the hands of the wealthy while enabling pastoral land use to develop at the expense of intensive crop-production and diversification. Even Munck, who looks more favorably than Crotty on the eventual turn away from land nationalization and on the movement of Ireland into the international scene, notes that European surpluses in beef and dairy products have tended to leave Irish farming in limbo (Crotty, *Farming* 104). Crotty emphasizes the fragility of the Irish "pastoral" economy ("Pastoral products—milk, cattle and sheep—account for 76 percent of Irish agricultural output, compared to 31 percent for the E.C. as a whole and 40 percent for the UK" [Crotty, *Farming* 38]); the milk, butter, meat, and bacon industry that Ireland has produced remains rocky after years of subsidizing. In a situation that guaranteed farmers high prices, the EC was forced to buy the surpluses logically produced by farmers chasing those guarantees. In order to maintain farm subsidies, the nonagricultural sector has been drained, growth in Ireland having occurred primarily in foreign-owned enterprises. Processing and marketing are controlled largely by major multinational corporations.

Overall, farmers make less than industrial workers on the island as agricultural profit margins continue to decline. Both Northern Ireland and the Republic have seen the consolidation of farms and the progressive disfranchisement of the small, marginal, and part-time farmer, so that in Ireland as much as in America the cards have been stacked systematically against anyone wanting to go into farming for the first time. During Ireland's twenty years in the EC, Brigid Nevin claims, "The public emphasis given to the special role of the family farm . . . cannot be seen as other than largely a rhetorical exercise, aimed at containing potential social unrest in response to the uprooting of traditional farming structures" (Nevin 111).

Brian Campbell echoes many commentators when he reminds us that the flip side of post–World War II multinational industry was, in Ireland, the use of EC money to enhance productivity and support the larger farms, as a result of which many smaller operators have had to give up farming (Campbell 22). On this point as elsewhere, the decline of the agricultural sector is attended by a flurry of figures and statistics. "'Agriculture' employed 51 per cent of the gainfully occupied population in 1926" according to Lee (117), but by the thirty years between 1955 and 1985, some seventy-seven thousand Irish people "left the land" (Nevin 111). What Crotty calls the "process of engrossing land by large farmers" had been encouraged by EC economic policies. In the Republic, dairy farmers figure prominently in this process of concentrating both wealth and the means of production. "The number of dairy farmers declined from 86,300 in 1983 to 57,200 in 1989," with only eight hundred farmers accounting for fully 8 percent of the milk produced. Between 1926 and the 1990s farmers owning fifty acres or less of land were virtually halved. Crotty argues that it would be in the best national interest for Ireland actually to make land available to small-and-medium-farmers (fifty-acre plots, say, or small herds of perhaps a dozen cows) rather than to sustain current high levels of unemployment and emigration. However, the CAP precludes any program except curtailed production to support prices, thus ensuring the unemployment and poverty of the Irish rural people and the decline of the rural environment (Crotty, *Farming* 43–46).

Similarly, Nevin reports that in the mid-1980s, of the small-and-medium-farmers who were still operating, one-third had "incomes of £3,000 or less per annum" while another 27 percent lived "on between £3,000 and £6,000." When Dublin city is excluded, 60 percent of the Republic's population live in rural areas, but only 6 percent of Ireland's people grow food. Nevin confirms that "there is a developing commercial sector of farming making rapid financial progress" while "subsistence" farmers are increasingly marginalized: small dairy producers have dropped from supplying 41 percent of the milk in 1966 to only 6 percent in 1982. In short, the "hegemony of larger farmers within . . . [Europe] has meant that the needs of small farmers have not been recognised or tackled." And as a result, even the traditional potato is now imported into Ireland, in 1982, for instance, to the tune of £12.3 million (Nevin 110, 114, 116, 117, 118, 122). Writing in the *Irish Times*, Shanahan confirmed that in 1990, "the last year for which figures are available, farmers' incomes from farming averaged £6,500, according to Teagasc, the research and advisory service. . . . Farm incomes fell by just over 10 per cent in 1991, according to the end-of-year figures from the Central Statistics Office. . . . There are roughly 149,000 farmers here and certainly fewer than 90,000 are commercial farmers in any sense of the word" (Shanahan 11).

To complement from the perspective of the North these dire readings of the southern Irish farm, we need only turn to the daily *Ulster News Letter* to find frequent articles with titles like "'Threat' to Farms" (29 February 1992, 11):

> The family farm in Northern Ireland could be wiped out if EC plans for reform of the Common Agricultural Policy go ahead, the Alliance Party has warned.
>
> Senior party member Addie Morrow, who owns a farm in Co Down, condemned the plans and said if they were carried out the whole rural community would be changed beyond recognition.
>
> Mr Morrow was proposing a motion attacking EC proposals which he claimed would have a 'devastating effect' on the traditional family farm.
>
> The need for reform was obvious, he said, but the consumer should realise there was a price to pay.

THIRD-WORLDING AND A DIALECTICAL PERSPECTIVE

The Irish Farm Association's chief economist, Con Lucey, has predicted that the depression in farming would continue during the 1990s: "Mr Lucey said the total number of people working in agriculture had declined from 189,000 in 1981, to 155,000 in 1991" (Dillon). Like the IFA, Strange's *Family Farming* argues that the agrarian community of the United States is caught up in a crisis that is still just a prelude to what is ahead. It was the implicit "fierce war of values" occurring within the totalization of farming that caught his attention during the 1970s when he founded the Center for Rural Affairs. The incremental shift from small-scale farming in the United States to industrial farming involves all of us, Strange argues, not only because of

During the early 1990s, the short-lived Midwest Center for Developing Artists advertised its productions using this photograph of a crucified ear of corn.

agriculture's role in the total economy, not only because of our pressing eternal need for sources of pure and wholesome food, not only because the government has intervened in the agrarian subculture with programs of subsidies and efforts to control the amount of food on the market, not only because people have been increasingly alienated from the land and from ownership of the land, not only because of American society's massive ignorance about agricultural production, and not only because when farm foreclosures reach a critical mass farmers routinely turn to violence. The fact is that the agrarian institution is undergoing a massive change, that the term "family farm" is increasingly meaningless during this period of reterritorialization and erasure of rural communities by corporations. Dangerously low commodity prices, dramatically high land prices and competition for that land, the economic routing of those who would like to become farmers (a violation of what Strange calls "opportunity rights"), the unrestricted use of elaborate technologies whose side effects may not yet be known—all of these issues become more dangerous to the society as a whole every year.

Strange's excellent book, which is nothing if not sensitive to the intense contradictions being faced by the farming community today, joins hosts of other sources in citing the catastrophic, rapid decline in numbers of family farmers in America and the percentage of the population engaged in farming. He chronicles the rise of land prices in the 1970s, the banks' insistence that farmers borrow against those inflated land values rather than the actual cash flow of the farm, the European advances in farming that undermined the markets for American goods, and the subsequent crash of values and farms alike. This story graphically lays out the third-worlding of the midwestern American farmer.

Agreeing with the usual hegemonic reading, Munck sees parallel issues within Ireland as "essentially regional problems" (Munck 107). He emphasizes the need for problems of failing farmers and agricultural support to be treated along with policies for rural regional development, stabilization, creation of job opportunities, and environmental control. But Irish historian Kevin Whelan diagrams the situation in a way that points to the determining role of a vertical administration:

> What are the bases of Irish regionalism? The most appropriate way of visualising this is as a series of allegiances, affiliations and attachment, built up in a nest hierarchy like a set of Chinese boxes. At the centre of these boxes is the family farm, the smallest but most potent vector of the territorial imperative in the Irish experience. . . . It is obvious that these small Chinese boxes are now increasingly stacked within ever larger boxes—those of the nation state, the EC, the global economy and media. . . . The problem of the region as conventionally defined is its increasing porosity to these territorially unrestrained influences." (Whelan 5, 12)

It is this frightening porosity to ever-larger structures of regulation that animates the writings of Irish Columban Father Sean McDonagh. McDonagh pointedly connects the so-called maldevelopment in the third world today[3] with the situation of Ireland during the famine, when families starved to death while haggards stood full of grain set aside for rent payments. McDonagh reminds us that in their anxiety to hold onto the land, Irish peasants literally starved to death. In "Knight in Shining Armour," McDonagh writes about the World Bank: "In order to generate foreign currency to repay creditors, it encouraged countries with large populations living in poverty to move away from supporting subsistence agriculture and concentrate instead on export-led growth, especially in the area of cash crops. The result is overproduction in commodities like tea, coffee, tropical fruits, cotton and tobacco, creating a glut in the world market. As a consequence, commodities prices have plunged, devastating local economies and leaving a legacy of famine and death, especially in Africa" (McDonagh, "Knight"). According to UNICEF, third world children also die by the "tens of thousands" because cash-poor countries cannot pay their debts and feed their children at the same time. McDonagh deplores the intervention of the IMF and the World Bank not only to insure loan repayments to developed countries but also, and more sinisterly, to engineer third world economies so that outstanding debts continue to grow at an exponential rate. It is not that World Bank officials are unaware of the damage they are causing but that a free market philosophy enables and actively mandates such unrestrained exploitation of the defenseless poor. Over the years, the mechanisms critiqued by McDonagh have been similarly analyzed by Noam Chomsky, John Kenneth Galbraith, Richard Douthwaite, Neil Middleton, Robert Lynd, Kieran Allen, Hilary Beckles, Samir Amin, Kristin Dawkins, Peadar Kirby, Wendell Berry, Wes Jackson, Marty Strange, and a host of other voices from many schools of thought. Adapted for the critical regionalism of this book, McDonagh's analysis suggests that what Osha Davidson has called the American Midwest's "broken heartland" must be viewed as part of an implicit structural adjustment policy effective in rural regions around the world.

The administration of such structural adjustment, direct and indirect, occurs as a result of the Bretton Woods mechanisms: the World Bank, the International Monetary Fund, and the General Agreement on Tariffs and Trade. Ursula Barry points out that within the Republic of Ireland "about half of the money borrowed by successive governments over the years was borrowed from foreign sources, such as the International Monetary Agency and the World Bank" (Barry, "Taxation" 15). In Ireland's setting of uneven development, Peadar Kirby reminds us that by the end of 1987, the per capita debt of Brazilians was only £500 (Irish), while each Irish man, woman, and child "owed IR£2,768 to foreign bankers": "Ireland owes far more to foreign bankers than do the most heavily indebted Latin American countries" (Kirby 20). Writing of the 1980s, Barry agrees: "The foreign debt per head in this country is about twice as high as that of Argentina, Mexico and Brazil—countries whose debt crises have been making world headlines." Much of this money is owed to America. Even the exchange rate of the dollar versus the punt makes a difference in this complex calculation: "Each time the dollar climbs by one cent against the Irish pound, it adds £3.5 million to the cost of Ireland's foreign interest payments" (Barry, "Taxation" 8, 9, 15). By the early 1990s, Ireland received substantial structural funding from the EC and so lessened its borrowing from the IMF, but Ireland still has a sizable and burgeoning national debt. Meanwhile, Ireland's economic boundaries have been redefined to allow big capital instant access to this country without the intermediary and possibly marginally more public mechanisms of the IMF or World Bank.

Which brings us to Ireland's agricultural role within the EU, specifically in relation to the Common Agricultural Policy (CAP). The CAP represents an agreement on European agricultural policy originally signed in 1958. Since then, the CAP has gone through much tinkering, but it has always been premised on a system of subsidies to regulate overproduction and keep European farmers competitive in the world market. Irish historian Joseph Lee usefully speaks about the CAP in the context of European unification by reference to a January 1972 Irish government White Paper called *The Accession of Ireland to the European Communities*. That document had explored the largely negative impact of unification on native industry, and he uses his analysis as a bridge to discuss Ireland and the CAP: "Whatever residual doubts might be detected in the careful phraseology of the White Paper about the capacity of 'traditional' industry [clothing, textiles, shoes] to confront change, no such reservations can be read between the lines about the huge gains expected to accrue to agriculture from the higher prices paid under the Common Agricultural Policy of the E.E.C. [European Economic Community]. An increase of no less than 150 percent in agricultural incomes between 1970 and 1978 was predicted" (Lee 463). Lee refers to critics of EC membership for Ireland: those "who held that accession would amount to the sale of the national birthright for a mess of common agricultural pottage, and that the jewel of Irish sovereignty was a pearl of too great price to be bartered for the flesh pots of Brussels, were bluntly told that Ireland could not lose what it had not got" (Lee 463).

Getting to the heart of much dispute over European integration—that is, whether Ireland should cede its sovereignty to another parliament—Lee praises the Foreign Affairs officials who wrote in the White Paper for their distinction, in Irish circumstances, between independence and sovereignty; he quotes their contention that the economic freedom of small countries "'is circumscribed to a very great extent by the complex nature of international, economic and trading relationships,'" a situation severely limiting national sovereignty as an effective tool (Lee 463). Hence, Ireland's dependency was well and fully recognized in official government documents on its 1972 entry into the EC. As recessionary measures became necessary to stabilize the entire EC economy, the needs of farmers were viewed as less and less important.

Lee's analysis addresses the Republic of Ireland only. To some extent, as the Republic goes, so goes the island; on the other hand, Northern Ireland's agricultural policy asks for separate treatment. Ulster's immediate fate has rested with the relationship between the EC and the United Kingdom. By 1992, twenty years on from the EC White Paper, all of Ireland was, of course, going through the initial phases of Single European Act (SEA) implementation. A program aired on the BBC on 26 April 1992, dealing with Northern Ireland's farmers and the Euro-changes being required of them, displayed an interesting slippage between discussion of farming in Ireland as a whole and what the North's agricultural policy was coming to be. Northern Ireland was represented as aggressive in its response to SEA changes, helping farmers to meet the challenge of an imminent loss of CAP subsidy checks under a substantial reorganization of the CAP, partly to meet U.S. demands for a more competitive situation for American farmers in the world market.

Herein lay a huge problem: President George Bush had been demanding EC reduction in farm subsidies. If Ireland did not comply with the demands of the Bush administration (particularly concerning the new European quotas on seed and vegetable oils imported from the United States), so the papers reported, the United States threatened permanently to block the General Agreement on Tariffs and Trade (GATT) negotiations that had long been stalemated. Australia joined the United States in its call for a removal of EC farm subsidies. While the GATT had promoted freer world trade,[4] the EC wanted to hold the line as much as possible on price-setting and subsidies. The CAP had discussed the wisdom of direct aid to farmers rather than maintaining higher "support prices," but the Bush administration saw this direct compensation as "an effective barrier to free trade" (Flynn 15). Bush called for a 70 percent cut in subsidies for EC farmers; in contrast, the 1992 CAP reform actually produced EC cuts of 30 percent ("Poor Odds" 89). On the midwestern front, a year later the *Cedar Rapids Gazette* (5 August 1993) printed a Joel Pett cartoon from the *Lexington Herald-Leader* that featured family farmers vainly trying to hold back a flood of "ubidie$ to Agri-Biz Giant$."

It is clear that for the purposes of cross-cultural studies, top-down administrative institutions—the World Bank, the IMF, the EU, and the North American Free Trade Agreement (NAFTA)—participate in and inscribe at many levels a single narrative for global fiscal culture. Many of the effects of structural symmetry across paired regions may be viewed in the instrumentality of the GATT. The GATT forces out less competitive suppliers and allows the ever-further consolidation of wealth in a global capitalist culture. As the *Economist* states: "The truth is that freer trade works by forcing economies to change. Disruption is the source of its benefits. The forces that would reduce farm employment would increase jobs not just in services (the biggest part of the economy) and construction, but also in capital goods, high technology, and other leading-edge manufacturing. The challenge for governments is to defeat resistance to these changes, partly by compensating losers in ways that do not retard growth (eg, by helping with retraining and relocation) and partly by mobilising support among the large majority of firms and workers who stand to gain directly from freer trade" ("GATT Will Build").

The last of several rounds of the GATT talks was the Uruguay round, begun in 1986 and continuing through 1994. Richard Douthwaite reminds us that each round was initiated by the United States to further a specific agenda. In the 1986 round, the United States wanted "to eliminate nontariff barriers to its exports" (for example, the EC refusal to purchase U.S.-grown, hormone-injected beef) as well as to "cut EC agricultural price supports" and "to let international banks operate freely" (Douthwaite 92–93). In 1992, after the passing of Sligo-born EC Commissioner for Agriculture and Rural Development Ray MacSharry's plan for agricultural reform in the EC, the *Irish Times* alleged that if the Uruguay round of the GATT talks deteriorated as a result of the new CAP agreement, the United States was expected to retaliate economically against Ireland. MacSharry "said that the US would target Irish products for special attention [on a projected "hit list" of products] because there was an Irish commissioner" for the EC. Alan Gillis, president of the Irish Farmers' Association, "called for a major E.C. diplomatic offensive to defend the right of European farmers to supply the food requirements of the internal market of 340 million consumers" (Shanahan, "How Fare").

MacSharry's new program guaranteed compensation to EC farmers for CAP cutbacks; this policy, maintained MacSharry, would not alter even under U.S. pressure. Beginning in July of 1993, Irish farmers would experience lower "intervention prices" for beef, butter, and grains; it was anticipated at the time of the agreement that consumers would benefit from these lowered rates: the farmer's margin would be reduced, sometimes significantly, in this plan. All areas of production had quotas defined (removing the possibility of increasing production to make more money); farmers had to gear up for greater efficiency on confined acreages and had to be prepared to accept EC premiums to compensate them for this restriction.

But would EC taxpayers continue indefinitely to support Irish farmers? One John Doyle (County Wexford) argued that farmers had been robbed not only of their autonomy but also of their ability to plan: "people are being forced off the land unnecessarily. The rural infrastructure in a country like Ireland or France is capable of supporting rural communities. But if this present trend continues this infrastructure will be unused, except for tourism purposes" (Shanahan, "How Fare"). By some lights, of course, the best farmers were already innovative, rolling with the punches, planning ahead. But by far the majority of farmers in Ireland were characterized as just "good operators" who were no more outstandingly adept at change than their counterparts in the Midwest. It was argued that Irish farmers would suffer because of the more competitive production standards being expected of them. What would happen to Irish farms in an unprotected market, when they were fully vulnerable to market forces? How would they cope without the CAP purchases of substantial percentages of otherwise unsalable crops? How would they learn to work as a team with processors, to create not a crop to be sold close to home but a value-added product to be marketed in the new Europe? Even if some unforeseen event unraveled the processes of European unification, these changes had been so fully propagandized by the EC that it would be hard to imagine an immediate re-restructuring of expectations held by the European small producer in any field. The need to connect with clients, to market effectively, and to compete at the commodity level remained a daunting and frightening challenge for many of Ireland's "good operators."[5]

At the same time, the GATT countries, which are constantly doing economic and regulatory battle with the EC, pushed for the lifting of trade barriers and controls in agricultural products. Thus, Argentina, Australia, Brazil, Canada, Chile, Colombia, Fiji, Hungary, Indonesia, Malaysia, New Zealand, the Philippines, Thailand, Uruguay (collectively, the Cairns Group), and the United States opposed the EC's barriers to imports from outside the Community and the EC's policy of unloading its surpluses in butter, beef, and the like in non-EC countries (Tansey). Owing to Ireland's overwhelming dependency on pastoral farming (milk, cattle, sheep) and to scandals during the early 1990s in the beef industry, as well as to a decline in milk prices, the entire situation of southern Irish agriculture looked increasingly unstable. And in Northern Ireland, the *Belfast Newsletter* for 17 January 1992 stated, "Farmers on Brink: Lean Times Ahead for Producers Warns UFU Chief."

> Hard-pressed farmers were last night told to brace themselves for another blow to their shrinking incomes. The warning to prepare for harder times ahead came as Government figures showed that farm income in the Province slumped by 10 per cent in real terms last year.
>
> Producers, already teetering on the brink of bankruptcy, viewed the forecast with anxiety.
>
> The average income of many sheep and beef farmers has already been cut to a measly £2,000 a year.
>
> The grim warning by Ulster Farmers' Union general secretary Vernon Smyth about leaner times came less than a week after he had said more than 15,000 farmers would have to look for a second job to make ends meet if controversial world trade proposals are accepted. (1)

Meanwhile the *Irish Farmers' Journal* reported on the World Family Farmers' Summit held in Tokyo in July of 1993. Organizations "representing 25 million farmers world-wide rejected . . . [another] MacSharry . . . deal on agricultural trade." The vote against the MacSharry plan was unanimous, all of the organizations predicting worldwide "rural depopulation," "attendant social and political difficulties," and environmental damage if the G7 did not reverse this decision on the Uruguay round of GATT talks ("IFA Active"). As it happened, the MacSharry plan was implemented, and the GATT talks were brought to an end, hailed by global government officials. The way had been paved for the World Trade Organization (WTO), whose effects, at the time of writing, were not discernibly at odds with the GATT it had replaced.

The Irish have produced a detailed critique of global trade and economic consolidation, and the vision underlying this critique can be read at the level of popular culture. One example will have to suffice here: in 1991, one of the nationalist murals in Derry's Bogside portrayed an emaciated man hanging from a cross bearing the slogan "World Trade Agreements." Marking Central America Week, the mural also depicted a map of Guatemala and El Salvador, superimposed over which were the corporate logos of Texaco, Olivetti, Pepsi, Volkswagen, Dupont, Shell, BP, and other major multinationals. When a photograph of this work appeared in a Sinn Féin calendar, the caption read "Making the Connections."

ASSEMBLING ADM

From the viewpoint of a negative dialectic and of critical regionalism, it is important to consider what the GATT talks and related CAP agreements looked like from the midwest. One measure can be found in a radio talk show on 16 October 1994, when a Republican senator from the state of Iowa told phone-in callers that the benefits of GATT for Iowa were clear. Without trade barriers, goods would sell more easily; he predicted twenty thousand more jobs and better pay for Iowans. The alternative to an export economy would have been, he said, to cut back production and related jobs by 40 percent. Another indicator may be found in the oscillating viewpoint of a multinational corporation that operates both in the Midwest and in Ireland—one that has a huge stake in the problematic goods that were the center of the CAP and GATT debate. Archer-Daniels-Midland (ADM) is such a corporation, a multinational production-consumption-inducement assemblage that advertises itself as the "Supermarket to the World" but is mocked by socialists as the supermarket to the rich. ADM reaches far and wide, leaps across both American and Irish political differences, helps to remake the world stage into a Heineken-Levitt conception of regions defined by supply and demand.

ADM is the result of a merger between an agricultural value-added company and the Midland Coop (a midwestern farmer-owned cooperative for marketing grain and purchasing all manner of agriculture supplies). The company is listed in *Moody's Industrial Manual* with a complex history of acquisitions. Linseed oil, soybeans, vegetable oil, mayonnaise, stock and poultry feed, cottonseed, sunflower seed, bakery flour, lecithin, malt products, corn sweeteners, pasta, pancake mix, and peanuts are among the elements now passing through the factories, processing plants, and grain elevators owned by ADM. As of the end of March 1991, ADM investors had logged in several record years. The published corporate report at that time proclaims, "ADM is the largest supplier of food ingredients to the U.S. companies that stock the supermarket shelves with the wide variety of food products enjoyed by the American consumer." It adds, "The food business, like most others, has become globalized and ADM is keeping pace. In the decade of the 80's, ADM substantially added to its overseas operations and expanded the grain acquisition and transportation capabilities necessary to support the processing operations." ADM supplies, for example, "over 25 percent of Japan's beverage alcohol demand." Its operations range all over the globe, from Eastern Europe to the Mississippi River valley. The corporation is particularly keen on its potential in the "1992-and-after European Community": "Malting barley varieties are now being developed to match more closely the characteristics of European types used in target markets." In the early 1990s, ADM acquired Pfizer's citric acid plants in Southport, North Carolina, and in Ringaskiddy, Ireland, while Arkady Feed Ltd. in Ireland is also an ADM subsidiary. With 1990 gross profits at $906 million, the company has been a model for the value-added side of agribusiness, operating globally and remaining remarkably resistant to the recessionary pressures affecting individuals and small business owners the world over. Companies like ADM thus wield tremendous global power. They have the capacity to manipulate the worldwide market, buying here and selling there to drive prices up or down, to create shortages, and otherwise to produce favorable conditions for their own profit pictures.

The current chairman of the board, Dwayne Andreas, was born to Mennonite parents in the small town of Lisbon, Iowa, where his family owned a grain elevator. Once an executive for Cargill (another dominant agribusiness firm), Andreas is the embodiment of the Levitt leader. He is quoted in the *New York Times* to this effect: "We endeavor to be on the Government's wavelength to see what they want done. Some years they want more soybeans. Some years they want to do something big in China. Who can do it for them? We're in 50 countries. We can do anything" (Weiss). It is interesting to speculate about the education that someone of Andreas's age might have received to have developed this optimistic attitude. One wonders if he ever began the school day by saying the 1930s civics book "Creed of Iowa": "I believe in Iowa, land of golden grains, whose harvests fill the granaries of the nation, making it opulent with the power of earth's fruitfulness. I believe in Iowa, land of limitless prairies, with rolling hills and fertile valleys, with winding and widening streams, with bounteous crops and fruit laden trees, yielding to man their health and wealth" (Moeller and Bowersox, frontispiece). In any event, Andreas has lived this creed. And he has done so while remaining centered in the Midwest: Decatur, Illinois, is the proud home of ADM's international corporate headquarters.

A friend of Ronald Reagan's whose international stature approaches that of Armand Hammer, Andreas gave substantial gifts to both the Bush and the Clinton 1992 presidential campaigns. Five presidents since World War II have been advised by Andreas, and when American businesses ventured into the Soviet Union in 1989, the consortium included Andreas as CEO of ADM—other companies represented being Chevron, Nabisco, Eastman Kodak, and Johnson and Johnson (Kraar). Andreas's friends have included Hubert Humphrey, Robert Dole (a major congressional supporter of policies benefiting ADM, such as ethanol and sugar subsidies [Abramson and Kuntz]), Lyndon Johnson, and Tip O'Neill (Henkoff 106). The ADM annual budget for advertising is between seven and eight million dollars, much "devoted to 'Face the Nation,' 'Meet the Press,' and 'This Week with David Brinkley'—shows that are de rigeur for Washington lawmakers" (Weiss). Asked to respond to a question about governmental affiliations, Andreas replied, "We have lived over many decades with dozens of different governments. It doesn't seem to make any difference to us. The kind of foods that we make are fundamental to life: margarine, cooking oil, protein for chickens, malt for beer, sugar for all possible uses, flour and all kinds of mixes for bread. They're fundamental. . . . They do not change with governments. Governments have to have our plants run. We are like a public utility except we're even more important than most public utilities, because we provide the bread and vegetable oil that people eat every morning of their lives. Governments come and go, but we survive" (Archer-Daniels-Midland, *Second Quarter* 5).

While corporations like ADM literally control the world's food supply, the individual midwestern farmer on the ground is unlikely to be in a position to market his produce effectively in the world at large. Would the small farmer attempting to plan for the transnational future do best just to buy stock in a company like ADM that not only has access to a global perspective but also is intimately involved in producing that market and that viewpoint? Perhaps; certainly, ADM's interests occupy the same position as American foreign policy when oilseeds are at stake. Consider the following excerpt from a leading Irish newspaper during the 1992 GATT debates:

$200M EXPORTS GET A REPRIEVE
AS US DELAYS TRADE WAR LIST

The American government has given Irish and other EC exporters three weeks breathing space in the threatened trade war which could hit up to $200m worth of exports from this country.

The US authorities have postponed publication of their revised hit-list of targetted Community products while talks are still ongoing to resolve the dispute over access to EC markets for American oilseed producers. . . .

The threatened trade war between the two economic superpowers is being discussed today at informal talks between Farm Commissioner Ray MacSharry and American Agriculture Secretary Ed Madigan at Dromoland Castle in Co Clare.

Sources say the Americans are unhappy with the peace proposals from the EC and that they are not bluffing about imposing a trade blockade if their oilseed producers are not compensated for estimated losses of $1 billion a year. . . .

Up to 1987, US oilseed producers enjoyed an unlimited access agreement with the EC. But they say the Community then unilaterally changed the rules by putting on an import tariff. A special GATT panel has twice since ruled against the EC action.

The Americans have rejected claims that Ireland is being hit because the Agricultural Commissioner is Irish. (Dillon, "200m," 5)

Of course, ADM spent the 1980s building its core businesses of oilseed, corn, and wheat processing toward the very sort of new value-added operations that the EC recommended to Irish farmers. The difference is that ADM does its own merchandising of such products both throughout the United States and with the aid of twenty-five or so foreign plants. The corporation owns grain elevators, railcars, trucks, and barges in great numbers to facilitate the movement of unprocessed and processed goods: ADM freight cars and corn-syrup-toting eighteen-wheelers crisscross the heartland. In the president's report for fiscal year 1990, stockholders learned that ADM's access to tidewater facilities in North Carolina and in Ireland would allow for even more effective worldwide transport of goods.

All of this information provides a context for what in the 1990s came to be called the Irish Greencore scandal—a footnote, if you will, to the Thatcher-Reagan era of privatization. The state-owned Irish Sugar Company gradually grew from 1975 through April of 1991 when Irish Sugar stock was floated under the new name of Greencore, the government holding 45 percent as its stake in this agribusiness company. Secret, perhaps illegal, deals made by Irish Sugar officials in 1989 came to light through court actions in July of 1991, causing an array of investigations into the running of the company, suspended as it was between the auspices of the state and the conventional corporate world. By 1993, the state had decided to complete the privatization process, and the multinationally successful ADM was the minister of finance's choice for purchaser.

Dain Bosworth's 1995 research report on ADM provides some useful background information about ADM's interest in the global sugar market. "Sugar," writes Bonnie Wittenburg, "is produced in about 100 countries, and is one of the world's most-protected farm commodities. Nearly all governments intervene in sugar trade because sugar is a staple commodity that is used in many products, its production requires a sizable investment, and it plays an important role in generating employment and foreign exchange."

Later in the report, while discussing international trade, Wittenburg adds that "business relationships in fast-growing developing nations typically require an ability to move quickly without a cumbersome bureaucracy at the home office," so that ADM "often teams up with a partner" in those markets—a situation that overall is "made for ADM" (Wittenburg, 1995, 13, 28).

Despite this positive assessment, in Ireland a number of issues arose among all the parties concerned: some expressed a certain amount of anti-American feeling; some wanted to offer the stock for sale to a consortium of Irish buyers; some preferred an outright investment by an American company rather than fostering Ireland's dependency on borrowed foreign capital; some simply deplored the passing of Irish indigenous firms into foreign hands; some still wanted to debate the merits or defects of privatization. The *Irish Times* editorial for 13 March 1993 reminded readers that Greencore had achieved its large successes at the expense of rural Ireland: "Its present commercial success required the jettisoning of factories in Tuam and Thurles, experiences which still leave a bitter taste locally" (11). The entire situation was complicated by the desire of Greencore's chief executive to work with ADM. It was understood through news reports that ADM had already purchased plants across Ireland (Southern Milling, Paul and Vincent, Arkady Feeds) whose production totaled 10 percent of the domestic animal feed market. After considerable debate and a passage of time that made ADM impatient, the government floated the shares to institutional bidders in Britain and Ireland. Various reports also drifted through the news: ADM had become angry at the coalition government's prolonged discussion of provisos to keep Greencore from being bought out by the American firm; ADM simply felt unwelcome in an essentially xenophobic situation.[6] In the course of a single week in May, however, the government announced the sale of its shares through Davy Stockbrokers, owned by the Bank of Ireland, and then had to admit that Davy had misprojected the sales, so that the bank was forced ethically to purchase major stock in Greencore. Would the bank hold the shares or sell? Prices plummeted, and eight international investors pulled out of the deal. Between the bank and Davy the losses were made up, and after two months the bank had unloaded its Greencore stock at a tidy profit of £2.4 million.

Throughout all of the journalists' efforts to explain these tortuous proceedings, the name of ADM surfaced as a highly desirable but not quite predictable icon of American business prowess. In contrast, the Dublin stock market came out looking like a hotbed of secrecy and speculation. Caustic journalist Dick Walsh agreed with one politician's opinion that "in certain professional areas—accountancy and law as well as stockbroking—the bulk of Irish business is done by a relatively small number of people." This sort of insiders' club, which in Ireland is called a "golden circle," was and would likely always be "far ahead of the State's official posse," regardless of the rules and regulations mandated by government in response to the Greencore event (Walsh, "These Things").

It seems clear that whatever was happening, ADM was not content to participate in a situation that it did not control. In fact, given ADM's legendary devotion to high fructose corn syrup, their effort to buy the agritrader business grounded in the competitor product, sugar, must be viewed merely as one of the hedges that ADM long ago trademarked. Owing to ADM's government connection, the United States has long maintained high prices for sugar and in the 1980s added a tight sugar import quota, both forcing sugar growers in the Philippines and Haiti out of business and making high fructose corn syrup a major growth area for ADM. It is a fact that government subsidies to corn farmers in the Midwest turn in ADM's hands into high fructose corn syrup, the major element in that American staple, Coca-Cola, all engineered around a sugar quota that keeps third world sugar expensive in comparison to American sweeteners (Barnes 20). As the 1993 Annual Report for Archer-Daniels-Midland has it, "In the unlikely event that government ceased to support sugar prices, sugar producers in the U.S. would drastically reduce production immediately and the fructose demand would double or triple. . . . If the EEC also dropped price supports for sugar, its sugar production, which has been artificially stimulated at taxpayers' expense, would probably drop by more than 6 million tons, increasing the demand and price of fructose" (7). Clearly, the wise corporate course is to own operations in the United States and in Europe and to be able to market both fructose and sugar. In 1994 and 1995, ADM was thus the largest stockholder of A. E. Staley's parent company, Tate and Lyle PLC, a British conglomerate that owns Domino, GW, and Redpath sugar. During a lengthy lockout of Staley workers in the early 1990s over job security, seniority, and shift hours, it was reported that ADM trucks took Staley products to market so the company could meet its contracts—despite the popular view of the two as competitors in the sweetener business. (Wittenburg reports that while ADM holds an estimated 31 percent of the high-fructose corn syrup market share, Staley holds 22 percent, thus giving ADM virtual control of over 50 percent of the market [Wittenburg, 1995, 15]). From the viewpoint of labor, the Staley lockout and ADM collaboration were part of a concerted union-busting practice in the Midwest. From the viewpoint of the Dain Bosworth investment group, "ADM is so big and efficient, and its product lines are so diverse, that it can benefit from almost any positive trend impacting agriculture worldwide" (Wittenburg, 1993, 1).

Similar coordinated hedging activities also hallmark ADM's oilseed business. Although annual reports expressed distress over the U.S. government's failure to negotiate a GATT agreement that would limit EU bin-busting subsidies to its growers and processors of oilseed, ADM was poised to benefit on both sides of the Atlantic, however the GATT was resolved. While Irish journalists saw the U.S. threat of trade war as an attack against the Irish MacSharry, what was not noted in those reports and what was not emphasized in the annual statements by ADM was the fact that the corporation owns oilseed plants in Germany. During the GATT debate, French farmers in particular were angered by the U.S. efforts to downscale European rapeseed (or canola) production. Endless discussions over rapeseed quotas filled European newspapers. The company's 1994 annual report reads,

> Consumers all over the world got a major setback when trade negotiators in Paris sat around a shiny table quarreling over which one should take the biggest cut in the production of oilseeds. The result was that the United States gave up its policy of being competitive in world markets for vegetable oil and the EU agreed to drastically reduce oilseed production. . . . Europe would . . . be allowed to produce oilseeds . . . [on idled acreage] for industrial purposes only. The result is obscene. The EU is now requiring processors to take perfectly good cooking oil . . . and turn it into diesel fuel. . . . Humanitarian considerations require the oil product from these acres be made available on concessional terms to people in need. (12)

Stop ADM's Union Busting!

The Archer Daniels Midland (ADM) agricultural products corporation will be at the UI this week conducting interviews for management positions. While ADM sells itself as a company that feeds starving people worldwide, the reality is quite different. ADM uses intimidation to keep it s own employees in line. ADM is also the largest stockholder of A.E. Staley's parent company, Tate & Lyle. Staley has locked out 760 members of United Paperworkers International Union (UPIU) from its corn processing plant in Decatur, IL since June 1993. Staley demanded 12-hour shifts and major cuts in wages and health benefits, while ignoring workers' concerns about job safety. When Local 7837 fought this concessionary contract, Staley locked them out rather than bargain in good faith. ADM has built a pipeline from its Decatur plant into Staley, so that Staley can continue to operate with management personnel and scab labor. Staley's goal from day one has been to bust the union, and ADM is helping them every step of the way. However, the Staley workers are not giving up the fight. We need to defend union jobs. Join the fight against corporate greed and for workers rights.

Support the locked-out Staley workers!

Dwayne Andreas reminds all those people going hungry this holiday season to take his advice: "feast off the labor of others" (and don't forget to apply for a job at ADM). (Decatur Free Press, Holiday Issue)

Informational Picket against ADM
Noon—1pm, Wednesday 15 March—Phillips Hall
Sponsored by the **International Socialist Organization**
Call 645-2945 for information-labor donated.

It's Our Solidarity versus Theirs!

This flier was circulated throughout the Midwest in March 1995 before the FBI investigation into alleged ADM price-fixing occurred. From the International Socialist Organization.

Conservative viewpoints such as those expressed in the *Economist*, however, felt that this agreement was just fine: they viewed rapeseed as nothing more than a weed that normally glutted world markets. As it happens, rapeseed is the source for European fuels that ADM is countering with its own soy-based biodiesel fuel (Wittenburg, 1993, 23). Again hooking into the American Midwest, ADM is also a key producer of ethanol.

Now, the inauguration of President Clinton immediately unfolded into a review of last-minute Bush regulations, including a ruling endorsing corn ethanol as a viable alternative fuel under the Clean Air Act; ethanol is reputed to contribute to smog production in warm climates. ADM is the major producer of corn-based ethanol in the United States, and the Midwest's corn farmers closely watch national legislation that would encourage or dissuade from ethanol use. So it is that the *Daily Iowan* reported on 26 January 1993 that "Farmers in the No. 1 corn-growing state once more found themselves defending ethanol after the Clinton administration slammed the brakes on an alternative-fuels program." During 1992, "Farmers waged an intense lobbying battle . . . to persuade then-President George Bush to retain corn-based ethanol's role in the nation's clean air plans" (Rosenfeld). Soon the Clinton administration's efforts to attack the ethanol program were strongly countered both by the Midwest's farmers and by ADM.

The tight linkages and overlapping agenda that mark the above narrative of cross-regional, transnational corporate enterprise do not depend on affiliations between business and specific political parties on either side of the Atlantic. Rather, the story more or less disregards politics, choosing to work with whatever groups enable the most profitable and encompassing capital growth possibilities. Viewed properly, ADM exists in a direct line of descent from the many British enclosure acts. In the era of the World Trade Organization, Iowa and Ireland equally and in parallel locksteps manifest administrative protocols of consolidation that complexly affect the life of everyone around the globe.

Cautionary evidence for this position emerged as this book went to press. During the summer of 1995, ADM and three other large global corn syrup dealers came under investigation by the FBI for alleged collusion involving high-fructose corn syrup, lysine (a critical feed additive that increases animal weight and a product for which ADM controls about half the world market), and citric acid (interestingly enough the area of ADM's recent growth in Ringaskiddy). Financial experts have opined that the alleged criminal activity involved not so much price-fixing for enhanced profits as "holding prices down to hinder competition" ("U.S. Antitrust" 4A). Surely the strategy of slashing prices to grab markets has been one hallmark of the emergent global economy. For the previous three years, so the reports go in all of the major American newspapers, Mark Whitacre, then president of ADM's BioProducts division, had been working undercover for the U.S. government, helping to gather audio and videotapes of hundreds of hotel-room meetings both in the United States and abroad involving several agribusiness concerns—including Cargill, CPC International, Staley, and, by implication, the British-based Tate and Lyle. If a former instance provides an example, the legal proceedings around this case will take years to unravel; a 1982 civil complaint against ADM took nine years just to reach judicial dismissal. Standing on its own, the picture of an ADM official carrying a briefcase tape recorder to dozens of international meetings is both troubling and comical; standing alongside the murky Greencore dealings as part of a portrait of contemporary agribusiness, the current investigation has wide-reaching implications for all farmers and consumers.

DELINKING

The welfare of the small farm and global corporate growth seem to be mutually incompatible. Richard Douthwaite, author of *The Growth Illusion*, argues that one thing binding capitalist culture to cancer, ideologically speaking, is their shared emphasis on growth for its own sake. Douthwaite is not an impressionist; his text uses abundant hard research strongly to support his contention that mindless economic growth has undermined the health and safety of the world while backfiring economically on all but the already wealthy. Douthwaite, a trained economist and former adviser to Caribbean governments, wrote *The Growth Illusion* in County Mayo, specifically led by the contradictions of Irish industrialization and emigration to pursue this transnational study of capital in our time. Douthwaite claims that

> the gains from trade are largely a myth fostered by those companies and countries in strong trading positions that stand to gain from bigger markets. International free trade inescapably leads to a levelling down. It means that salaries and wages will tend to converge at Third World levels, and social security provisions in industrial countries will have to be cut, since these are an overhead which economies cannot bear if they are to compete successfully with countries without them. Only the owners of the surviving transnational companies and of natural resources will escape the general impoverishment. Already the islands of prosperity are growing steadily smaller in an otherwise sick, dilapidated and hungry world. The quest for corporate growth has much to answer for. (Douthwaite 95)

One of the best writers on development today, Douthwaite provides a balanced view of the dangers posed both to industrial and to developing nations by unrestrained growth. While the only antidote to recession is generally construed to be unlimited expansion, Douthwaite has shown that there are no longer grounds for pursuing the ignis fatuus of bigger and better.

Economic downturn, he argues, needs to be opposed not by growth but by a flexible, dynamic concept of human development at many and varied cultural registers. Douthwaite is well worth quoting at length:

> As a result of an invitation from the Department of the Environment to submit its views on what the Irish position should be at the 1992 Earth Summit (the United Nations' conference on environment and development to be held in Brazil), the environmental organization Earthwatch prepared a paper it subsequently circulated to other organizations. This argued that the Irish countryside was the creation of the farming community and that if that community continued to be displaced by larger-scale, less labour-intensive methods, the consequences for the environment would be severe. The reason for the decline in rural populations, the paper said, was that high-labour, low-input Irish family farms could not compete with highly mechanized, energy-intensive farms elsewhere, particularly those on the prairies of the United States. . . . However, if taxes on fossil fuels were imposed in response to the threat of global warming, small Irish farmers would become much more competitive again. The flight from the land, which had reduced the number of farmers by half over the previous fifteen years, would be stemmed, and traditional farming methods, and the countryside they created, might be retained. . . . [E]nergy taxes might deliver all the benefits of protectionism while avoiding its artificial, bureaucratic restrictions. (Douthwaite 282–83)

Douthwaite's interest in global energy taxation might well be connected with other proposals put forward by critics of an unlimited growth ideology, including the delinking of regional/peripheral economies from IFI administration and the governmental regulation of agribusiness size.

For my purposes in a project devoted to symmetries and assemblages, Douthwaite's analysis finds a direct and timely counterpart on the midwestern front. In *Iowa: Perspectives on Today and Tomorrow* economist and writer Robert James Waller closely questions the premise, widely held and at the heart of contemporary life, that continued, sustained, endless economic growth is not only desirable but necessary. In contrast to the expectation of "high-intensity purchasing" that runs American industry, Waller asks us to recall a time on the prairies when the winter winds pierced the homemade clothing of farmers struggling to maintain shelter and put food on the table (Waller 232–35). Waller decidedly rejects a purely sentimental back-to-naturism, but he asks us to honor the quest for self-sufficiency that brought immigrants to the heartland throughout the nineteenth century. He demonstrates the perils of looking for endless growth, both the hazards to the environment and the danger to social sanity; he notes the national upsurge in violent crimes, suicides, and addictions, which he correlates with a mindless growth ideology (Waller 232–35). The argument that Waller makes for human as opposed to economic development echoes wonderfully with Douthwaite's and reinforces the many structural homologies linking the rural regions in question.

Like Douthwaite and Waller, Strange also concludes that bigger is not always better, that a growth economy increasingly reveals its drawbacks. Social and environmental costs find their way into the public mind more and more frequently, but very few seem to agree on how to combat the move toward larger farms in more eroded rural communities. The debt-growth cycle receives much of Strange's attention, and he convincingly provides the figures to demonstrate the viability and even necessity of a more heterogeneous farming system. Strange also alerts us to the tendency to romanticize the family farmer while overlooking the increasing gap between private and public good that bad agricultural policies and tax codes have more or less forced on many operators (those who have to use chemicals to produce more to pay for the land, and so on). Soil conservation and clean water, alternative goals from those of a "worn-out" industrial ideology, must be explored. In fact, Strange makes a case for reconciling "farm policy with its historic rural values"—"self-reliance, frugality, ingenuity, stewardship, humility, family, neighborhood, and community." His suggestions for positive change, which echo those of Irish rural analysts, include "a national land policy to prevent concentration in farm ownership and to make land more available to those with the ability and eagerness to use it well" (Strange 245, 244, 249).

It is encouraging that the Leopold Center for Sustainable Agriculture at Iowa State University, along with the director of the Iowa Farm and Rural Life Poll at ISU have called for a rejection of superfarms in favor of highly efficient family farms. They have publicly named the problem: "Our heavy dependence upon corn and soybeans and the vagaries of international markets coupled with tight profit margins have forced farmers to expand beyond the efficient size"—a complex network trapping farmers in ever-greater land purchases. "One of the goals of the Leopold Center for Sustainable Agriculture . . . is to develop alternative farming systems that will maintain family farms as viable economic units" with optimal production and control rates (Duffy, Lasley, and Keeney). The center contends that both consumers and rural communities are suffering from an inflexible and yet increasingly interdependent system.

To this chorus of voices, Stephen Krasner adds the insight that cross-regional global relations of rich and poor will remain conflictual unless the opposing sides can find a way to achieve "disengagement" (Krasner 269–70). In this argument, Krasner nods toward dependency theory, which retains an imaginative and partially actualized force in describing the relationship between so-called peripheral zones and so-called core nations. "If," Krasner states conditionally, "the world capitalist system is milking the periphery through unequal exchange, perverting its political development . . . and undermining its cultural autonomy with bourgeois Northern products and advertisements, then the most desirable course of action is to sever or restrict relations with the center." Krasner favors a third world seeking of "collective self-reliance" (Krasner 301, 304), which Crotty and other analysts have also proposed for Ireland.

From an Irish perspective, Kieran Allen ably brings into focus the fact that, *pace* Crotty, a separable, self-contained national economy can no longer be spoken of or aimed for in the current world economy. As a revolutionary socialist, Allen argues that "workers must aim to transform the whole world economy, not retreat from it" (*Southern Ireland* 26). I would put this point differently, perhaps less anachronistically, if you will. I would argue that given the current nature of transnational investment and international monetary exchange as well as the documented conflict between global first world and third world interests, both workers and intellectuals would do well to produce a powerful analysis of the causes and consequences of recession and collapse in the late twentieth-century world economy. It must be widely recognized and made a matter of common knowledge that changes in that economy take place across many registers and at many levels. The very concept of a critical regionalism depends on the ability of local cultures to exert their own pressure toward self-determined structural responses.

By way of proposing a solution, Crotty says that Ireland has "a unique opportunity to serve the Third World. . . . As the only western country that has had the same historical experience of capitalist colonialism as all the countries of the Third World, Ireland has the opportunity—indeed, the duty—to provide for that half of the world's population resident in the Third World, the essential, and hitherto missing, precedent of a former capitalist colony so reorganising its resources that it can provide adequately for all its people" (Crotty, *Farming* 74). Strange agrees that we literally cannot "solve" farm problems without looking at other parts of the world-system than our own. Rural regions face a set of problems driven by exports, utopian aspirations, trade realities, local expectations about normality, and engineered cycles of boom and bust. We need to reconnect cousin regions and to think in classrooms and at dinner tables, in boardrooms and in legislatures, the effects of corporations across distant territories. Can metropolitan populations join farmers in picturing a process of delinking and relinking in imaginative assemblages? While the world order constructs its own ever-enlarging ensembles, can we deploy the assemblage as a tool for social determination and rural change? Can we discern creative interspaces presided over by an agrarian imaginary that is not bankrupt but evolving?

The Agrarian Imaginary

All the perversions of the soul
I learnt on a small farm.
How to do the neighbours harm
by magic, how to hate.
MICHAEL HARTNETT, "A SMALL FARM"

One of the more startling aspects of family farming is its ideological consistency, at least in its public face, across decades, miles, cultures, and nations. The values professed by small farmers assume transregional ideological force, grounded as they are in a particular economy of desire, hope, and gratification. In fact, the recurrent struggle to sustain or restage the agrarian imaginary in zones linked by migration and by economic cycles has produced strikingly parallel representations of farm life. Consider that a text about farm crisis in the American heartland is likely to have a precise analogue in the literature of rural Irish life: it is not enough to suggest aesthetic influence to explain this phenomenon, even when we are thinking in terms of a pervasive Hollywood influence on international film. Nor is heritage alone a determining force, especially given the midwestern mixture of Irish migrants with Scottish, English, Welsh, Bohemian, Norwegian, Swedish, German, Caribbean, Vietnamese, Mexican, and other populations. Rather, the parallel honing of film and fiction in, say, Iowa and Ireland has been complexly overdetermined by multiple historical, economic, psychological, and aesthetic conditions of production. To read these representations adequately requires not only the sort of induced insider-outsider viewpoint created in this study through pairing homologous regions, not only an insistently depriveleging negative dialectic that moves between a lateral migratory axis and a top-down global administrative axis, not only recognition that every representational moment—whether utopian or tragic—carries its own opposing shadow-text. Rather, or in addition, the conscious act of pairing texts is an ensemble activity; this work helps to foster bridges across the noetic, cognitive, and information gaps that exist even, or especially, in the days of the information highway. Putting pressure on ideological consistencies between regions and strategically forcing symmetries can broaden our collective insight, reinforce our belief in the value of intuitively discerned design, and suggest that critical regionalist assemblages may provide models for counteradministered transregional linkages.

This chapter explores parallel texts of small farming that register the profound internal damage suffered by the family on the farm—especially by the patriarch whose authority is eroded by a multinational corporate symbolic order. The struggle for economic survival and the quest for self-actualization are depicted as mutually incompatible in narratives from both Ireland and the heartland. This situation prompts the evolution of a specific theoretical category to designate the dialectic of desire explored below.

A THOUSAND ACRES

A Thousand Acres (1992), the best-selling novel for which Jane Smiley won the Pulitzer Prize, is abundant in themes and fertile in interpretive possibilities surrounding the issue of agrarian upheaval and patriarchal strife. Smiley's epigraphic note from Meridel Le Sueur bears quoting here: "The body repeats the landscape. They are the source of each other and create each other. We were marked by the seasonal body of earth, by the terrible migrations of people, by the swift turn of a century, verging on change never before experienced on this greening planet." On that apocalyptic note, Smiley begins her story of crisis in the heartland. The narrator, Ginny Cook Smith, tells the story of her father's precipitous decline from being the county's premier farmer (at least in his own mind, presiding as he did over three daughters, newly painted farm buildings, admirably drained fields, debt-free property, and rich crops) to being its latest scandal: alcoholic, unhoused, abject, field-wandering.

This father's dispossession does not occur owing directly to debt, disease, or the machinations of international financial institutions coming to rest on his sizable chunk of black Iowa earth; rather, one afternoon Daddy—a term of endearment that, by the end of the story, resonates with pain and fear—abruptly divides his land between two of his three daughters and begins to act out publicly the peculiar, twisted, secretive tyranny that has defined his adult life and that is paced by a growth-driven economy. As the narrative unfolds, the unity of Daddy and his thousand acres becomes clear, his unmistakable though unacknowledged sense of unworthiness ultimately fracturing the place that is indistinguishable from his body and being.

By some lights, the father's problems are purely his own—his abuse of his daughters after the death of their mother and his relentless, silent control of them as much a function of what we might view as his personality as they were connected in any way to the macroeconomic situation of an Iowa farmer in the late twentieth century. But it is never far from the minds of Daddy and his neighbors that in more western states one could find "farms that dwarfed my father's in size, thousands of acres of wheat or pastureland rolling to the horizon, and all owned by one man" as well as "unbroken rows of tomatoes or carrots or broccoli miles long, farmed by corporations" (Smiley 131)—an image taken up in the endless games of Monopoly that the family plays through the long summer evenings. In fact, owning massive acreages and having well-drained fields is far more important in the community's eyes than functional parenting; the desire for economic growth long ago overrode more publicly avowed familial pieties having to do with the healthy growth of the child. As Ginny's sister Rose observes when recalling in a rage the father's sexual abuse of the sisters, "the thing is, he's respected. Others of them like him and look up to him. He fits right in. However many of them have fucked their daughters or their stepdaughters or their nieces or not, the fact is that they all accept beating as a way of life" (Smiley 302). Despite Daddy's years of denied abuse and unresolved conflicts, the folks of Zebulon County prefer to view him as a betrayed father undone by an ungrateful Regan and Goneril. And yet Ginny is caught between the two systems of desire that have unhinged her father. Even at the end of the story, when Rose has died of cancer and Ginny has forever left the farm to wait tables in St. Paul, she recalls that "a distant view of my father driving a green tractor across a green field had always moved me" (Smiley 317).

Inside the contradictory cartel mentality of the family-on-the-farm, other forces are literally at work on their bodies. The women in Smiley's novel succumb to mysterious miscarriages, lymphatic cancer, precipitous declines in health and happiness—all owing, as it turns out, to the accumulated nitrates and atrazine in the well water. And the apparent life-failure of these particular sisters is partly owing to chemical runoff from the fields and partly owing to the silences that surround them—family sins, old grudges, lively envies, unspoken interfamilial angers and hatreds, complex and ongoing betrayals:

> Every life I knew of in Zebulon County was marked by conflict and loss. Weren't our favorite conversations about just these things—if not how some present tangle was working itself out, then how past tangles prefigure the present world, had made us and our county what it was? And didn't it always turn out with these conversations that the fact that we were prospering, getting along, or at least feeling our life strong within our flesh proved that everything that had happened had created the present moment, was good enough, was worth it? (Smiley 248)

Always, the economics of life on the farm surface in the narrative: Ty's decision to write huge checks to cover the cost of a new hog complex; the cost of a "brand-new, enclosed, air-conditioned International Harvester tractor with a tape cassette player" (Smiley 17); the fact that "in 1979 the market value of my father's land was $3200 an acre, at the very pinnacle of land values in Zebulon and in the whole state." That fiscal picture changes drastically as the story of Ginny's family unfolds. In the late 1970s, the farm economy was booming in Iowa, and land values were high enough to justify massive loans to midwestern farmers for expansion and improvement. During the court case in which Daddy and Caroline attempt to sue Ginny and Rose for possession of the thousand acres, the local banker Marv Carson explains that Ginny's husband has contracted for the first $125,000 of an eventual $300,000 loan "with the farm as collateral."

The Des Moines lawyer said, "Mr. Carson, many would consider it remarkably risky for a family operation to take on this kind of debt. Don't you?"

"Oh, no. I feel good about it."

The Des Moines lawyer raised his eyebrows.

"Hogs are an excellent investment. Profit is going to be in hogs. The idea of being debt-free is a very old-fashioned one. A *family* can be debt-free, that's one thing. A *business* is different. You've got to grasp that a farm is a business first and foremost. Got to have capital improvements in a business. Economy of scale. All that." Marv was grinning. Clearly, he considered that he was giving everyone in the courtroom a well-deserved lesson. (Smiley 324–35)

By the time that the story ends, the farm crisis is in full swing, and the agriconsolidation of the Midwest almost accomplished in its 1980s version. Leveraged buying has turned a land boom into a bust, and real estate prices have plummeted. Bankrupted family farmers are being replaced by large businesses.

Ginny's husband Ty tells her, when he comes to St. Paul to arrange for their divorce, that he is on his way to Texas to seek work with a "big corporate" hog operation (Smiley 339). He explains, "Marv Carson wouldn't give me a loan to plant a crop this year. I didn't have any collateral except the crop itself, and they decided to stop making those kind of loans, with the farm situation the way it is."

"I heard it was bad."

"Bob Stanley shot himself in the head. Right out in the barn. Marlene found him. That's been the worst."

"They lost the farm?"

"He knew they were going to. That's why he did it. Marlene's working in Zebulon Center now, as a teacher's aide in the elementary school."

My mouth was dry. I took a sip of the Coke. (Smiley 339)

Ty explains that in his own case he had been unable to keep up with loan payments. Finally, Ty had traded his four-year-old pickup truck for an eight-year-old Chevy Malibu and headed out of Iowa. In the terms that Smiley's narrative provides, these failures speak volumes. In terms of the critical regionalist dialectic proposed in this book, it is immensely relevant that the Coke Ginny turns to for relief probably contains high fructose corn syrup processed by ADM.

The endless implied discourse—how one farmer financed his new combine and how another bid for and won adjacent acreage when his neighbor lost the mortgage—coincides with and reinforces the "wisdom of the plains. Pretend nothing happened" (Smiley 22). And it is precisely that silence— the still-exploding legacy of the family farm decorum—that Ginny critiques for Ty:

> "The thing is, I can remember when I saw it all your way! The proud progress from Grandpa Davis to Grandpa Cook to Daddy. When 'we' bought the first tractor in the country, when 'we' built the big house, when 'we' had the crops sprayed from the air, when 'we' got a car, when 'we' drained Mel's corner, when 'we' got a hundred and seventy-two bushels an acre. I can remember all of that like prayers or like being married. You know. It's good to remember and repeat. You feel good to be a part of that. But then I saw what my part really was. . . . You see this grand history, but I see blows. I see taking what you want because you want it, then making something up that justifies what you did. I see getting others to pay the price, then covering up and forgetting what the price was. Do I think Daddy came up with beating and fucking us on his own?" Ty winced. "No. I think he had lessons, and those lessons were part of the package, along with the land and the lust to run things exactly the way he wanted to no matter what, poisoning the water and destroying the topsoil and buying bigger and bigger machinery, and then feeling that all of it was 'right,' as you say." (Smiley 342–43)

Perhaps needless to say, Ty is not convinced by Ginny's reflections. But the reader, especially one engaged in cross-cultural exploration of agricultural regions, can discern Ginny's shrewdness in refusing to absolve Daddy and the local mythology from all guilt when the corporations move in to take over their land. *A Thousand Acres* shows us that responsibility is not a question of either/or but of both/and: at the very least, the family farmer's willingness to buy into a lifestyle that privileges productivity at any cost enters into complicity with the mid-1980s incorporation of the region, encouraged as it was by tax laws that saved money for larger farmers by allowing bigger deductions to incorporated farms and assigning more favorable tax rates to them. Ginny's body becomes one with Daddy's and with the land, all seamlessly infected not only by chemicals but also by ideologies that enable the end of the very traditions that they believe they privilege.

Smiley makes clear that Daddy's demise is emblematic of agricrisis as a whole; she has Ginny tell us, "The Boone Brothers Auction House was plenty busy that spring, and for years to come, riding on the surging waves of the land as it rolled and shifted from farmer to farmer. . . . Our thousand acres seems to have gone to The Heartland Corporation" (Smiley 368). The sisters' houses are razed during corporate expansion and alteration, and Ginny is left with a $17,000 property-sale tax bill. Ginny adds that "although the farm and all its burdens and gifts are scattered, my inheritance is with me, sitting in my chair. Lodged in my every cell, along with the DNA, are molecules of topsoil and atrazine and paraquat and anhydrous ammonia and diesel fuel and plant dust" (Smiley 369).

A similar textual paradigm and cultural dissonance shadows John McGahern's acclaimed novel of the same vintage as Smiley's, *Amongst Women* (1990). From the outset, we are aware that the Daddy-figure, Moran, is the center of the story, his family, and the land they call "Great Meadow." His three daughters, despite feeling some resentment at Moran's control of their lives, nonetheless greatly value the sense of pride in their self-defined status as local aristocrats of their village world. The tragedy in McGahern's narrative has less to do with the loss of land than with the gradual dawning on the father of his children's withdrawal from the way of life associated with that place and that farm. Rather than stay on at home, they prefer, daughters and sons, to migrate to Dublin city, England, America. The central tension in the novel has to do with the father's constant surveillance of and control over his dwindling domain. Holding his children for as long as he can in a state of suspended claustrophobia, he finally watches them drift away.

As in Smiley's narrative, the "untutored and uncaring outside world" is oblivious to the drama of this man's life. When Moran alters his ancient routine to go to the town bank—he wants to "get the manager's advice on whether to sell or keep certain government bonds he held" (McGahern 174)—this former IRA hero and local patriarch is treated like a nonentity.

And despite the family's outrage at their father's marginalization by the younger, modernizing community, neither wife nor daughters complain to the bank. From being central to a world full of tradition and custom-bound ways of doing business, Moran has moved to the periphery of an administered theater in which bankers take center stage. "He had never in all his life bowed in anything to a mere Other," McGahern writes (178), but Moran's day has come and gone. Although the daughters pronounce that he would always live on in them, it is clear that Moran's era has, like Daddy Cook's day, not only passed by but also become visible merely as a transitional moment in the development of global capital.

Not coincidentally, that experience from the 1990s is depicted in Jim Sheridan's film *The Field* (1990), which shows Ireland in the 1930s and is based on a 1965 play by John B. Keane.[1] The emerald-green field produced by carrying seaweed fertilizer over rocky hills, the walled-in grazing land for the McCabe family's precious cattle, the luxurious color created from a palette of sweat and blood—this field that is clearly Ireland in miniature is about to be sold by a bitter widow, herself an outsider, to a Yank whose family Bull McCabe views as having deserted the Connemara community during the famine. A stranger of the worst kind, no better than the travelers who have "lost their footing" on the land and thus are cursed to wander eternally, the cinematic American with his cashmere coat and shiny umbrella returns to the home of his forefathers eager to cover the field with concrete, pull limestone out of the hills, build good roads, attract industry, and provide employment for the men of the village.

The outsider's plans conflict with McCabe's lifelong priorities. We learn that McCabe had chosen to harvest hay while his mother lay dying; we learn that McCabe's older son, the heir to the field, apparently unwilling to preempt his younger brother's right to stay in the community, committed suicide at the age of thirteen. When the Yank confronts McCabe and buys the beloved bit of land, the Bull beats the American's head against a rock until he dies. When McCabe's remaining son decides to run away with a traveler's daughter, denying the earth that is sacred to his father, McCabe-cum-Lear drives all of his animals over the cliff into the sea. His son, attempting to stop this madness, is also dashed on the rocks below, and McCabe becomes an ersatz Cuchulainn, battling the waves as though they were enemies attacking his son, his land, his cattle, and his world. In the mythic space and time of the film, the conflict of local priorities and multi-national expansionist economics can end only in disaster.

For an American midwesterner to understand McCabe's obsession with the field, which even in the milder narrative of the original play motivates the Bull to murder the man who bids against him for the property, it is necessary to invoke the concept summarized in the Irish word *ceantar*, which means both an area and its people. It is no exaggeration to say that in the Irish language as spoken in the preindustrial Gaeltacht, there was no conception that a people could be deprived of its land. Even in times of warfare, when hostages were taken away from their homes, it was unthinkable that an entire group could be shifted to another place. In *The Field*, the plot of land itself is not so much a possession as a conduit between Body and Land, part of each, an organ or limb. There *is* no outside here except the Returning Yank, who can occupy both interior and exterior at once only because of his money. He is not totally unadmirable, but he lacks sensitivity to Ireland and its ancient coping responses in regard to capitalist colonization. He wants to contribute, as much as today's multinationals and with the best will in the world, to the dispossession of Irish people and the alteration of indigenous culture.

McCabe, like Smiley's Daddy and McGahern's Moran, is a socially estranged and angry figure butting heads with history in a dark fever that continues to unfold from the original play text into the movie, from actual history to contemporary folklore. The film, Fintan O'Toole has asserted, not only adapts the play but also distills "80 years of images" from Irish theater (O'Toole, "Field"). As a summary statement about the many ways in which drama has shaped and articulated the conditions of twentieth-century Irish life, Sheridan's film echoes the Lear story as unerringly and inevitably as do *A Thousand Acres* and *Amongst Women*. In such cases, real-life farm crisis finds its central image in the figure of the patriarch, driven by cultural imperatives but woefully unaware of his own needs and desires, who creates his own tragedy in dialectic with macroeconomic change.

The relation of the 1990s film to the earlier play as well as to the real-life story that underpins it tells a lot about the progress of international growth-based capitalism. O'Toole observes, "Keane's play is very much a reflection on the change that was happening in Ireland in the late 1950s and early 1960s, the change from a traditional and rural society to a modern and industrial one. The plan to turn the Bull's cherished field into an industrial quarry is a powerfully simple statement of the clash of one way of looking at the world and another" (O'Toole, "Field"). I would add that more than an encounter of rural and industrial, or of Irish and American viewpoints, both play and film dramatize local responses—including aesthetic ones that seek in Shakespeare a shape to which to cling amidst global conflagration—to planetary forces of change. This is not to undervalue the "specific social tragedy" that the play initially explored. In fact, the event that stands behind this play has to do not only with a century of dispossession and famine, to which O'Toole refers, but also with a dispute during the late 1950s in Keane's home village in Kerry, a mini "land war" between Dan Foley (the model for the Bull McCabe) and Moss Moore. Michael O'Regan reports that the dispute involved the townland of Reamore, close to Tralee, when County Kerry was "economically and socially devastated" by emigration and unemployment. In this environment, and in a nation where land of any size was seen as "gold dust," Foley and Moore fell out during 1957 over the siting of a boundary ditch. By November of 1958, Moore had been found strangled to death. Although Foley was never charged with the crime and always protested his innocence, many in Kerry believed him guilty of murder. O'Regan adds that the houses of both Foley and Moore "are in ruins."

Rather than depose the local history embodied in this play, I want also to endorse the work done under Sheridan's direction, the cross-cultural inquiry into a global system with oppressive implications for all of us. When we compare Keane's play and Sheridan's film with Smiley's novel, we discover that these parallel deployments of the Lear figure enable us to hold in one breath devastating losses and compensatory hungers, all modulated within and through a will to power that corporate life cannot fail to accommodate and make use of. In all three—*A Thousand Acres*, *The Field*, and *Amongst Women*, the children of a strong father literally undergo arrested development and are silenced by the father's fierce presence. The contradiction between the needs of personal development and the protocols of economic development could not be more overt.

The abuses and tragedies that occur in these narratives find a useful context in Marshall Berman's classic study, *All That Is Solid Melts into Air*. Berman rightly identifies the nineteenth century as a pivotal moment, when modernization processes were far advanced but when people could still live also in memory, straddling the world of the past and that of the present/future. It is this zone that the rural literature of Ireland and the Midwest is most eloquent in examining, extending from the 1840s to our own day this complex process of "living in two worlds" (Berman 17). Whether Keane shows us the last-straw scenario of the migrant's return or Smiley unfolds the familial impact of agribusiness reorganization in the heartland, a key portrait is of the farmer-father whose pride and desire were surely used by what Berman calls "bureaucratic materialism" to create the very conditions that not only would render that farmer smaller than life but would actually remove him from ownership of the land. Capital has unerringly intervened at the level of the father's drives for power and linked them to its own requirements for unlimited growth.

These stories are about the migrating population's imaginary and how it has been colonized by the corporate symbolic in uncanny, disturbing ways. It is perhaps for this reason—the degree of disturbance in the father gone awry—that many farm crisis stories dispose of the father altogether in a representational address to the real and recurring problem of agrarian suicides during economic strife. On opposite sides of the Atlantic, twinned tales return us to the world of Hamlin Garland and Huck Finn, where space and place, growth and stasis, do battle in and through the name of the dead or emotionally moribund patriarch.

We might recall Elmer Powers's farm diary of the Great Depression in Iowa. On 21 November 1932 he reports a death without missing a beat, "I dressed turkeys for the Thanksgiving trade. Bill husked corn all day. The weather was quite warm and Bill says the fields are in fair shape again. Rumor says a prominent banker shot himself this morning. Supposedly too many complications to attempt to find a way out" (Grant and Purcell 24). In April of 1936, he adds with a mixture of defensive remoteness and mystery, "Another farm tragedy occurred this morning. A farmer living about the edge or to one side of our community, a middle-aged man, committed suicide by hanging himself in his barn. He was well known, much liked, a good farmer and had a nice family. He was about to lose his farm to the mortgage company and I suppose that is what drove him to commit such a rash act. I do not know if this is just a singular incident, or if it is still one of the suicides that should be connected with the number of them several years ago, or if it is the beginning of another wave of troublesome loads that finally become more than farmers can bear" (Grant and Purcell 100). Moving from one downswing in the economic cycle to another, we find a famous case in point occurring in 1985 when a farmer in Lone Tree, Iowa, about to be dispossessed of his home, walked into the bank holding his mortgage, shot the manager dead, then returned home and killed both his wife and himself.[2] Such derangement and the acute depression of farmers became a matter of concern throughout the Midwest in the 1980s, and organizations like PrairieFire organized to counsel people whose day on the land was passing. Even the local southeastern Iowa news in October of 1991 reported that during the 1980s, the suicide rate for farmers in the American Midwest was roughly twice that of a comparable population of white males in other occupations in the United States. Experts suspected, the commentator added, that this unusually high suicide rate was related to the farm crisis.

On the other side of the Atlantic, there have been frequent reports out of rural Britain that suicides have increased dramatically: "To the outsider, Shropshire, with its round hills and fields separated by ancient hedges, appears an area of assured contentment. But last year, 27 of the 40 suicides in the county were farmers" ("When the Only Way"), a fact attributed to subsidy cuts and rising interest rates in the region of Britain most similar to both Ireland and the heartland. Although the issue of why members of the general population commit suicide at any given historical moment is immensely complicated, it is worth noting the 1987 report that the suicide rate in the Irish Republic had risen 400 percent from fifteen years earlier ("Fourfold Increase"). Most of the victims were reported to be young and middle-aged men. At the twenty-third annual meeting of the Psychological Society of Ireland, this quadrupling was reiterated along with the statement that the 1990s were seeing a leveling off of this rise (Hogan, "Suicide Rise"). But reports in 1993 denied a plateau in such deaths (Ryan). In an article called "Priest Says 9 Young Clare People Committed Suicide in Six Days," *Irish Times* agricultural correspondent Sean MacConnell shifted attention from the city to the countryside. Father Harry Bohan, a rural activist, attributed the rash of deaths all over Ireland to the undermining of families by the government; he also commented on the "hopelessness" of

This headline from the *Irish Times*, 19 March 1993, reveals only one moment in an escalating unemployment crisis for both rural and urban Irish youth. Courtesy of the *Irish Times*, Dublin.

unemployed young people throughout the island (MacConnell, "Priest Says").

By the autumn of 1994, the same paper told of "Farmers and the Suicide Factor"; "It was reported earlier this year that Ireland had one of the highest rates of suicide in Europe and that farmers accounted for 18 per cent of the total. According to the survey men who kill themselves, when categorised by their occupation, comprise more farmers than any other sector of society." Joan Fitzpatrick, chair of the Irish Farm Association's Farm Family Committee, responded that "every farmer knows someone who has taken his or her life, but . . . they are not anxious to attract attention to this or discuss it." Depression, isolation, lack of "pleasurable pursuits," a reluctance to communicate, the trend toward having only one generation on the land, and uncertainties over CAP and GATT all were mentioned as contributing to suicides in the Irish heartland (Foley). It is worth noting that in Ireland, suicide is taboo, a forbidden action that some have found to be equaled only by the act of selling off the family farm. Consider this 1992 *Irish Times* commentary:

> It came down casually in the conversation.
>
> They were from the heartland of Tipperary. I was from Galway. Same rural background. Same love of hurling. Same love of land.
>
> 'So, what are you doing in The Great Capital?' I asked.
>
> 'The buildings. He's a carpenter. I'm a bricky. Yourself?'

'I'm trying my hand at journalism.'

'Go down every weekend, do you?'

'Down?'

'Home. To the farm.'

'No. The farm is gone. Sold.'

I wish I had a camera.

'You sold the farm?' the black-haired one said, looking over at me from the stool beside his companion.

'Yes,' I said.

He went on looking at me for several seconds, then turned back to his pint.

'Jesus.'

'Christ,' the red-haired one added.

I said nothing. After several seconds the red-haired one said: 'Well, it's none of our business.'

. . . It has been said that suicide ranks as the greatest taboo in modern Ireland. That may be so in Ireland as a whole, but in rural Ireland, in the Ireland of milking parlours and cattle marts there is as great a taboo. It's called selling out. And in the minds of many rural people there is little difference between the two. (Monahan)

The most dire representations of the agrarian imaginary occur when the macrosystem's needs come into overt conflict with the values that the father on the farm endorses. The various "Daddys" who run amok in the world's heartlands may be viewed as symptoms of the logic of consolidation as it impacts directly on spaces long associated with an ideologically consistent, apparently fixed way of life. Eventually, economic development protocols push the father to the breaking point in a recurrent story that is predicated on the patriarch's control of both utilitarian and emotional relations. It seems fair to speculate that when the father on the farm perceives his inutility, he may well exit from the scene of convention and commerce. An overview of rural literature and experience suggests further that IFIs have replaced the patriarchal phallus as transcendental signifier. Meanwhile, the narrative of the family farm unfolds into a conception of lack and reassemblage expressing these conflicts. Smiley's Daddy, like the Bull McCabe, displays the inchoateness of an imaginary in crisis, traversed by an invasive administrative symbolic order. At the level of sensation and drive, IFIs suck up surplus value and occupy the locus of creativity—a representation that may help to explain the social stalemate so often encountered when we think about agriculture amidst seemingly overwhelming social change.

Libidinal Economy and Alternative Jouissance

It is here that Joseph Lee's harsh analysis of families in Ireland finds a place in relation to the worldwide farming system. His analysis is Gramscian, focusing on the hegemony of the IFI symbolic order. Traditional Ireland, according to Lee, "was a society that devoted much of its energy to skilfully socialising the emigrants into mute resignation to their fate" (Lee 644). Lee emphasizes that those who were propertied and desired to remain so perpetuated the mass exodus as not only an option but also an expectation. In this regard, middle-class interests won out above nationalist aspirations, family values, and agricultural mores (Lee 644). He argues, too, that after the famine, when this system of thought and class benefit was in place, the emphasis on late marriages as a way of controlling the number of births also "protected the property interests of the farmer, whose children dominated the clergies, Catholic and Protestant, which preached these necessary values" of premarital abstinence and selfless emigration (Lee 645).

Much of what Lee deplores seems to emanate from what Arensberg called the Irish system of "familism." In this configuration of the rural family, individual members automatically became part of the farming workforce. Recalling the situation of agrarian crisis that Arensberg monumentalized into an ancient way of life, one can nonetheless observe the inherent misrecognition that occurs when people are viewed not only as commodities but also as utilitarian entities at the disposal of the father's ego. In this closed system, the resulting alienation actually reinforces rural collapse. Similarly, in the Midwest, as Cayton and Onuf comment, family members, land, and crops have historically and increasingly been turned into commodities both within small-scale agriculture and at the corporate level (34). The commercialization of the family farm has had prodigious consequences, not only for food production and rural values but also, tellingly, for stylizations of desire down on the farm. To put the case in terms of ineluctably mixed metaphors, an analyst's willed migration from one subjective position to another enables a view of experience from the edges and play-accommodating expansion joints installed as part and parcel of cross-cultural mirror-staging. A practice of constant relocation makes visible, however fleetingly, the larger system from which reification, standardization, and instrumentalism drop like leaves from a tree. The reciprocal images we trace and deplore have been able to colonize the family structures of rural societies separated by thousands of miles.

What the many farm narratives seem to tell us is not simply that the agrarian imaginary is bankrupt or that we need collectively to regress to a macromirror-stage in order to escape the brutal drives to which the fathers have acquiesced, but that the model of the biological family has been coopted into automatic compliance, forced migration, and powerful pecking orders to such an extent that we need to rethink what constitutes the family itself. Perhaps beyond instrumentality lie alternative configurations of identity, role, and performed being. This is the work of Robert and Donald Kinney, where the absence of the father paves the way to a queer desire that depends not at all on blood connection, that disavows the land, that is provisionally willing to cooperate with the family order but refuses to be forced, and that has become simply bored with the global system's relentless takeover bids. The story that results frees the elements of the family farming story in the path of a queer desire aiming to empower those it touches to move toward self-determination. Whether that personal energy is best expended in saving the farm, in supporting the matriarch, in lighting out for the territory, or in self-consciously furthering the deterritorialization prerogatives of capital remains to be seen.

Robert and Donald Kinney are twin brothers born in Iowa who make experimental videos, including a farm piece called *Demons* (Monozygote Productions, 1994). From their perspective, a patriarchal culture deposits misogyny and homophobia in the same social zones. Their work eloquently explores this linkage as well as the ease with which the heteronormative family is being dismantled by time and circumstances. *Demons* is based on Japanese filmmaker Kinedo Shindo's piece called *Onibaba*, in which, in order to survive, an impoverished peasant woman and her daughter are reduced to murdering wounded samurai and selling their armor in order to survive. The women's predatory behavior enacts the social oppressions that have reduced them to a level where survival needs and sexuality become part of a single, chaotic exercise of drives and personal power. On the occasion around which the film grows, the daughter seeks to escape her horrible existence by having sex with a samurai who wears a gorgeous mask. In a complicated effort to win the daughter back, the mother dons the mask, which becomes stuck to her flesh. When it is hacked off, it leaves behind leprous sores. In the midst of this grotesquerie and squalor, it is the sheer force of the old woman's will that both frightens and enlightens.

Restaging this script, the Kinneys tell the story of an Iowa widow named Allie who lives with her teenage son, Dip, on an impoverished farm during the early 1960s. The video reveals the primitive, ugly quality of their emotionally stunted, brutally hard lives. On the one hand, corporate prospectors try to persuade Allie to sell her debt-ridden property; on the other, she fights to keep the farm by insisting that Dip stay on as her unpaid farmhand. As the Kinneys state it, "The popular representation of midwestern reserve and work ethic is revealed here as a kind of impoverishment that is both claustrophobic and relentless while their labor operates as a matrix from which the drama unfolds" (*Demons* fanzine, 10). Their sad, quiet life is interrupted when Gray, the brother of Dip's dead father, arrives and is allowed to live in a tiny trailer on their land. Gray insinuates that he has been in a mental asylum because of his homosexuality; he proves an attraction to the frustrated and isolated Dip, and they become lovers.

The issue in *Demons* is not whether Dip is gay; what the video privileges is not identity or coming out but rather resistance to the familist rural lifestyle constituted by the prevailing economy. The Kinneys themselves might well argue for increased tolerance in the heartland, but in this piece their focus is much more turned to the interaction of family and external administered society, the mutual contamination, pain, suffering, and rage produced in that complicated nexus. Frantic to keep her son on the farm and thus enable her to maintain her meager existence, Allie soon offers herself to Gray as a replacement lover. Rejected, she dons a mask—in this case the head of a dead pig—in the hopes of frightening Dip back home as he runs through the night toward a tryst with Gray. The Kinneys' treatment emphasizes that Allie is motivated almost entirely by a desire to survive; to do so, she conforms to the hegemonic values of her region, class, and society, and yet "this collusion with a force authored by a system that also marginalizes the role of women sets up within the narrative a tragic circumstance that destroys Allie, Dip and Gray" (*Demons* fanzine, 14). That these people are all trapped and circumscribed by a joyless, narrow, impoverished, and exploitative social structure for which homophobia is merely "pragmatic" and morality a form of passive aggression emerges in every aspect of the video—its bleak colors, its bare interiors, its dark tones and grainy contrasts. According to the Kinneys, *Demons* shows how "the issue of homosexuality exists within a knot of circumstances and issues that include gender, economic survival, knowledge and sexual desire" (*Demons* fanzine, 15). To put it another way, the Kinneys strikingly reinforce Smiley and Keane, Garland and McGahern, Suckow and Durcan to insist that the autonomy of desire in the present economic circumstances is purely a fiction.

How did the father on this particular farm die? Far from committing suicide, at least directly, he drunkenly fell into the pigsty, where the animals ate away his face. Similarly, Allie's face is deformed from wearing the pighead mask: matriarch and patriarch become equally distorted and interassimilated by the demands of their appalling environment. In *Demons*, as in *Onibaba*, the mother polices the offspring's sexual pleasure in order to assure herself that younger hands will be available to do the work necessary for her own survival. It is clear that no return to the normative family will solve the problems of these people, any more than a simple acceptance of Dip's apparently opportunistic homosexuality will render the farm free of debt and their mutual lives open to some minimal pleasures. Rather, the Kinneys dramatize the dire effects on the agrarian imaginary of the desperate need to stave off corporate buyers.

At the same time, the family farm ethos has typically been the bastion of heteronormative, child-rearing culture, and the nostalgic tale surrounding the family farm depends on this seamless productivity. In presenting the story of Dip and Gray, the *Demons* video abruptly broadens the scope of the environmental possibilities for the constitution of the family and of desire down on the farm—at least as these have been dominantly represented in film and fiction over the past 150 years. But the Kinneys, never sentimental, make clear that liberating alternative forms of jouissance will not turn the tide of corporate buyouts. No unilateral shift in behavior will do; the entire system, top to bottom, must be scrutinized.

The Kinneys thus begin from the space of marginalized desire in order to highlight the shocking decay of human life under an administrative regime. They help us to see that in addition to starting at that point of pro-

hibited or policed desire and rethinking it, we need to imagine a space-
between or interbeing that liberated energies can inhabit while they reassemble mulitiplicitously. Perhaps it is possible to discover in the libidinal
energies of all split-off aspects of desire elements of the uncanny that can
be introjected as/by others interested in economic refiguration. Thus one
region can offer to its twin not a utopian third space but rather a critical
regionalist platform on which to explore reclaimed desires. The view from
the inside and the view from the outside would both become part of the
resulting assemblage, a stance that brings me to propose a new category for
cultural studies that grounds itself in mirroring and in liberating jouissance.

OBJET PETIT I

Lacan's Seminaire XVI was his seven-hundred-page response to the May
1968 uprising in the French universities. Marcelle Marini summarizes, "Focusing on the Other and the *objet a*, Lacan analyzed and combined Pascal,
Marx, and the logic of the link" between identity and the *a.*, with connections to both jouissance and the Phallus. He cited his reading of Marx at
age twenty, especially attending to the fifth chapter of *Capital.* "Marx, he
said, had invented 'surplus-value [plus-value]' and *he* had invented the *objet
a.* He stated that he was going to construct the *plus-de-jouir* so as to isolate
the *objet a*, and he was going to do so by homology (and not analogy, what a
nightmare!) with 'surplus-value'" (Marini 215–16).

One ancient question of family farming as Ireland and the heartland
have known it is whether an individual's multiplicitous desire can be indefinitely contained by the father's desire for surplus value. Another question is
whether the will to consolidation can utterly occupy the space of the father.
The bankruptcy of the farming system is purposefully connected by Smiley,
Keane, the Kinneys, and others with the father's lack as well as with the
semantically similar lack of the father. In methodological response to this
puzzling set of issues, I want to put forward a composite category for cultural studies, the function of which will be to remind us to keep in focus the
operations of IFIs while we also concern ourselves with issues of individual
agency and collective everydayness within a comparative framework. The
category that I propose spans what we often regard as intuitive creativity
(the making of disparate connections) and all that is most counterintuitive,
even totalitarian, about how our world is ordered.

This new category I would call *objet petit i* in partial reference to what Lacan calls the *objet petit a*. Lacan was, of course, one of the West's great cross-cultural spokespersons for Lack.[3] According to him, in an ever-unsuccessful effort to complete a sense of identity, human beings routinely struggle to keep their perception of gnomonic self-absence at bay. In infancy, the self is experienced in desired proximate somatic objects. As the child matures, the objects of desire become less and less amenable to the illusion of solidity and integrity. Lacan calls this combination of mastery and loss the "*objet petit [a]utre.*" This perception of "castration" or damage abjects the whole texture of relations. Displacement, compensation, projection, transference all express this situation. "The *objet a*," Lacan avers, "is something from which the subject, in order to constitute itself, has separated itself off. . . . This serves as a symbol of the lack" (Lacan 103).

Summarizing the observer's experience, Lacan says, "You never look at me from the place from which I see you. . . . Conversely, what I look at is never what I wish to see" (Lacan 103). Rephrased in the terms of a comparative cultural studies, this negatively inflected state of visuality is the same space projected and mapped by the cousin regions of international marketing and by whatever structural paradigms we can cobble together first by looking from one space, then from the other, gaze and eye contravening and constructing one another by turns. In the shifting elsewheres charted by seeking the Midwest from Ireland and vice versa, we discover the factitiousness of the world's heartlands in the face of historical manipulation and cynical contemporary administration.

If Lacan is correct, and the *objet a* marks all that the subject is not, then we can agree with Zizek when he adds that the domination by a master signifier, by patriarchy, say, produces not only representation but also "some disturbing surplus, some leftover." The "remnant" is also the *objet petit a*, and various discourses exist to cope with it (Zizek, *Looking* 130–31), precisely because of its negative rather than positive condition. Many of those discourses are institutional. Lacan, of course, defines not only an *autre* but also an *Autre*, not only the fetishized organ but also the law and its symbolic ground—for our purposes, the *objet Administration*.

I contend that *objet petit i* is mobilized as the bifocal, oscillating, dialectical glance that respects but defies boundaries and taps into outsiderly desires to assert uncanny cross-regional twinnings. If the emblem of lack for

Lacan is the eye, or the *objet autre*, I would say that the emblem of lack for a critical cross-regionalist methodology is the culture's administrative twin, often transmuted by desire into a utopian phantasm. It is the shuttling, the weaving of desire between regions that creates our shared cultural field, that makes up a fantastic adventure narrative, and that may forestall the entropy of total administration.

The paradox of an identity that can never be achieved or escaped challenges us to consider at what level of community and in what interactional terms we may be able to shift the balance from exploitation to enhancement, from commodification to something like mutual benefit. Imaginary worlds, the processes of migration between heartland-peripheries, and the desire to leave recessionary violence behind all stand in for the *objet petit i*, Ireland and Iowa in their moments of representative assemblage. Thus *objet irlandaise* comes into focus for this immersed outsider, and the "i" in question slides into continuity with the subjective I, the viewing eye, and what we might call *objet iowa*. Insofar as any form of perceived lack may be viewed in this psychohistorical maneuver as both castration anxiety and agricultural anxiety, cross-regionalism need not, of course, be limited to places with names that begin with "I"; my examples frame *objet petit i* with a context rich in cross-cultural methodological possibilities. Again, Lacan argues that the subject is doomed always to seek an unconscious that is not inside but utterly exterior, not in the past but in the repressed future other. Thus Zizek describes the situation of the analysand who "is confronted with a scene from the past that he wants to change, to meddle with, to intervene in"—finding out along the way that this particular "intervention was from the beginning comprised, included" (Zizek, *Looking* 57–58). This situation is why we can adapt the concept of *objet petit a* to a macrological, social sphere whose administration exerts a totalizing force.

When Bhabha looks for a "third space of enunciation" or when Haraway speaks of the necessity for mutual articulations, the trajectory of that search leads us toward *objet petit i*. The dimension-between in which all of the oscillations and exchanges take place is the crucial zone for cultural studies. As such, *objet petit i* connotes a different way of looking, understanding, and being than we currently employ in much cultural studies work. The desire in question is both deeply mutual and heterogeneous; it enables many more regional interanimations than it deflects; it enjoys the introduction of consensual spaces-between. *Objet petit i* signs our desire for the other insofar as that yearning maps the constant dialectic of terms and boundaries that bring us into being, a dialectic that operates within and among the interstices mapped by a viral and self-replicating administrative culture. In short, *opi* is itself an ensemble concept. It is a psychocultural counterpart to the GATT and to the likes of ADM. In a way, this comment returns me to Lacan's return to Marx and the situation of 1968. Where Marx saw the proletariat as the "irrational" constitutive kernel (Marini 23), we might pose the family-on-the-farm (specifically its situation of forced labor through genealogy) as a version of that kernel. The family system brings the farm as such into functioning existence by subsuming the child's *a* into that of the Father (*A*). That outlaw desire barely domesticated is both the founding element and the wild card, as *Demons* shows us. *Opi* recuperates and restages the concept of lack in the concept of the assemblage; it reminds us of the possibilities for delinking that hover within mirroring; it shows us the nomadic underside to administered culture. And it helps us to see that the parallel economies of global capital and personal development are not reversible. To intervene at the level of the drives on the organizational register of capital, we have to reassemble society, not just critique it.

In Anglo-American culture, the end of the twentieth century has been about learning to tolerate and embrace diversity: gay and straight, black and white, female and male, walking and wheelchaired, native and foreign. Alex Callinicos suggests that the entire late twentieth-century controversy over political correctness has been mobilized in order to deflect attention from ongoing oppression. In fact, he prefers to discuss oppression rather than difference. What I am after is a discourse and a methodology for cultural studies that, making use of a variety of creative assemblages, can imagine ways of addressing both diversity and power struggles. We must learn to construct spaces that will allow for all manner of differences in desire and expression without compromising a collective impulse to push against consolidation from above. A critical-regionalist methodology provides one key to allowing a useful confrontation between marxist doctrine and psychoanalytic insight. As top-down consolidation has threatened individual autonomy and personal growth over the past two centuries, we have learned to accede to and even to privilege size and money over individual jouissance. At the top, it would seem, all desire has been deflected into a greed that impinges on the pleasure and livelihood of most of the world's population. We need consciously to produce assemblages that sanction and protect the jouissance of the family—however we might choose to describe its configuration—both off and on the farm.

SIX

Fielding Dreams, Eating Peaches

Determining what drives economic growth or decline
depends as much on storytelling as on data.
DONALD N. MCCLOSKEY

What has prompted me to strengthen and formalize certain connections between the Midwest and Ireland is my sense of a partly repressed, partly scripted identification of one region with the other's desired object, the use of one region to speak the other's fear of abandonment, loss, and mourning. Given the history of Irish migration, it is not surprising to find that relay of desire, a multilevel *opi*, operative in many meditations on movement and separation. Further, the case can be made that desire arises most notably at the threshold of the assembled state rather than in states of phantasmatic singularity (Deleuze and Parnet 97). Thus a critical regionalism focuses on conjunctions of history and imagination in order to recover energies at the level of the collective drives.

Kelly Oliver, relying on the work of Julia Kristeva to critique Deleuze and Guattari, attempts to reconceive of the family romance to avoid the problem of the negative father—whom we might identify with McGahern's Daddy, say, or with Smiley's—and to make room for an imaginary good father.[1] The oedipal fixation on paternal power thus becomes muted in favor of more multiplicitous connections of parent and child, the social order and individual development. In fact, the father manifests in Oliver's developmental scenario as pure energy available for directing utopian impulses conjured in the spaces between split subjects. For the purposes of a cross-regional macropsychology, previously prohibited jouissance finds its way into the public realm at the nexus of the familial imaginary and the administrative symbolic. But first we have to finish mourning, to complete decathexing the family farm mythos in its inherited, nostalgic form. The new farm may look like the old one, but it won't *be* the old one; it must be reconstituted, critical-regionally, as a becoming-farm able to look at itself with the eyes of a twinned other. Entering a third space of *opi*, viewers can experience an uncanny linkage formed by utopian projections, economic cycles, consolidation protocols, and active mythmaking. Virtual migration between administratively linked regions creates such a negative space that ceaselessly deprivileges the two given geopolitical zones in favor of mutual desire. In that interzone we can interpret anew regional literature and film.

The films triangulated in this final chapter pose symbolic resolutions not only to individual regional issues but also to global manipulation of local economies. The principal narratives in this assemblage complete one another, are parts of one story that returns to us, if you will, from both the past and the future. Posed as critical regionalist artifacts the films cannot be reduced to a naive and univocal statement or meaning. They remain open to new constructions. They cannot be used up by history but are reactivated by it as thresholds. Taking their places as twins within the global or world system, the American Midwest and rural Ireland continue symbolically to generate an excess, an unmet desire for satisfaction beyond that offered by the world economic system.

One further prefatory note: there is a lot of discussion today, especially in third-worlded spaces, about delinking from global capital mechanisms and their indifferent exploitation of this space and that. I argue here that the process of delinking is facilitated by being preceded by a purposeful mirroring, which provides support for the collective narcissistic register of a given region's cultural identity. In the narcissistic border realm, where fantasy can engender change as well as collective action, one encounters Guattari's "group-subject," which aims for recuperation of its logic in relation to other fields. As Guattari argues in *Psychoanalysis and Transversality*, only when collectivity has been achieved can individuals self-determine.[2]

The kind of delinking that Guattari would approve moves toward revolutionary action through the agency of individual groups that would create "unorthodox, transverse relations" within larger groups and institutional settings. Guattari claims that this directional reinforcement can create a "structural redefinition" across both individual and group subjectivity (Bogue, *Deleuze* 86). Analogously, I would argue that within a capitalist system that reaches across regions and into the heartlands of every geomass, transverse networks may be able to loosen the hold of that structure on individual regions and begin to embody the desires of local subjectivities. The loop that connects deterritorialization with reterritorialization in the international capital machinery creates in its processes and contradictions the possibilities for creative instances of delinking and provisional regrouping closer to the rural collectivity's libidinal needs. Because the Deleuzoguattarian conception of nomadic desire runs indifferently through the worlds of people, animals, and plants, it provides the materials for new integrations of farming modalities. The nomadic unit is a chance component fortuitously traversing nature and culture. Aleatory likenesses, strategically unfolded, offer reflective possibilities to a critical transregionalism intent on *being* reflective, on insistently and even therapeutically mirror-staging comparable spaces and places.

Thus, even though we can never recuperate the family farm as we have nostalgically shaped it, we can take the opportunity of mirroring to understand something of what the autonomous, perfected, even grandiose rural condition might be (Ireland seen through the eyes of midwesterners and vice versa). And we can observe what we value in those mirages of wholeness, what we have lost by entry into a global symbolic order. It may still be the case that the patriarchal system that we figure as capitalism could be engineered to enable delinking at various operative levels, so that different forms of community could be reclaimed or depicted.

As Adorno affirms, "A gaze averted from the beaten track, a hatred of brutality, a search for fresh concepts not yet encompassed by the general pattern, is the last hope for thought." The "freedom from exchange" that Adorno seeks may well depend on the ability of the worldwide farming community to create new connections, new assemblages from their partial selves. This is why Adorno insists on the almost zen position that nothing exists in isolation; refusal to "affirm individual things in their isolation and separateness" (Adorno, *Minima* 67–68, 71)—refusal to view only the heart-land, only Ireland—constitutes the first step on the way toward recuperating a measure of autonomy, however compromised. Through negation, through contradiction, through strategic pairing, we can try to detect whatever atoms have resisted being swept up in the totality. This unsystematized material revels in assemblage, in bricolage. The "waste products" and "blind spots" of which Adorno speaks include everything "cross-grained, opaque, unassimilated" (Adorno, *Minima* 151). In some way that the theorist aims to understand, these excess materials and residues have been able to move, at least provisionally, "outside" the world economic system.

BLACK SOX, FAMILY VALUES, IMMIGRATION, INDUSTRIALIZATION

My linked cinematic narrative begins with a historical moment. In 1919, it was alleged that eight members of the Chicago White Sox, including Joe Jackson, conspired to throw the World Series and then profit by betting on a Chicago loss. To this day, it is not clear which of the players actively conspired and which ones were technically innocent. What motivated this GUBU[3] act of public fraud, and who was really to blame? Some would point to the players' rage against their nonsimpatico owners. Baseball and American culture scholar Eric Patterson reports that although the men had attempted to set up a National Brotherhood of Professional Players, the cooperative system lost out to private ownership of teams, and the Black Sox scandal, by discrediting players, enabled that consolidation of power. At the same time, in 1922 "the Supreme Court officially defined the game as an 'exhibition' and not as a business," a move that disallowed prosecution of the two major league team owners under antimonopoly laws, however overwhelming their control over the world of baseball. The players had lost their autonomy and become pawns in a play-for-profit sports industry that was nonetheless accepted by millions of fans as quintessentially American and self-identifying. As the hero of W. P. Kinsella's *Shoeless Joe* recalls his father maintaining, Joe Jackson was "innocent, a victim of big business and crooked gamblers," a player paid like a "peasant . . . while the owners became rich" (6, 9). Taking the proffered money without actually throwing the series, Joe Jackson becomes an emblem for a manipulated proletariat, displaced from Europe and seeking its fortune in the New World, trying to become American, destined to be sold out one way or another.

That said, Patterson maintains that baseball provides a key to American culture. First, the game is associated with rural imagery, particularly through the agency of the farm team, and takes a prominent place in American nostalgic pastoralism; in fact, a case could be made for this game as the intersection of rural and urban values from the earliest days of industrialization to the present. The urban pastoral mode receives underscoring from the relationship between baseball and immigration to the United States: "The new institutions of mass culture were important for all newcomers to the city (loyalty to a baseball team, for example, could provide a sense of identity), but particularly so for immigrants from abroad." As Patterson sees it, migrants quickly realized that baseball enacted and represented American values, from individual enterprise to "fast, efficient teamwork" and on to social and geographical mobility. According to this logic, Joe DiMaggio and Lou Gehrig stand for a host of ethnic players who came to symbolize America's possibilities (Patterson).

The Black Sox scandal saw the game of baseball, this collective forum for heartland values where every player is created equal, sullied by a self-degrading and illegal corruption that big business then capitalized upon. The controversy also split Americans into two camps, those who believed that the eight indicted players were guilty and those who felt they had been framed. In the film version of Kinsella's fiction, *Field of Dreams* (1989),[4] the protagonist says that he wants to help the long-dead Shoeless Joe, somehow "to let him play, to right an old wrong." The Kinsellas (both character and author) are not the first to seek a form of fictional restitution for the disgraced Black Sox players. Resounding in and with *Field of Dreams*, John Sayles's film *Eight Men Out* (1988) joined previous filmic representations of the White Sox's shame. In American folklore, the World Series had traditionally been more sacred than any other sporting event; despite the White Sox's association with Chicago, the midwestern home of American racketeering, the violation of the ritualistic World Series has demanded repeated, formal, aesthetic mediation and collective atonement.[5]

Despite the strong association with American identity and midwestern values, the game of baseball in its early days was tremendously diverse; it assimilated not only immigrants, not only natural athletes, but also borderline personalities, ruffians—a wide range of individuals. Viewed in this context, Joe Jackson was a product of a nomadic rural culture and of the contradictions simmering there among a heartland ideology, a totalizing market economy, and the emergent desire for individual autonomy. Removed from the family unit into an urban world of atomized moral agency and substantial corruption, Jackson was not prepared to make the kinds of fiscal and ethical decisions presented to him. While loyalty to the group would have shaped his early rural life, that ideology was countered by the heavily striated, "acquisitive individualism" (Cayton and Onuf 53) in which baseball played a pivotal role. On the one hand, loyalty to a team enabled recent immigrants to become American in their sensibilities; on the other, the business interests that were taking over the game reinforced the individual's struggle for money and power.

One place where these contradictions come home is *Angels in the Outfield* (1951).[6] In this film, sadly remade by Disney in 1994, a major league baseball team starts a winning streak with heavenly help. In general, the movie is eminently dismissable in both renditions for reasons suggested by the *Saturday Review*: the film "doesn't take long to get bogged down in the worst kind of corn, involving nuns, miracles, and a heavenly ball team. By the time the movie is over the entire cast is believing profoundly in these ball-playing angels." The profanity-wielding, fist-swinging, public-alienating manager is repeatedly caught between his own knowledge of socially acceptable morality and an abusive temper. His bad humor is a case study of an individual caught in the industrializing of baseball—all posed against the pathos of a story about a little orphan girl with an Irish name who loyally prays for the team that grants her a large portion of her American identity. Notably, the incorporeal helpers do not materialize for viewers but rather for Bridget, who is the only one able to see the nine angels as they stand beside the human players. It takes no stretch of the imagination to interpret this story of a dispossessed and displaced hybrid American child who finds herself both a family and a winning team through the power of desire and prayer: the story urgently recuperates absent parents, religion, and morality against the consolidating economy's transformative pressures. And *Angels in the Outfield* transfers its energy intact to the much later *Field of Dreams*.

The writer of *Field of Dreams*, W. P. Kinsella, is a Canadian national who suggests that one Eno Cinnsealagh provides a measure of Irish ancestry for his family.[7] That said, Kinsella denies being influenced by Irish culture; he reads mostly contemporary American fiction. Certainly, it would be difficult to find a more relentlessly American novel than *Shoeless Joe* (1982). That story takes place in the heartland and invests itself in things timelessly American—the family, the farm, baseball, a rugged individualism that defies rebuke. The narrative claims as its starting point the shocking divestiture of Shoeless Joe Jackson. Kinsella's hero, named Ray Kinsella, says, "Instead of nursery rhymes, I was raised on the story of the Black Sox Scandal, and instead of Tom Thumb or Rumpelstiltskin, I grew up hearing of the eight disgraced ballplayers: Weaver, Cicotte, Risberg, Felsch, Gandil, Williams, McMullin, and, always, Shoeless Joe Jackson" (Kinsella 7). That is, the imaginary into which his urban father indoctrinated him had everything to do with Jackson's rural ways and their unjust cooptation by the metropolis.

The film tells the story of a couple, Ray and Annie, who move to Iowa to run a farm. When a mysterious voice tells Ray to plow under a significant part of their cornfield in order to construct a baseball diamond (in the film, land sells for $2200 an acre), Ray feels a visceral need to do so, even though it will require all of his savings to build the field and even though he needs the acreage in corn to meet his mortgage payments. Soon enough, the couple is about to lose its farm, joining the ranks occupied by Richard Gere in farm crisis film *Miles from Home* and hosts of real-life midwestern farmers. In Kinsella's story, the obligatory malign banker threatens foreclosure on the mortgage and demands that the family plant corn where the ballfield stands. But the family refuses to do so, entranced by the events that have followed their irrational construction of the diamond amidst the corn.

The voice's repetitive directives send Ray on a multiple quest; in addition to suffering from a midlife crisis, Ray needs a way out of the farm crisis, and he wants to recover the American dream. One might add that Ray, like the film, suffers from an overdose of stereotypes, including the fact that baseball becomes his panacea. Not that his vision of the baseball diamond in the cornfield goes unchallenged. Annie openly questions what he sees, despite her underlying support for his dream. When Ray tells her that the voice said, "If you build it, he will come," she asks him:

"If you build what, *who* will come?"

"He didn't say."

"I hate it when that happens."

Could this voice be an acid flashback, she queries. Or, as he claims not to have done acid during the 1960s, a "flashforward"? Whatever the case, she accedes to Ray's obvious need to construct the baseball diamond. The almost immediate appearance of a youthful Shoeless Joe vindicates the vision but does not complete the plot. In this Iowa of humorless American gothic, Ray passes radiantly into his dream, into the diamond zone in which he meets not only Shoeless Joe but other ancient players, as well as his own father as he was before Ray's birth, an eager player in the minors, still hoping to make it big in his passionate innocence and love of this identifying American pastime.

When the voice tells Ray to go further, to drive to Chicago, to locate the disaffected writer Terence Mann (in the book, the writer is none other than the reclusive J. D. Salinger), and to go with Mann to rediscover an elderly doctor who once played ball under the name of Moonlight Graham, Ray responds vigorously. The point, it seems, is not simply to enable Ray to make peace with his Dad by playing ball in the field that Ray built for him. (When Ray was a boy, in an unforgivable moment he told his father that he "could never respect a man whose hero was a criminal." If Ray is to move forward into his own maturity, he has to do penance in some way for that remark.) Nor is the point merely Ray's giving Shoeless Joe and his friends another chance to play ball. Despite what we may think for a time, the point of the narrative is not the bringing of a great writer out of seclusion, enabling him, if he desires, to speak again, as in the 1960s, for a generation in search of truths to live by. It is not even that Ray forestalls middle-age slump by doing something so "illogical" and "crazy" that it sets him apart from the rest of us. No, beyond all of this and in echo of the imbedded tonality of *It's a Wonderful Life*, Ray and his family magically reclaim the rural American dream in the midst of fiscal disaster. When Mark, the evil banker, shows up to foreclose on the farm, he cannot see the baseball diamond or the men on it. When Mark sees Terence Mann, he asks sarcastically, "Who's this, Elvis?" The cinematic Mark consigns miracles to tab-loids and runs his life on a cash-only basis.

The stick figure version of Mark in the film has a more compelling role in *Shoeless Joe*. There we are provided with details of Mark's economic deal-ings. Owning apartment buildings and several thousand acres of land, Mark has a partner stereotypically named Bluestein. The two villains of the piece want Ray's quarter section even though, or rather because, they have al-ready purchased a good deal of the county. Ray muses that their farmland "is planted and harvested by a crew of hired hands headed by a foreman who wears a black hat and looks a lot like Jack Palance." He adds, "It is curious that at one time the land barons owned prairie ranches as far as the eye could see. Their authority was eventually undermined, and the farmers took over, dividing the land into checkerboards. . . . Now a new breed of land baron is buying out the farmers one by one." Mark opines that Ray is an "anachronism" on his measly quarter section (Kinsella 61, 62). It takes him a while, but Ray is finally able to figure out that Bluemark Properties, Inc., has bought up 10,240 acres of "prime corn-growing land," with the exception of his tiny farm (Kinsella 162). There follows an inevitable con-frontation between Ray, toting a gun, and Mark and his partner.

Although the Kinsella family is on the brink of eviction, Ray and Annie's young daughter Karin tells the bankers they can relax because "people will come." In the narrative, Salinger/Mann prophetically fills in the dream-scenario of what will be. "The people who come here will be drawn." He stops, searching for words. "Have you ever been walking down the street and stopped in midstride and turned in at a bookstore or a gallery you never knew existed? People will decide to holiday in the Midwest for reasons they can't fathom or express." (At this point, in real life, in a movie theater in Iowa City during the summer of 1989, my then twelve-year-old son turned to me and smiled with delight. He loves Iowa City; it's a great place to be a kid.)

> "They'll turn up your driveway, not knowing for sure why they're doing it, and arrive at your door, innocent as children, longing for the gentility of the past, for home-canned preserves, ice cream made in a wooden freezer, gingham dresses, and black-and-silver stoves with high warming ovens and cast-iron reservoirs.

"'Of course, we don't mind if you look around,' you'll say. 'It's only twenty dollars per person.' And they'll pass over the money without even looking at it—for it is money they have and peace they lack.

"They'll walk out to the bleacher and sit in shirtsleeves in the perfect evening, or they'll find they have reserved seats somewhere in the grandstand or along one of the baselines—wherever they sat when they were children and cheered their heroes, in whatever park it was, whatever leaf-shaded town in Maine, or Ohio, or California. They'll watch the game, and it will be as if they have knelt in front of a faith healer, or dipped themselves in magic waters where a saint once rose like a serpent and cast benedictions to the wind like peach petals. The memories will be so thick that the outfielders will have to brush them away from their faces. . . . I don't have to tell you that the one constant through all the years has been baseball. America has been erased like a blackboard, only to be rebuilt and then erased again. But baseball has marked time with America. . . . It is the same game that Moonlight Graham played in 1905. It is a living part of history." (Kinsella 211–13)

Put aside, if you will, the utter improbability not so much of Salinger's coming to Iowa as of the master of reticence talking in this unrestrained, semiconfessional fashion. Be aware only that the dream that he details comes to pass in the novel, and cars from Ohio, from New York, and from across the nation line up—in the movie we go aerial to see in the gathering darkness a glinting zigzag of headlights off into the infinite distance—to pay their money and see the retroshow. But there's something more than a little disturbing about a melodrama that ends with its protagonists taking such a big cut off the capitalist top. For one thing, the line of cars echoes scenes in 1930s depression films in which displaced people are actually leaving their bankrupt farms behind. For another, Salinger bizarrely evokes a terrifically selective view of America, a place of "apple-cheeked children and collie dogs" (Kinsella 212), where all the people have been discreetly subjected to Lake Woebegone whitewash. When Shoeless Joe asks Ray, "Is this heaven?" I have to smirk cynically at Ray's answer: "No, this is Iowa."

In this version of "Iowa," the players are steeped in familial love and that old cinematic and sports standby, male bonding. Ray had deeply offended his father before his death, but now Ray can play ball with him in a re-claimed past before the national loss of faith that centered in the Black Sox scandal. Now the displaced relationship of progenitor and child allows Ray to have the superior self-knowledge that will allow him to play ball with absolute innocence. Terence Mann, who had spent his alienated days in Chicago writing conflict resolution interactive software for children, moves out of virtual reality into a magical realist form of atonement. The atone-ment itself is not separate from baseball; it actually *is* baseball. As Mann says, even though he has the antiwar movement, the civil rights movement, the Bill of Rights, the anticensorship movement, these things are "not enough" because he also needs baseball. Legislation and activism pall be-fore the collective effort to have fun and to do it with decency and generos-ity. It is important that in this film the past is never lost, and history is not irrevocable.

And yet the film is not entirely an exercise in melodramatic wish fulfill-ment; if it were, Ray would have achieved power over the bank's threat of foreclosure more directly, and he would not have risked his mortgage in the first place to satisfy the whim of an auditory hallucination.[8] That is to say, Ray's cultural identity would be fixed; he would be the Iowa farmer pure and simple, without having access to other social registers and experi-ences beyond the predictably stereotyped. In this case, Ray would be a clone of the character played by Richard Gere in *Miles from Home*. But Kinsella chooses not to present a realist fiction at all, the aim of which can only be to garner sympathy for rural folks trapped in impossible economic circum-stances. Rather than negate clichés by realistically humanizing his charac-ters and their circumstances, *Field of Dreams* turns to oscillating viewpoints as an antidote to reified perception. We see across Iowa's farmland into an alternative universe that coexists with that space or into a liminal space between past and present; we see through Karin's innocent eyes as well as through Annie's skeptical ones; however provisionally, we have access to more than one form of reality and perception. The recession of the 1970s and 1980s, brought about by IFIs' production of insatiable debt structures for enterprise and development, coexists in the narrative with a pre-World War II, pre-Bretton Woods, pre-global form of capitalism. Beneath the lack that *Miles from Home* displays for us we discover in *Field of Dreams* that even fiscal failure, when placed within a perspective that oscillates among registers of social meaning, mobilizes our psychohistorical yearnings for and recognition of relinkings toward atonement and collectivity.

MAGIC REALISM AND ARIEL DORFMAN

Distinguished writer and critic Ariel Dorfman has done perhaps the most sustained critique to date of *Field of Dreams*. He sees the film as an enactment of self-deceptive America's erasure of the past, its preemptive rewriting of history to leave out the awkward bits. Having offended his dead father, Ray now brings him to life to make everything okay again (Dorfman, Rosenstone, and Beller 174). This eradication process does not trouble the filmmakers because they retain both marketing (people will pay to visit the field) and baseball as the historic, replaceable core of American values.

Certainly, Dorfman's analysis applies in spades to *Field of Dreams*. I agree profoundly with his conviction that we should not seek escape from history but should form collectivities and move into history toward social change (Dorfman, Rosenstone, and Beller 178). But as it stands, Dorfman's approach overlooks not only the underlying fictional text of *Shoeless Joe*, with its fuller attention to farm crisis than the film, but also the psychocultural implications that the film's larger cultural context implores us to recognize. What seems to me most interesting about *Field of Dreams* is the implicit emblematic intersection among moments of oppression and deprivation: Irish migration, rural crisis, big business coming down on the proletariat players. Certainly, Dorfman is more than sympathetic to this terrain. In fact, he compares Kinsella's film to Sayles's *Eight Men Out*, the message of which he sees as "if you're poor in America, you're screwed, they're going to manipulate you and use you, no matter what" (Dorfman, Rosenstone, and Beller 184). To this reading, I would want to add the specificity of the rural situation, the cross-regional assemblages in which the story aspires to find a place, and, of course, the invocation not just of magic but of something like magic realism in the heartland.

Any number of definitions have been offered for magic realism, but very few would debate the assertion that the magic realist register is where you can perceive something beyond accepted cultural encoding. By these lights, there exists an agrarian imaginary in which one can see the baseball players; notably, there are people living in the heartland who cannot. From a midwestern perspective, the magic of the field links it to the multilayers that describe colonial and postcolonial spaces, arenas that have been hidden for self-protection. Dorfman looks on as a consumer and critic, from above, and this viewpoint creates a situation of blaming the victim rather than producing an analysis that uncovers the reasons for behaviors—the cyclic economic crisis that cranks out a series of stories in which hope and despair alternate, in which dead fathers come back not so much to make things right as to indicate what has been lost.

To this end, it is worth noting another aspect of the novel that the film bypasses. Ray also has a twin brother and has for this reason become attentive to "uncanny coincidences" (Kinsella 30). He frequently confuses his memories with his brother's, partly because the two must somehow come together if they are ever to perceive their father, not again but, as it were, for the first time. The novel tactfully dramatizes a return to the mirror-stage and a reconstruction of shared drives at that point of mutual regression. (Note that Ray feels as "weak as a kitten" [Kinsella 168] when his father appears on the field and says it's as though he's about to commit a crime.) The twins, like paired administrative regions, experience something like "magnified sense perception" (Kinsella 201) and wholeness of being once they are able to see through one another's experience. And all of this comes about within Ray's ability to imagine the world as if the Black Sox scandal has never occurred, as if his forebears had never left Ireland. Insofar as Iowa is "the right time" and "the place" (84) for such a feeling, Kinsella writes a story about the malleability of history yet to be critically constructed.

In the fragmented but powerfully expressive ensemble joining the American Midwest and Ireland, where the phenomenology of the magic realist text is at home, we can readily unfold a subversive reading of even so benign or so bankrupt a film as *Field of Dreams*. Critical-regionally, we can imagine the perception of channels not yet entirely controlled by the powers that be. In this shared region, ordinary semantic systems collapse and create another order of meaning even while Ray's American dream floats in a time of actual and impending farm crisis.

In the section of *A Mass for Jesse James* called "American Dreams," Fintan O'Toole specifically notices that Ireland is what he calls "multi-layered" (O'Toole, *Mass* 126). Among its layers of experience we can locate the United States as an extension of Ireland. That is to say, America is part of the mnemonic present of Ireland, and American soil is where Irish ideas have recurrently blossomed. Similarly, Saldívar states that a writer like García Márquez gains power from "his ability to create themes in which different modes of production, social formations, and ways of ethnographic and historical representation overlap . . . as the ground for conflict, contradiction, and change" (Saldívar xiii). Although Kinsella is by no stretch of the imagination a writer of García Márquez's complexity, he does make an effort toward unfolding the local narratives hidden under or about to be swallowed by a combination of conservative censorship and corporate gloss. To do so, he adopts something of the immigrant viewpoint that Frank Capra brought to his down-home American films. This is also a residue of a transplanted colonial longing that unfolds as a space-between, a smooth or nomadic space entering the territory of bureaucratization and there setting up a disturbance. Within the larger representational context established here, Kinsella's writing can draw on chains of association that take us deep into the agrarian imaginary. It is in this kind of space that *opi* is most likely to be generated in the form of a yearning for full knowledge of the links between and among individual subjectivity, regional inscription, and the powerful manipulations of IFIs.

But it is important to distinguish between the modest work done by Kinsella's story *per se* and the life that the story took on outside of its film version. *Field of Dreams* actually made ordinary Iowans do things that they might not otherwise have done, a situation that bears looking into. In a curiously American turn of events, all of the attention that the book and film brought to Shoeless Joe's disgrace helped to recuperate the player's image. During 1989, the AP wires reported, "SHOELESS JOE COULD STILL ENTER HALL," that is, despite the Black Sox crisis he could even now be inducted into the prestigious Baseball Hall of Fame. To this end, a resolution was made in the South Carolina General Assembly to request that Shoeless Joe's name be formally cleared by the baseball commissioner, and other locales in America followed suit. Certainly, stranger things have happened, and what is very clear is that Kinsella's fantasy of ghostly restitution is shared by a large enough portion of middle-aged America that the hapless Jackson—not to mention Pete Rose—could well be exonerated someday.

Similarly, in July of 1991, Kinsella returned to Iowa City and visited the Field of Dreams in Dyersville, Iowa, still cornfree. "Author Finds Visit 'Quite a Thrill,'" reported the *Iowa City Press-Citizen* (12 July 1991: 1). Indeed, Kinsella is quoted as saying, with all the aplomb of an architect who marvels over the massive efforts that result from his drawing of blueprints: "To see all of these people running around like ants, all from a few pages that I wrote, is quite a thrill." A few days later, on July 25, Iowa City's local newscast took us to the Iowa field, where Kohei Otomo, then Japan's number one rock star, who models himself on Elvis, came to film a rock video. Dressed in a white baseball uniform, Otomo told the interviewer in Japanese that for him the field represents "American freedom, strength, and the vastness of the land"; playing there is like a personal dream come true for him. He believes that he is probably the only Japanese person to have played with the ghost players there.[9] The newscaster informed us happily that *Field of Dreams* was an international success. And he added that it is nice to see that the corn is so high this year, so lush. What the newscaster had in mind was the fact that in 1988, during the filming of *Field of Dreams*, when five thousand Iowans participated in the filming, the drought was so severe that the corn was still quite short when shooting began. Because the script calls for head-high corn, in which the otherworldly White Sox materialize, the producers, who had come in from California, had to flood the farm for eighteen days to force-grow its crop. What the film gives us is a synthetic Iowa, one that exists in an ideal space where it rains when it should. But that gesture produced in the Dyersville residents a desire to maintain the field in its fictional state. According to Kinsella, people have told him that they feel there is magic in the Dyersville field. At his press conference in Iowa City, he claimed, "I always wonder about these people. There are no gods. There is no magic." And yet, before the 1991 rush of attention to the field, the farmer who owns it placed a coffee cup in front of his house, with a sign saying "Keep the Dream Alive." As in the film, this farmer actually did need the space for corn income, especially in that period of several years' drought and prolonged economic recession. What came across in his press conference as the rather cynical flatness of Kinsella's personal perspective did not disable cultural uses of his writing that, despite their triviality, displayed the rural hunger for a threshold beyond the present that

Is This Heaven?... No, It's...

DYERSVILLE
IOWA

HOME OF

FIELD OF DREAMS™

"Field of Dreams" Movie Site

The Academy Award nominated movie, "Field of Dreams" was filmed on two farms 3.3 miles northeast of Dyersville, Iowa. Open daily 10 a.m. to 6 p.m. April thru Nov. 1. Souvenir Shop.

"Field of Dreams" tourism brochure for Dyersville, Iowa, 1993. Courtesy of Dyersville Area Chamber of Commerce.

would free ordinary people from the absolute control of their lives by global economic forces.

By September of 1991 the first Field of Dreams celebrity game took place. Reggie Jackson was there, the child star from *The Wonder Years*, somebody from *Cheers*, Bob Feller, Bob Gibson, Larry Drake from *L.A. Law*, Lou Brock, Joe Pepitone, Iowa Governor Terry Branstad, and other notables of that caliber. They played ball. A tour bus carried people out to the field.

A GLORIOUS DAY ON FIELD OF DREAMS

Field of Dreams, IA.—Build it and they will come, the voice said.
Boy, did they ever.

About 1,000 people came to Iowa's legendary Field of Dreams near Dyersville Monday to watch two dozen sports, movie and television luminaries play a baseball game. To do it, they paid $50 a ticket (even for small children), left their cars in a school parking lot and rode school buses over a few miles of country roads to get to the game.

Ask any of them and they'll tell you it was worth it. (Hovelson)

And in August of 1993, a year before the IRA and Ulster Volunteer Force ceasefire, Northern Irish boys and girls visiting Iowa through the Project Children program took a day trip to the Field of Dreams and walked along the adjacent rows of corn. Regardless of political and economic realities, utopian desire can still be activated by the concept of the heartland. What's needed is to reimagine the follow-through.

EATING THE PEACH

What to do with a backyard in Iowa in the midst of a recession is fairly clear in the aesthetic of Kinsella. Plow the corn under and build a baseball field. Let nostalgia have its head. In Ireland, where nostalgia is just as much a team sport as in the heartland, what to do with a backgarden may not be as clear-cut, but it is certainly instructive for a critical-regionalist approach. Around 1980, an English correspondent and independent filmmaker named Peter Ormrod had worked at Radio Telefís Eireann (RTE) and while gathering stories for a magazine show called "P.M." he discovered a County

Longford resident named Connie Kiernan who, with his brother-in-law Michael O'Donoghue, had compensated for the closing of a Japanese electronics factory by constructing a wall of death behind his home. Brian McIlroy describes the wall as a "60' high barrel tower," built in tribute to the 1964 Elvis Presley movie, *Roustabout* (Clinch; McIlroy 78–79). That is to say, when the worldwide recession hit their part of rural Ireland, Kiernan and his mate expressed the devastating retreat of the multinationals by imitating an American movie from the mid-1960s. They built the wall "just three feet from the back wall of the cottage where Connie's wife Marcella sat huddled with their new-born baby while her brother and husband hurtled around and around horizontally, oblivious to the ear-splitting racket." They had spent £3,000 and six months (October 1977–April 1978) building it. As Kiernan said, "many's the man who's spent more on drink and had nothing to show for it" (Smyth).[10] Hoping that a backer would learn about his venture through RTE, Kiernan waited by the phone after Ormrod's broadcast but was disappointed that no one rang him with an offer of support. According to John Kelleher, then a controller at RTE, Kiernan "was psychologically devastated by the lack of response to the track—he couldn't believe it. The problem with people like Connie is not that they're in poverty, or that they're starving, but that what they totally lack is the means of expressing what they have to offer. So you have these very young people channeling their talent into something crazy." He added, "It's hard to get a word out of Connie. He's had little education, his income is low, he's a grease monkey. But he channels his energy into doing something quite strange. Under other circumstances, he might have designed buildings or harnessed bridges, but instead . . . he did what Elvis did" (Harti).

Not only did this remarkable cross-regional assemblage find its way onto RTE, but Kiernan's environmental sculpture had further aesthetic consequences when, several years later, Ormrod recalled Kiernan's story and decided to base a film on it. That film was *Eat the Peach* (1986).[11] On release, *Eat the Peach* won an award at the 1986 Taormina Festival in Sicily. It did well in Finland and throughout Europe. Kelleher and Ormrod were disappointed that it did not become a major seller in the global market. Even so, their film was the first "Irish-made, Irish-financed commercial movie to reach U.S. cinemas," having done so under the endorsement of Jonathan

All they wanted was a chance to ride high

EAT THE PEACH

Cover illustration for press-pac of the Irish film *Eat the Peach* (1986). Courtesy of David Collins, Samson Films, Dublin.

Demme (Guthmann 23). United International Pictures distributed it in 1987 in the United States. Above all, *Eat the Peach* was a hit in Ireland. As Eoin Edwards wrote in the *Cork Evening Echo*, "I literally fell out of the cinema, body drained of all energy and feeling a deep sense of satisfaction." He continued, "The film is full of sketches of life as we know it in Ireland today. Smuggling, political canvassing etc. abound and result in some of the funniest pieces of film to have appeared on our big screens for a long while. If you thought *Beverly Hills Cop* was funny, as the saying goes 'you ain't seen nothin' yet.' All this without the stage Irish we sometimes have to suffer" (Edwards). Ultimately the film grossed half a million pounds in Ireland (Farrell 27).

Both the Irish film and its American counterpart are ostensibly grounded in the domestic struggle for survival; both center on a family composed of one slightly crazed and obsessed dad, one shrewd but puzzled woman, and a little girl in whose eyes we read the closest text that we can find of transatlantic innocence, a troubled wonder at what the ideologically controlled adults are really up to as they tear up their land and build athletic sites where vegetables had been growing. In comparison to *Field of Dreams*, *Eat the Peach* tells us what building things in the backyard looks like, to echo a popular song used in the film, a bit further down "the road to who knows where." Instead of crowds of multinational investors wending their way to the industrial boglands, we find the much sadder registering of failure. In place of any projection that says the likes of "If you build it, he will come" or "Go the limit," we confront the folly of the enterprise undertaken by the film's heroes. In fact, together *Field of Dreams* and *Eat the Peach* map once again the unevenly developed, intricately related dual aspects of the boom and bust economic cycle that paces their represented cultures.

In *Eat the Peach*, the desire was to portray Ireland as a highly specific site of previously unrepresented economic forces. To say all of this is quite different from arguing that Connie should have built a baseball field. *Peach* in fact aimed to portray a language of Euro-forces controlled by shadowy IFIs. *Eat the Peach* marked a critical moment of coming of age for Irish film; Irish viewers had hungered for precisely the kind of self-depiction that the film provides for them—accurate, funny, nuanced, caught economically between the devil and the EEC. Toward this end, the story of *Eat the Peach* went through several stages of conception, writing, and rehoning—each one a significant negotiation of cultural issues.

The original fictional representation occurs in an early treatment of *Eat the Peach* called "My Wall of Death: A Story" by Peter Ormrod.[12] The script identifies a factory worker named Con who works on a polystyrene cutter in County Longford. He has two children, Michael and Catherine, and he lives in a farm cottage. His wife is anxious to interest him in a "Spanish style" bungalow plan from a book. Con and his friends find pleasure not in bungalows but in bikes: they ride their motorcycles at top speed along the bogland roads of County Longford. They go to a bar to play pool, and the TV is switched to "an early Elvis Presley movie. . . . In it Elvis plays the role of a fairground hand whose ambition is to ride the wall of death." Ormrod's narrator describes the wall of death event as "spectacular."

That night, Con cannot sleep. "Something had touched him, somehow the images from the Elvis Presley film registered in his mind." The very next day Con arranges to have the kitchen garden and shed area plowed up to produce a pit while his wife is at work. When she returns, Nuala is too enraged to speak; she gathers up her clothes and the children, and she calls her father to come get her. Undaunted, Con proceeds to work with his friend Michael, illegally cutting down pine trees on Forestry Commission Land. Soon a dozen skinned tree trunks form a circle around the pit. When Nuala returns the next day, Con haltingly explains the attraction of Elvis's derring-do and the lack of anything like a wall of death in Ireland. When Nuala acquiesces to the novel plan, Con and his friends celebrate with some six-packs. Trouble is brewing in Granard, however, in the form of a town planning committee. The wall of death is a "planning infringement." Town father Peadar O Hegarty speaks out vigorously against Con's structure: "Look now if everyone was to build a similar construction in their back garden where would we be then. Indeed where would the country be for that matter." While O Hegarty threatens Con, a reporter calls a London subeditor on the *Sunday Mirror* to place this "novelty item" in the paper: "You know the Irish wall of death rider who stopped his bike at the top to ask someone the time."

When the wall is completed, Nuala and the children watch from the overlooking balcony while Con tries it out on his old Honda 250. The same Honda, later brought into their house, leaks fuel, which a water heater pilot light ignites, and the house burns down. Again Nuala's father arrives to take his daughter and grandchildren to his home. But the work proceeds, and the planning committee calls Con in to talk. Now that Con's work has been covered in an English paper, O Hegarty is civil; "This town needs men like you, who have initiative. There's precious little about these days." In fact, the committee has brought in a would-be promoter to manage the wall of death. On its first truly public tryout, the wall works well; Con rides it to the top amidst great vibration all along the balcony. Later, RTE comes to film Con riding the wall. Con wears a "new silver bomber jacket" with cowboy hat and boots. Con and Nuala hope that with proper audiences they can make enough money to build a real house and workshop. But after the RTE coverage, even though the phone number of the box near Con's caravan had been announced, no one calls to sponsor the enterprise. Nonetheless, when we next see Con and Nuala, a year's time has gone by and their new house is almost finished. Con has worked at a factory around the clock. The wall has been used for firewood. But Con's dreams have taken a new shape—he is constructing a helicopter, even though "it doesn't fly yet."

The screenplay for *Eat the Peach*, dated 1985 and composed by Northern Irish playwright Stewart Parker, is considerably longer—a full 115 pages. According to John Kelleher, Parker wrote two early drafts of the film. The screenplay reflects critical conceptual changes that directly address the motivations, values, and economic crisis underlying Ormrod's story and the original events on which the story was based. The film is to open with a "pan across Irish border countryside, mainly tracts of bog, mis-shapen fields, untidy hedgerows, criss-crossed by narrow roads. In the background, the border hills." As Stephen Kruger notes in the study sheets that he prepared for British classes viewing *Eat the Peach*, the film takes place "in a part of Ireland that is not often seen by the rest of Europe." Speaking about the Irish landscape, Ormrod comments that outsiders "think it's some kind of green paradise. In fact it's a big brown desert" (34). Ormrod says, "People in Ireland have a saying 'No good will come from the Bog,' and when I went to see the place, I could see what they meant. It is the weirdest place, just miles and miles of undifferentiated brown peat."

Con and Michael have become Arthur and Vinnie; County Longford has been shifted toward the contested terrain of the island's frontier—specifically Milltown, County Monaghan. The two men work at Murakami Industries, a textile factory about to announce its closure in Ireland,[13] located near "a battered sign 'Site for EEC Advance Factory.'" The Japanese executive speaks of declining trade and of "local communication difficulties (TRADE UNION OFFICIALS SHIFT A LITTLE UNCOMFORTABLY)." Liam Kennedy remarks, "The opening scene of the acclaimed Irish film *Eat the Peach* (1986) shows a group of Japanese businessmen closing down their branch-plant in one of the midland counties, a reminder that the overall increase in employment in multinational firms masks the fact that some companies during this time were either contracting or ceasing operations. In part this was due to world recession and competitive pressures but it also reflected the inescapable fact that products, and the investment projects associated with them, have a life cycle: an initial period of vigorous growth, a mature phase and eventually one of decline. Corresponding to this sequence is an employment profile." Parker's use of adjectives throughout the opening scenes strikingly sets the mood for the economic crisis portrayed at every level of behavior and decision making: in addition to the "untidy" hedgerows and "battered sign" we find a "rotting" barge, a "disused canal," a village that is "grey, run-down, untidy" and boasts "an amazingly ugly modern church." The canal itself is signed as follows: "Milltown Marina. Projected Opening: 1987. This project is financed by a grant from the EEC Regional Development Fund." The lock house stands "badly in need of paint," and even the calculator that Arthur uses is "battered." (The film summarizes this ambiance in a weathered signboard that says "Regional Development Authority," which Arthur and Vinnie tear down for plywood.)

Eat the Peach thus places itself ambiguously, in relation, if you will, to many possible thresholds—on the periphery of collapsing multinational space, with a tenuous and technomythic connection to Japan, and on the frontier of Northern Ireland and the Republic. In a scene when the protagonists, functioning as smugglers, are mistaken to be IRA operatives, the film charts the toppling together of political and economic regimes. And Parker's description evokes information about recessionary gloom that was everywhere in the Irish media of the early 1990s: for example, one journalist quotes Father Colm Kilcoyne, who spoke at a national conference in September of 1991: "He was talking about the 'bereavement' of the West [of Ireland], the separation of its people from their aspirations, the disillusion and anger which have followed the collapse of that region's dreams of multinational money and EC grants *in secula seculorum*" (O'Toole, "Million Miles" 5).

It is into this atmosphere of resonant decay that Sean Murtagh drives in a campaign car set up with "loudspeakers blaring to the empty land." That nearby is a northern border town, its boundaries marked by customs officials, sits comically with the country and western music advertised and played in the film. Parker writes: "The camera works impressionistically: we feel we could be in a western—here and there we see a Stetson, are aware of cowboy-style boots." In fact, this scene introduces Boots Finnegan, a character excellently played by Niall Toibin in the film and described in a review in the *Independent* (4 December 1986) as a "would-be Colonel Parker figure." One reviewer tells us that Boots is "taken from a known stereotype in Ireland. There really are people who say, 'Hi, Man,' and 'You all take care,' because they've seen it in the movies" (Garrett). A *Gunsmoke*-style Joey the Lips, Boots enacts his identity in relationship to American frames of reference. One reviewer calls him "pure imitation J. R. Ewing—as ludicrously displaced as a surfer on the Siberian tundra" (Guthmann 24).

In the screenplay, too, Vinnie and Arthur, freshly unemployed again, turn to smuggling goods over the border.[14] Evoking something like the desert and something like an idealized Midwest as portrayed by James Fenimore Cooper, Parker directs, "The width and flatness hint of the prairie, but here there is no good pasture, no rich grain harvest; just a desultory emptiness, with old railway tracks and the remnants of the abandoned canal system." It is Vinnie's perspective on this barren landscape that the viewer is asked to rely on for suture: "Vinnie is walking moodily round to the back of the house, surveying the general mess,—some redundant posts, bits of rusted corrugated roofing, an old chicken run, a few half-derelict out-houses. The ground for the most part is rough clumps of grass, and stony. Focus away from ground until Vinnie stops and we find from his p.o.v. an oasis of order and productivity amid chaos, carefully 'fenced' with makeshift bits and pieces to keep out the rabbits: this is Nora's vegetable garden. Everything is coming up in neat rows, labelled, with the seed packets still readable. Large-ish stones have been neatly bedded-in to form pathways." Vinnie's point of view continues to inform our vision, from the moment when he mends a stretch of chicken wire to the morning scene at the factory where helicopters wait to take away the Japanese executives.

A peculiarity of the screenplay eliminated from the film is the introduction of Mrs. Downing, a fortyish woman attracted to Vinnie. Her husband, an asbestos insulation businessman of some sort who has left her and moved to the Bahamas, had been one of the proprietors of the "new Ireland." Sad, lonely, self-pitying, and intensely aware of the loss of poetry and music that Ireland has suffered, Mrs. Downing reads to Vinnie from "The Love Song of J. Alfred Prufrock," thus supplying the critical explanation of the film's title: "Do I dare to eat a peach?" In fact, Mrs. Downing asks "Vincent," "Have you ever eaten life's peach?" In what was intended as a come-hitherish scene, Mrs. Downing, played by Sarah Miles in the early rushes, asks Vinnie to feel the "swollen" fruit in her hand, the "tender flesh." In a telling conflation of Joyce's Mr. Duffy and Prufrock, she explains to Vinnie that the speaker in Eliot's poem is "afraid of life, you see. He's never really lived. He feels like an outsider—locked out from the feast of life." She seduces the surprised Vinnie, who is actually enjoying the peach she has offered him while she smooths his hair. While the melodramatic elements in *Field of Dreams* run their predictable course, the melodrama in the Parker script

Arthur and Vinnie in the bogland. Still from *Eat the Peach* (1986). Courtesy of David Collins, Samson Films, Dublin.

The Wall of Death. Still from *Eat the Peach* (1986). Courtesy of David Collins, Samson Films, Dublin.

has been gathered into the portrait of the emotionally bankrupt, moribund upper-class woman. That the Mrs. Downing character was partly filmed and then eliminated speaks well for the filmmakers and their responsibility to an Irish audience. The ponderous Eliot backdrop and Big House theme cannot explain the Irish experience of uneven industrial development, of economic marginalization, and of incredible potential perversely thwarted by multinational and governmental interventions.

In the screenplay, Nora and Vinnie, much like Annie and Ray in *Field of Dreams*, debate the issue of the male's irrational need to take a risk, to do something significant. But the venture has been shown on television and ignored by the public. After waiting for the never-never phone call from a potential angel, Vinnie rides the wall one last time, and Parker calls for a reprise of the TV crew filming the ride, until the wall "becomes a small cylinder in the surrounding landscape, with a toy figure spinning round inside it." Some time later, like all the other abandoned enterprises that the screenplay details, the "Great Wall of Death" sign is carried off by children.

Later, Vinnie again goes into business, with the help of a government grant for a hothouse, growing tomatoes. Even this enterprise would be recognized by an Irish audience as doomed to failure. As Liz McManus explains, "derelict glasshouses . . . used to litter Connemara. Relics of the great tomato-growing experiment that failed. Homegrown vegetables bit the dust in a big way when we joined the EC." At the same time, using plans that a Japanese friend sent them, Vinnie and Arthur are building a helicopter. "CONTINUE PULL-BACK—TO GIVE IMAGE OF THE THREE SITTING AROUND, WITH THE CANAL BEHIND, THE DERELICT BUILDINGS, THE EMPTY VILLAGE, THE WIDE LANDSCAPE—AN OPTIMISM BEING RE-ASSERTED DESPITE THE ODDS—"

The scene bears comparison with *Miles from Home*. In the final moment, the character depicted by Richard Gere takes off for Canada to escape capture and prosecution for burning down his foreclosed farm. Speeding along the back roads to Canada, he passes two farm kids walking in the Iowa dust. One remarks, "He's either way ahead or he's way behind." Even more precisely, the final scene of *Eat the Peach* is fleshed out by *Field of Dreams*, the magical realist plenitude of the latter and the losses of the former are both sides of the same international coin. As filiated locales, Ireland and the Midwest are caught in a productive mirroring that allows one to fill in the interpretive blanks for the other. By this means, we seek access to the limen that spans rural areas and offers them a productive meconnaissance, an interzone beyond the structures of administered society, the terrain for a critical cross-regionalism and a cultural studies eager for canny material change.

INTRODUCTION: CULTURAL STUDIES AND CRITICAL REGIONALISM

1. During the early 1990s implementation of the Single European Act, the traditional name European Community (EC) was altered to European Union (EU). In this volume I retain the EC denomination in quotations and references that precede this name change, but I use the abbreviation EU for more recent instances.

2. The Levitt school of thought assumes that there is no questioning the bottom line, that local companies ought not be encouraged simply in order to sustain a living for inhabitants of given regions, or so that unemployment and a perception of human obsolescence do not create mass despair. In fact, Levitt's breezily clinical language tacitly refuses conditions of human suffering in those often third world zones of cheaper production to which he gestures.

3. As Deleuze and Guattari point out, Pierre Boulez originated the vocabulary of smooth and striated. They explain that "smooth space is constantly being translated, transversed into a striated space; striated space is constantly being reversed, returned to a smooth space" (474).

4. Deleuze and Guattari create their own semiappropriated, semioriginal vocabulary of the molar and the molecular, of the desiring machine and interbeing. I use the Deleuzoguattarian idiom as a starting point to talk about forms of relatedness in culture and in history; I do not maintain any but the most tenuous connec-

tion to the intricacies of the system discussed in *Anti-Oedipus* and *A Thousand Plateaus;* my purpose is to designate zones of relating and becoming in which readers and writers can intervene without being constrained by the evocative but somewhat counterintuitive lexicon construed by Deleuze and Guattari.

5. Frampton attributes the term *critical regionalism* to Alex Tzonis and Liliane Lefaivre (Frampton, "Some Reflections" 78). I am indebted to Desmond Bell for his evocative references to Frampton's work in an article called "Cultural Studies in Ireland and the Postmodernist Debate." He queries, "Can we however talk of a critical regionalism in the territory of social theory?" This is an important question, which is still being answered by an Irish cultural theory that remains, I would say, largely to be created. Bell does find the ground laid "for the emergence of a genuinely postnationalist but anti-imperialist, adversarial critical studies practice in Ireland."

CHAPTER ONE: AGRICULTURAL ASSEMBLAGES

1. Riley also provides some useful demographic figures, showing that in 1850, 4,885 people born in Ireland lived in Iowa; in 1869 that number had jumped to 28,072, and by 1870 there were 40,124 Iowans who were born in Ireland; Sage cites the source for these figures as the 1940 U.S. census. He provides a decade-by-decade chart that shows a significant dropping off in the number of Irish-born Iowans after an 1880 high of 44,061 (Riley 100; Sage 93). It is worth noting Allan Bogue's point that "To the census-takers, the children of immigrants, born in the United States, were, of course, native-born" (*From Prairie* 16).

2. Conversation with Gabrielle Mullarkey, Iowa City, June 1991.

3. A more detailed census of Irish settlers in Garryowen and other Iowa towns can be found in "Irish in Iowa."

4. Compare the regional mapping of child-disciplinary styles reported in February 1995 on the CBS morning show: midwestern parents perceived themselves as being more rigorous than mothers and fathers in the northeastern states, and they also regarded their children as better behaved.

Robert N. Cline, senior vice president of Creswell, Munsell, Fultz, and Zirbel advertising agency in Cedar Rapids, Iowa, one of the largest advertising companies in the world, characterizes the parental generation in Iowa (age 35–50) as being "mainstreamers," that is, in the general category of the outer-directed middle-majority that makes up 70 percent of the U.S. population. However, within that large national group, these target Iowans are distinguished from the "Aspirers" and the "Succeeders," their more achievement-conscious peers. As Mainstreamers, Iowa middle-agers are family-oriented, interested in spectator sports, committed to being socially acceptable, and fiercely brand-loyal. Their main goal is security; their principle motivations for buying products are conformity and family responsibility. (I thank Robert Cline for this information.)

5. I am indebted to William Murray for discussions with me about his writing and the Irish experience.

Chapter Two: Transmuting Geographies

1. Holy Cross had been active for five hundred years and then abandoned for two centuries before a recent restoration (Fr. James O'Connor, *Catholic Mirror*, 15 April 1976, 5).

Chapter Three: Recycling the Heartland

1. Meeting of the Society for the Study of Midwestern Literature, Modern Language Association, December 1994.

2. James Joyce turned to Mark Twain's epic narrative when he was seeking analogues for his own hero in *Finnegans Wake* (Ellmann 699n).

3. Perhaps the most eloquent evocation of what was lost in soil quality and quantity owing to the avaricious agricultural methods of America's frontier period occurs in two films written and directed by Pare Lorentz, *The River* (1937) and *The Plow That Broke the Plains* (1936)—both produced to support the New Deal policies of agricultural reform.

4. Compare the Iowa Board of Immigration's promise of untold glories in the climate and soil of the state: "The spring, summer, and fall months are delightful. Iowa is noted for the glory and beauty of its autumns. That gorgeous season denominated 'Indian Summer,' cannot be described, and in Iowa it is peculiarly charming. Day after day, for weeks, the sun is veiled in a hazy splendor, while the forests are tinged with the most gorgeous hues, imparting to all nature something of the enchantments of fairyland" (*Iowa* 35).

5. Compare Suckow, *Folks*, 712. Fred Ferguson's parents had built a stone cottage on the farm next to the white main house. "It had been a big job to get those stones hauled from the quarry more than fourteen miles away. But mother had wanted a stone house. She had wanted it to be like the old homes in Scotland, about which *her* mother had told her."

Chapter Four: The Political Economy of Consolidation

1. For the record, his other two examples are "the collectivization of Soviet and Chinese agriculture, and the creation of *ujamaa* village co-operatives in Tanzania."

2. Crotty was an Irish agricultural economist who taught at Trinity College, Dublin, and was born in Kilkenny, where he was at one time a farmer. He was a consultant for the World Bank, the United Nations, and other organizations and worked in the Caribbean, South America, Africa, India, Southeast Asia, and the British Isles.

3. Kieran Allen significantly links the analyses of anti-EC economist Raymond Crotty, Sinn Fein president Gerry Adams, and academic marxists Nicos Poulantzas and F. H. Carduso as all agreeing, from radically different viewpoints, on the neo-colonial and at least partly third world status of Ireland through the 1980s.

4. It has been argued that NAFTA (the North American Free Trade Agreement that unites America, Mexico, and Canada) and the EC represent a move beyond the often-stalled GATT as a way to promote free trade. Hence, America, Canada, and Mexico have agreed to enhance trade among the NAFTA members, just as the EC has removed tariff barriers and borders for its members. Whether or not regional FTAs work to promote free trade in the long run is discussed in "The Trouble with Regionalism," *Economist* 27 (June 1992): 91.

5. An April 1995 speech by then Iowa Secretary of Agriculture Dale Cochran precisely mirrored this prodding of the farmer toward value-added marketing and global awareness of competition. On this occasion, Cochran inaccurately maintained that unfair advantages accrued to European farmers because of CAP subsidies. This strategy of blaming foreign competitors was based on misleading information.

6. During 1993, I spoke with the public relations officer for ADM, who, after talking with a superior, was authorized to say only that the company put in a bid and it was not accepted. She suggested that there were incorrect reports in the Irish newspapers about ADM's role in the situation.

CHAPTER FIVE: THE AGRARIAN IMAGINARY

1. *The Field*, 1990. Directed by Jim Sheridan. Starring Richard Harris, John Hurt, Tom Berenger, Sean Bean, Brenda Fricker, Frances Tomelty, John Cowley, Sean McGinley, Jenny Conroy. The original play differs considerably from the film. The outsider who wants to buy the field happens to be from England rather than America. The ending is far less reminiscent of *King Lear*, with the Bull getting his field and also keeping both land and family intact.

2. For detailed information about the Lone Tree murder, see *Lone Tree: A True Story of Murder in America's Heartland* (New York: Crown, 1989).

3. In the discussion of Lacan, I am indebted not only to Marini's translations of Lacan's seminars but also to Ellie Ragland-Sullivan's *Lacan and the Philosophy of Psychoanalysis* (especially pages 21–23), as well as for conversation with Ragland-Sullivan about Lacan and culture.

1. Oliver shares this preoccupation with recovering the good father with a number of recent theorists, perhaps most notably with Andrew Samuels.

2. Citing Guattari, Ronald Bogue writes: the repression of the State "effects 'an imaginary territorialization, a fantasmatic corporalization of the group' in phenomena such as 'racism, regionalism, nationalism'" (*Deleuze* 87).

3. GUBU is an Irish acronym meaning "grotesque, unbelievable, bizarre, and unprecedented."

4. Directed and written by Phil Alden Robinson, starring Kevin Costner, Amy Madigan, Gaby Hoffman, Ray Liotta, Timothy Busfield, James Earl Jones, Burt Lancaster, Frank Whaley, and Swier Brown.

5. These atonement films take their place within the extensive genre of American baseball films, which includes Ray Enright's *Alibi Ike* (1935), Sam Wood's *The Pride of the Yankees* (1942), Roy Del Ruth's *The Babe Ruth Story* (1948), Busby Berkeley's *Take Me Out to the Ball Game* (1949), Sam Wood's *The Stratton Story* (1949), Lloyd Bacon's *It Happens Every Spring* (1949), Alfred Green's *The Jackie Robinson Story* (1950), Lewis Seiler's *The Winning Team* (1952), Harmon Jones's *The Pride of St. Louis* (1952), Robert Aldrich's *The Big Leaguer* (1953), Robert Mulligan's *Fear Strikes Out* (1957), George Abbott's *Damn Yankees* (1958), John Hancock's *Bang the Drum Slowly* (1973), Michael Ritchie's *The Bad News Bears* (1976), Barry Levinson's *The Natural* (1984), Ron Shelton's *Bull Durham* (1988), and David S. Ward's *Major League* (1989).

6. Directed by Clarence Brown, starring Paul Douglas, Janet Leigh, Keenan Wynn, Donna Corcoran; based on a story by Richard Conlin.

7. Interview with Kinsella, 11 July 1989.

8. As one local cartoon phrased it, "If You Build It, You Are Dumb."

9. It is interesting that many Japanese tourists have also been anxious to visit the actual field portrayed in the Irish film *The Field*.

10. Ormrod covered the story on the TV and then eighteen months later stopped in to see Connie. Connie explained his hopes of having become a celebrity; after he waited up all night for a call, he refused to ride the wall again, and it quickly went to ruin (Smyth). Smyth includes a picture of Connie and Michael in 1978.

11. Directed by Peter Ormrod, produced by John Kelleher and David Collins, and starring Stephen Brennan, Eamon Morrissey, Catherine Byrne, Niall Toibin, Joe Lynch, Tony Doyle.

12. I am indebted to John Kelleher for allowing me access to Peter Ormrod's "My Wall of Death," to the screenplay written by Stewart Parker, to the original screen kit and stills, and to his files of international reviews of *Eat the Peach*.

13. Niall Toibin tells a joke about an Irish junior minister who goes around the country to various functions, having dinner with local politicians, raising funds for various enterprises, "opening a factory one week and closing it the next."

14. John Fairleigh says that Stewart Parker gathered smuggling stories on the border as part of his work on *Eat the Peach* (conversation with John Fairleigh, October 1992).

▨ SELECTED BIBLIOGRAPHY

Abbey of Our Lady of New Melleray. *Cistercians of the Strict Observance.* Peosta, Iowa: Trappist Monastery, Our Lady of New Melleray, 1952.

Abramson, Jill, and Phil Kuntz. "Antitrust Probe of Archer-Daniels Puts Spotlight on Chairman Andreas's Vast Political Influence." *Wall Street Journal,* 11 July 1995, 16A.

Adorno, Theodor W. *Minima Moralia.* Translated by E. F. N. Jephcott. London: New Left Books, 1974.

———. *Negative Dialectics.* Translated by E. B. Ashton. New York: Continuum, 1973.

Akenson, Donald Harman. *The Irish Diaspora.* Belfast: Institute of Irish Studies, 1994.

Alexander, Christopher, et al. *A Pattern Language: Towns, Buildings, Construction.* New York: Oxford University Press, 1977.

Allen, Kieran. *Is Southern Ireland a Neo-Colony?* Dublin: Bookmarks, 1990.

Allen, Robert C. *Enclosure and the Yeoman.* Oxford: Clarendon Press, 1992.

Amin, Samir. *Delinking: Towards a Polycentric World.* Translated by Michael Wolfers. London: Zed Books, 1990.

Appignanesi, Lisa, ed. *Postmodernism: ICA Documents.* London: Free Association Books, 1989.

Archer-Daniels-Midland. Annual reports, 1990–94.

———. *Second Quarter Report to Shareholders,* 1 March 1993.

Arensberg, Conrad. *The Irish Countryman: An Anthropological Study.* 1937. Rpt., Garden City, N.Y.: Natural History Press, 1968.

Arensberg, Conrad, and Solon T. Kimball. *Family and Community in Ireland.* 1940. Rpt., Cambridge, Mass.: Harvard University Press, 1968.

Arrighi, Giovanni, Terence K. Hopkins, and Immanuel Wallerstein. *Antisystemic Movements.* London and New York: Verso, 1989.

Bailey, Leon. "Theodor W. Adorno: Reflections from Damaged Life." *Issues in Radical Therapy* 12, no. 3 (1986): 9–11, 44–49.

Barnes, John A. "Anatomy of a Rip-Off." *New Republic*, 2 November 1987, 20–21.

Barry, Ursula. "Salvation for the Irish Economy?" *An Gael*, March 1990, 12–13.

———. "Taxation and Debt." In *Who Owns Ireland? Who Owns You?* edited by Carmel Jennings, et al. Dublin: Attic Press, 1985.

Bell, Desmond. "Cultural Studies in Ireland and the Postmodernist Debate." *Irish Journal of Sociology* 1 (1991): 83–95.

Bell, Sam Hanna. *December Bride.* 1951. Rpt., Edinburgh: Mainstream, 1990.

Bello, Walden. *Dark Victory: The United States, Structural Adjustment, and Global Poverty.* London: Pluto Press, 1994.

Berman, Marshall. *All That Is Solid Melts Into Air: The Experience of Modernity.* New York: Penguin, 1982.

Berry, Wendell. *The Unsettling of America: Culture and Agriculture.* San Francisco: Sierra Club, 1977.

Beuys, Joseph. *Report to the EEC on the Feasibility of Founding a Free University for Creativity and Interdisciplinary Research in Dublin.* Edited by Caroline Tisdall. London: Free University Press, 1975.

Bhabha, Homi K. "The Commitment to Theory." In *Questions of Third Cinema*, edited by Jim Pines and Paul Willemen. London: British Film Institute, 1989.

———. "The Other Question: Difference, Discrimination, and the Discourse of Colonialism," In *Out There: Marginalization and Contemporary Cultures*, edited by Russell Ferguson, et al. New York: New Museum of Contemporary Art; Cambridge, Mass., and London: MIT Press, 1990.

Birdwell-Pheasant, Donna. "The Early Twentieth-Century Irish Stem Family: A Case Study from County Kerry." In *Approaching the Past: Historical Anthropology through Irish Case Studies*, edited by Marilyn Silverman and P. H. Gulliver. New York: Columbia University Press, 1992.

Bognar, Botond. "On the Critical Aspects of Regionalism." *A & U: architecture and urbanism* 234 (1990): 11–18.

Bogue, Allan G. *From Prairie to Corn Belt: Farming on the Illinois and Iowa Prairies in the Nineteenth Century.* Chicago and London: University of Chicago Press, 1963.

Bogue, Ronald. *Deleuze and Guattari.* New York and London: Routledge, 1989.

Bourdieu, Pierre, and Löic Wacquant. *An Invitation to Reflexive Sociology.* Chicago and London: University of Chicago Press, 1992.

Bowie, Malcolm. *Lacan.* Cambridge, Mass.: Harvard University Press, 1991.

Bracher, Mark. *Lacan, Discourse, and Social Change: A Psychoanalytic Cultural Criticism.* Ithaca and London: Cornell University Press, 1993.

Brennan, Teresa. *History after Lacan.* London and New York: Routledge, 1993.

Brienza, Susan. Discussion of *Huckleberry Finn* and *Finnegans Wake.* James Joyce Symposium, University of California at Berkeley, July 1989.

Buck-Morss, Susan. *The Origin of Negative Dialectics: Theodor W. Adorno, Walter Benjamin, and the Frankfurt Institute.* Sussex: Harvester, 1977.

Callinicos, Alex. *Against Postmodernism: A Marxist Critique.* New York: St. Martin's, 1990.

Campbell, Brian. "Voices from the Edge." *Captive Voice* (Spring 1992): 22–24.

Cayton, Andrew R. L., and Peter S. Onuf. *The Midwest and the Nation: Rethinking the History of an American Region.* Bloomington and Indianapolis: University of Indiana Press, 1990.

Clancy, Patrick, et al. "Introducing Sociology." In *Ireland: A Sociological Profile,* edited by Patrick Clancy et al. Dublin: Institute of Public Administration, 1986.

Clinch, Minty. "Bowie meets the Muppets in Labyrinth, and the Irish fight back in Eat The Peach." *Midweek* (U.K.), 4 December 1986, 19.

Commins, Patrick. "Rural Social Change." In *Ireland: A Sociological Profile,* edited by Patrick Clancy et al. Dublin: Institute of Public Administration, 1986.

Coulter, Carol. *Ireland: Between the First and the Third Worlds.* Dublin: Attic Press, 1990.

Craig, Maurice. *The Architecture of Ireland from the Earliest Times to 1880.* London: Batsford; Dublin: Eason, 1983.

Crotty, Raymond. *Farming Collapse: National Opportunity.* Naas: Amárach-Ireland 2000, 1990.

———. *A Radical's Response.* Dublin: Poolbeg, 1988.

Danaher, Kevin, ed. *Fifty Years Is Enough: The Case against the World Bank and the International Monetary Fund.* Boston: South End Press, 1994.

Davenport, Michael, with Sheila Page. *Europe: 1992 and the Developing World.* London: Overseas Development Institute, 1991.

Davidson, Osha Gray. *Broken Heartland: The Rise of America's Rural Ghetto.* New York and London: Anchor-Doubleday, 1990.

Dawkins, Kristin. *NAFTA, GATT, and the World Trade Organization: The Emerging New World Order.* Westfield, N.J.: Open Magazine Pamphlet Series, 1994.

Day, Graham, and Gareth Rees, eds. *Regions, Nations, and European Integration: Remaking the Celtic Periphery.* Cardiff: University of Wales Press, 1991.

Deane, Seamus, ed. *The Field Day Anthology of Irish Writing.* Derry: Field Day Publications, 1991.

Deane, Seamus. "The Production of Cultural Space in Irish Writing." *boundary 2* 21 (Fall 1994): 117–44.

Deleuze, Gilles. *Cinema 2: The Time-Image.* 1985. Translated by Hugh Tomlinson and Robert Galeta. Minneapolis: University of Minnesota Press, 1989.

Deleuze, Gilles, and Claire Parnet. *Dialogues.* Translated by Hugh Tomlinson and Barbara Habberjam. New York: Columbia University Press, 1987.

Deleuze, Gilles, and Félix Guattari. *A Thousand Plateaus: Capitalism and Schizophrenia.* Translated by Brian Massumi. Minneapolis: University of Minnesota Press, 1987.

Demons. Iowa City: Monozygote Productions, 1994. Videotape.

Dillon, Willie. "Depression in Farming Set to Continue: IFA Warning." *Irish Independent*, 31 December 1991, 7.

———. "$200m Exports Get a Reprieve." *Irish Independent*, 29 July 1992: 5.

Donaldson, Peter. *Worlds Apart: The Development Gap and What It Means.* New edition. London and New York: Penguin, 1986.

Doran, Séan, Margaret Greenwood, and Hildi Hawkins. *The Real Guide: Ireland.* Edited by John Fisher and Jonathan Buckley. Englewood Cliffs, N.J.: Prentice-Hall, 1990.

Dorfman, Ariel, Robert A. Rosenstone, and Jonathan L. Beller. "Popular Films and Historical Memory." In *Learning History in America: Schools, Cultures, and Politics*, edited by Lloyd Kramer, Donald Reid, and William L. Barney. Minneapolis and London: University of Minnesota Press, 1994.

Douthwaite, Richard. *The Growth Illusion: How Economic Growth Has Enriched the Few, Impoverished the Many, and Endangered the Planet.* Dublin: Lilliput Books, 1992.

Doyle, Lynn. *The Spirit of Ireland.* 1935. 4th edition. London: Batsford, 1946–47.

Duff, Charles. *Ireland and the Irish.* New York: Putnams, 1953.

Duffy, Michael, Paul Lasley, and Dennis Keeney. "The Real Economic Folly in Farming." *Des Moines Register*, 30 July 1993, 15A.

Durcan, Paul. *Daddy, Daddy: Poems.* Belfast: Blackstaff Press, 1990.

Editorial. *Irish Times*, 13 March 1993, 11.

Edwards, Eoin. "*Eat the Peach* Not to Be Missed." *Cork Evening Echo*, 18 March 1986, 7.

Edwards, Ruth Dudley. *An Atlas of Irish History.* 2nd edition. London and New York: Methuen, 1981.

Elias, Gillian. *A Cistercian Monk's Life Yesterday and Today.* Coalville, Leicester: Mount Saint Bernard Abbey, n.d.

Ellmann, Richard. *James Joyce.* Revised edition. Oxford: Oxford University Press, 1982.

Emery, Mary Lou. "Reading 'W.H.': Draft of an Incomplete Conversation." In *Wilson Harris: The Uncompromising Imagination*, edited by Hena Maes-Jelinek. New South Wales: Dangaroo Press, 1991.

Evans, E. Estyn. *The Personality of Ireland: Habitat, Heritage and History.* Cambridge: Cambridge University Press, 1973.

"Farmers on Brink: Lean Times Ahead for Producers Warns UFU Chief." *Belfast Newsletter*, 17 January 1992, 2.

Farrell, Paul. "Take One—The Irish Film Industry Starts to Roll." *Success* (June 1987): 26–28.

Fitzgerald, Gretchen. *Repulsing Racism: Reflections on Racism and the Irish.* Dublin: Attic Press, 1992.

Fitzpatrick, David. *Irish Emigration, 1801–1921.* Dublin: Economic and Social History Society of Ireland, 1984.

Flynn, Sean. "EC Stopped in its Tracks as CAP Plan Faces Problems." *Irish Times*, 6 March 1992, 15.

Foley, Anthony, and Dermot McAleese, eds. *Overseas Industry in Ireland.* Business and Economics Research Series. Dublin: Gill and Macmillan, 1991.

Foley, Catherine. "Farmers and the Suicide Factor." *Irish Times,* 19 September 1994, 12.

Foster, Hal, ed. *The Anti-Aesthetic: Essays on Postmodern Culture.* Port Townsend, Wash.: Bay Press, 1983.

Foster, R. F. *Modern Ireland: 1600–1972.* New York and London: Viking Penguin, 1989.

"Fourfold Increase in Suicide Rate." *Irish Times,* 3 July 1987, 1.

Frampton, Kenneth. "Luogo, Forma, Identita Culturale." *Domus* (May 1985): 6–24.

———. "Some Reflections on Postmodernism and Architecture." In *Postmodernism: ICA Documents,* edited by Lisa Appignanesi. London: Free Association Books, 1989.

Free for All. David Powell, contributor. Edited and researched by Chris Rushton and Jennie Walker. London: Filmit, 1992.

Friel, Brian. *Faith Healer.* London and Boston: Faber and Faber, 1980.

Garland, Hamlin. *Crumbling Idols.* Chicago and Cambridge: Stone and Kimball, 1894.

———. *Iowa, O Iowa!* Iowa City: Clio, 1935.

———. *Main Travelled Roads.* New York and London: Harper and Row, 1899.

———. *A Son of the Middle Border.* 1914. Rpt., New York: Macmillan, 1928.

Garrett, Robert. "'Eat the Peach' Inspired by Real Irish Folk Hero." *Boston Globe,* 31 July 1987, 42.

Gates, Paul W. *Landlords and Tenants on the American Frontier.* Ithaca and London: Cornell University Press, 1973.

"GATT Will Build the World." *Economist,* 27 June 1992, 10.

Gómez-Peña, Guillermo. "Border Culture: A Process of Negotiation Toward Utopia." *La Linea Quebrada* 1 (1986): 1–6.

———. *Warrior for Gringostroika: Essays, Performance Texts, and Poetry.* Saint Paul: Graywolf Press, 1993.

Grant, H. Roger, and L. Edward Purcell, eds. *Years of Struggle: The Farm Diary of Elmer G. Powers, 1931–1936.* Ames: Iowa State University Press, 1976.

Grant, Richard, and Donald Lyons. "The Republic of Ireland in the World-Economy: An Exploration of Dynamics in the Semiperiphery." In *Semiperipheral States in the World-Economy,* edited by William G. Martin. Westport, Conn.: Greenwood Press, 1990.

Graves, Charles. *Ireland Revisited.* London and New York: Hutchinson, n.d.

Grossberg, Lawrence, Cary Nelson, and Paula Treichler, eds. *Cultural Studies.* London and New York: Routledge, 1992.

Guthmann, Edward. "Irish Film Industry Blossoms With 'Peach.'" *Los Angeles Times,* 14 August 1987, 23–24.

Gwynn, Stephen. *Ireland: Its Places of Beauty, Entertainment, Sport, and Historic Association.* London, Bombay, and Sydney: George G. Harrap, 1927.

Hamilton, Carl. *In No Time at All.* Ames: Iowa State University Press, 1974.

Hannan, D. F., and R. Breen. "Family Farming in Ireland." In *Family Farming in Eu-*

rope and America, edited by Boguslaw Galeski and Eugene Wilkening. Boulder, Colo.: Westview Press, 1987.

Harbison, Peter, Homan Potterton, and Jeanne Sheehy. *Irish Art and Architecture from Prehistory to the Present*. London: Thames and Hudson, 1978.

Harl, Neil E. *The Farm Debt Crisis of the 1980s*. Ames: Iowa State University Press, 1990.

Harris, Wilson. "Fossil and Psyche." *Explorations*. Denmark: Dungaroo Press, 1981.

———. "History, Fable, and Myth in the Caribbean and Guianas." *Caribbean Quarterly* 16 (1970): 1–32.

Harti, John. "Backyard Genius Gives 'Eat the Peach' Magic." *Seattle Times/Seattle Post-Intelligencer*, 2 August 1987, 42.

Harvey, David. *The Condition of Postmodernity: An Enquiry into the Origins of Cultural Change*. Oxford: Basil Blackwell, 1989.

Haukos, Mark. "Thesis Retrospective, 1987–89." Unpublished manuscript in the possession of Cheryl Herr.

"Heineken Offers Brewer's View." *Sunday Business Post*, 28 June 1992, 20.

Henderson, Gertrude. "An Epic of Early Iowa: Father Trecy's Colonization Scheme." *Iowa Catholic Historical Review* 3 (October 1931): 3–13.

Henkoff, Ronald. "Oh, How the Money Grows at ADM." *Fortune*, 8 October 1990, 105–16.

Hill, John. "Images of Violence." In *Cinema and Ireland*, by Kevin Rockett, Luke Gibbons, and John Hill. Syracuse: Syracuse University Press, 1988.

Hoffman, M. M. *Arms and the Monk! The Trappist Saga in Mid-America*. Dubuque, Iowa: Brown, 1952.

Hogan, Dick. "Another Time, Another Place." *Irish Times*, 16 April 1994, Weekend, 3.

———. "Suicide Rise Shows Signs of Levelling Off, Conference Told." *Irish Times*, 14 November 1992, 2.

Hood, Neil, et al. Department of Trade and Industry. *Multinational Investment Strategies in the British Isles: A Study of MNEs in the Assisted Areas and in the Republic of Ireland*. London: Her Majesty's Stationery Office, 1983.

Horton, Loren N., ed. "The Character of the Country: Excerpts." *Palimpsest* 57 (September–October 1976): 158–60.

Hovelson, Jack. "A Glorious Day on Field of Dreams." *Des Moines Register*, 3 September 1991, 1.

Howe, Stephen. "Where Dreams Come True." Review of *America* by Jean Baudrillard. *New Statesman and Society* 1 (18 November 1988): 39.

Hurt, R. Douglas. *American Agriculture: A Brief History*. Ames: Iowa State University Press, 1994.

"IFA Active at Tokyo Family Farmers Summit." *Irish Farmers' Journal*, 17 July 1993, 38.

International Monetary Fund. *Staff Papers* 39 (March 1992).

Iowa: The Home for Immigrants: Being a Treatise on the Resources of Iowa, and Giving

Useful Information with Regard to the State, for the Benefit of Immigrants and Others.
1870. Rpt., Iowa City: State Historical Society of Iowa, 1970.

Irace, Fulvio. "Kenneth Frampton." Interview. *Domus* 661 (May 1985): 6–7.

Ireland in the European Community: Performance, Prospects and Strategy: Summary of Main Points. Dublin: National Economic and Social Council, [1992].

"Irish Film Acclaimed in London." *Evening Press,* 5 December 1986, 15.

"The Irish in Iowa." *Palimpsest* (February 1964). Special Issue.

Jameson, Fredric. *Late Marxism: Adorno, Or, The Persistence of the Dialectic.* London: Verso, 1990.

———. *Marxism and Form: Twentieth-Century Dialectical Theories of Literature.* Princeton: Princeton University Press, 1971.

———. "Postmodernism, or The Cultural Logic of Late Capitalism." *New Left Review* 146 (July–August 1984): 53–92.

———. "Third World Literature in the Era of Multinational Capitalism." *Social Text* 15 (Fall 1986): 65–88.

Jencks, Charles A. *The Language of Post-Modern Architecture.* 4th edition. New York: Rizzoli, 1984.

Jenkins, Iain. "Europe's Dream of Money Union Starts to Splinter." *Sunday Times,* 12 April 1992, 26.

Joyce, James. "The Dead." In *Dubliners.* Introduction and notes by Terence Brown. New York and London: Penguin, 1992.

Keane, John B. *The Field.* New revised text. Cork: Mercier, 1991.

Kearney, Richard. "A Blot on the Edge of Europe." *Fortnight,* January 1992, 10, 12, 14.

Kelleher, John. Personal interview at Windmill Lane Pictures, Dublin, 12 April 1991.

Keller, John. "Kelleher Incentives Plea after Irish Peach Smash." *Screen International,* 29 November 1986, 16.

Kelly, Alan. "Who Gains from Third World Debt?" Review of *The Debt Boomerang* by Susan George. *Socialist Worker* (May 1992): 8.

Kennedy, Liam. *The Modern Industrialisation of Ireland, 1940–1988.* Dublin: Dundalgan Press, 1989.

Kinney, Robert, and Donald Kinney. *Demons.* Iowa City, 1994. Fanzine.

Kinsella, W. P. *Shoeless Joe.* New York: Ballantine, 1982.

Kirby, Peadar. *Has Ireland a Future?* Cork and Dublin: Mercier Press, 1988.

Kirwan, F., and J. McGilvray. *Irish Economic Statistics.* Dublin: Institute of Public Administration, 1983.

Kolakowski, Leszek. *Main Currents of Marxism: Its Origins, Growth, and Dissolution.* Translated by P. S. Falla. Oxford and New York: Oxford University Press, 1978.

Kraar, Louis. "Top U.S. Companies Move into Russia." *Fortune* 170 (31 July 1989): 165–71.

Krasner, Stephen D. *Structural Conflict: The Third World Against Global Liberalism.* Berkeley, Los Angeles, and London: University of California Press, 1985.

Krause, Linda. "The New Brutalism." *Circa* 53 (September–October 1990): 28–31.

Kruger, Stephen. Study Sheets: *Eat the Peach*. Film Education, Faculty of Humanities, Holland Park School, London W.8. For U.I.P., n.d.

Lacan, Jacques. *The Four Fundamental Concepts of Psycho-Analysis*. Edited by Jacques-Alain Miller; translated by Alan Sheridan. New York and London: Norton, 1981.

Lash, Scott, and J. Urry. *The End of Organised Capitalism*. Oxford: Oxford University Press, 1987.

Lee, Joseph J. *Ireland, 1912–1985: Politics and Society*. Cambridge: Cambridge University Press, 1989.

Levitt, Theodore. "Advertising: The Poetry of Becoming." *Harvard Business Review* (1993): 134–37.

———. "Futurism and Management." *Antioch Review* 49 (1991): 29–38.

———. "The Globalization of Markets." *Harvard Business Review* 61 (1983): 92–102.

———. *The Marketing Imagination*. New edition. New York: Free Press; London: Collier Macmillan, 1986.

———. *Thinking About Management*. New York: Free Press/Maxwell Macmillan International; Toronto: Collier Macmillan Canada, 1991.

Lloyd, David. *Anomalous States: Irish Writing and the Post-Colonial Moment*. Durham: Duke University Press, 1993.

Longley, Edna, ed. *Culture in Ireland: Division or Diversity?: Proceedings of the Cultures of Ireland Group Conference*. Belfast: Institute of Irish Studies, Queen's University of Belfast, 1991.

Lucas, John. *England and Englishness*. Iowa City: University of Iowa Press, 1990.

Lynd, Robert. *Home Life in Ireland*. London: Mills and Boon, 1909.

MacConnell, Sean. "The Bottom Line Is That Farmers Are Going to Have to Be More Efficient." *Irish Times*, 3 June 1992, 12.

———. "Priest Says Nine Young Clare People Committed Suicide in Six Days." *Irish Times*, 13 November 1992, 1.

———. "US Would Target Irish Goods, Warns MacSharry." *Irish Times*, 8 June 1992, 2.

Madsen, Peter. "'Postmodernism' and 'Late Capitalism': On Terms and Realities." In *Psychology and Postmodernism*, edited by Steinar Kvale. London, Newbury Park, and New Delhi: Sage, 1992.

Maguire, John, and Joe Noonan. *Maastricht and Neutrality: Ireland's Neutrality and the Future of Europe*. Cork: People First/Meitheal, 1992.

Manifold, D. Letter to Editor. *Irish Press*, 13 July 1993, 15.

Marini, Marcelle. *Jacques Lacan: The French Context*. Translated by Anne Tomiche. New Brunswick: Rutgers University Press, 1992.

Massumi, Brian. *A User's Guide to Capitalism and Schizophrenia: Deviations from Deleuze and Guattari*. Cambridge, Mass., and London: MIT Press, 1992.

Matthews, Alan. "The CAP Crisis: Overspecialisation, Overcapacity are Roots of Farmers' Problem." *Irish Times*, 13 July 1991, 9.

McAllister, Jimmy. "The Scale of Global Hunger." *The Captive Voice: An Glór Gafa* (Spring 1992): 5–6.

McDonagh, Sean. "IMF, World Bank Taking Resources from Third World to Benefit First." *Sunday Business Post*, 5 July 1992, 14.

———. "A Knight in Shining Armour with a Disastrous Record." *Irish Times*, 15 September 1992, 12.

McGahern, John. *Amongst Women*. New York: Penguin, 1990.

McIlroy, Brian. *World Cinema 4: Ireland*. Wiltshire: Flicks Books, 1988.

Merton, Thomas. *Cistercian Life*. Mount Melleray Abbey, Cappoquin, Co. Waterford: Cistercian Book Service, n.d.

Middleton, Neil. "Buried Deep in GATT is a Serious, New Threat to Sovereignty of the Poor's World." *Irish Times*, 7 August 1993, 8.

Minh-ha, Trinh T. "Outside In Inside Out." In *Questions of Third Cinema*, edited by Jim Pines and Paul Willemen. London: British Film Institute, 1989.

———. *Woman, Native, Other: Writing Postcoloniality and Feminism*. Bloomington and Indianapolis: Indiana University Press, 1989.

Moeller, Hugh C., and Fred C. Bowersox. *Constitution and Government: Iowa and the Nation*. New revised edition. Mason City, Iowa: Klipto Loose Leaf Co., 1938.

Moloney, Stephen J., O. Cist. *The History of Mount Melleray Abbey*. Cork: Paramount Printing, 1952.

Monahan, Leonard. "The Heartland That Is Never Left Behind." *Irish Times*, 10 June 1992, 14.

Monastery Seasons. Trappist newsletter. 1970–91.

Mullarkey, Gabrielle. "The Importance of Being Iowish." (Middlesex) *Irish Post*, 8 November 1991, 4.

Mulrennan, Frank. "MacSharry Bares His Soul on CAP." *Farming Independent*, 17 March 1992, 8–9.

Munck, Ronnie. *The Irish Economy: Results and Prospects*. London and Boulder, Colo.: Pluto, 1993.

Murphy, Eithne. "Ireland's Economic Welfare in a Barrier Free Europe." In *Across the Frontiers: Ireland in the 1990s: Cultural-Political-Economic*, edited by Richard Kearney. Dublin: Wolfhound, 1988.

Murray, John J., ed. *The Heritage of the Middle West*. Norman: University of Oklahoma Press, 1958.

Murray, W. Cotter. *A Long Way from Home*. Boston: Houghton Mifflin, 1974.

———. *Michael Joe: A Novel of Irish Life*. 1965. Rpt., Dingle: Brandon, 1991.

National Economic and Social Council. *Economic and Social Policy, 1980–83: Aims and Recommendations*. Dublin: Stationers' Office.

National Planning Board. *Proposals for Plan, 1984–87*. Dublin: Mount Salus Press Ltd., 1984.

Nelson, Jane Taylor, ed. *A Prairie Populist: The Memoirs of Luna Kellie*. Iowa City: University of Iowa Press, 1992.

Nevin, Brigid. "Agriculture." In *Who Owns Ireland? Who Owns You?* by Carmel Jennings et al. Dublin: Attic Press, 1985.

New Ireland Forum. *A Comparative Description of the Economic Structure and Situation, North and South.* Dublin, 15 December 1983.

New Melleray Abbey: Cistercians of the Strict Observance. Dubuque, Iowa: New Melleray Abbey, n.d.

Newman, Michael. *Socialism and European Unity: The Dilemma of the Left in Britain and France.* London: Junction Books, 1983.

Nusbaum, Eliot. "A Matter of Taste." *Des Moines Register,* 3 November 1994, T1.

O'Carroll, J. P., and John A. Murphy, eds. *De Valera and His Times.* Cork: Cork University Press, 1983.

O'Clery, Conor. "Fields of Dreams." *Irish Times,* 15 February 1992, Weekend, 1.

O'Connor, James. "Monastery Seasons." *Catholic Mirror,* July 1975–June 1978.

———. "Mystery of Human Suffering." *Catholic Mirror,* 1 September 1977.

O'Flanagan, Patrick, Paul Ferguson, and Kevin Whelan, eds. *Rural Ireland, 1600–1900: Modernisation and Change.* Cork: Cork University Press, 1987.

Oliver, Kelly. *Reading Kristeva: Unveiling the Double-Bind.* Bloomington and Indianapolis: University of Indiana Press, 1993.

"One Third Drop in Farming Population." *Irish Democrat,* 25–31 June 1992, 16.

O'Regan, Michael. "An Irishman's Diary." *Irish Times,* 14 April 1990, 11.

Organisation for Economic Co-operation and Development. *Innovation Policy: Ireland.* Paris: OECD, 1987.

Ormrod, Peter. "My Wall of Death." Unpublished manuscript on file at Windmill Lane Productions.

O'Sullivan, Patrick. *The Irish in the New Communities.* Volume 2 of *The Irish World Wide: History, Heritage, Identity.* Leicester and London: Leicester University Press, 1992.

O'Toole, Fintan. "The Field." *Irish Times,* 14 April 1990, 11.

———. *A Mass for Jesse James: A Journey Through 1980s Ireland.* Dublin: Raven Arts Press, 1990.

———. "A Million Miles from Nostalgia." *Irish Times,* 12 November 1991, 5.

Paolozzi, E. *Lost Magic Kingdoms, and six paper moons from Nahuatl,* Exhibition Catalogue, Museum of Mankind, London, 1985.

Parker, Stewart. "Eat the Peach: Screenplay." Unpublished manuscript, loaned to the author by John Kelleher, 1985.

Parliament Buildings: Stormont. N.p.: Her Majesty's Stationery Office, n.d.

Parnell Centennial: 100 Years in Little Ireland. Deep River, Iowa: Brennan, 1987.

Patterson, Eric. "The American Dream of Baseball." *Living Marxism* (August 1989): 44.

Pinder, John. *European Community: The Building of a Union.* Oxford and New York: Oxford University Press, 1991.

Plowden, David. *A Sense of Place*. Norton: State Historical Society of Iowa, 1988.

"Poor Odds, High Stakes." *Economist*, 27 June 1992, 89–90.

Ragland-Sullivan, Ellie. *Jacques Lacan and the Philosophy of Psychoanalysis*. Urbana: University of Illinois Press, 1986.

Rees, Jim. *A Farewell to Famine*. Co. Wicklow: Arklow Enterprise Centre, 1994.

Review of *Angels in the Outfield*. *Saturday Review*, 22 September 1951: 30.

Riley, Glenda. *Frontierswomen: The Iowa Experience*. Ames: Iowa State University Press, 1981.

Rogers, Earl M. "Fiction with an Iowa City Setting: An Annotated Checklist." *Books at Iowa* (April 1986): 10–26.

Rosaldo, Renato. *Culture and Truth: The Remaking of Social Analysis*. Boston: Beacon Press, 1989.

———. "Where Objectivity Lies: The Rhetoric of Anthropology." In *The Rhetoric of the Human Sciences: Language and Arguments in Scholarship and Public Affairs*, edited by John S. Nelson, Allan Megill, and Donald N. McCloskey. Madison: University of Wisconsin Press, 1987.

Rose, Gillian. *The Melancholy Science: An Introduction to the Thought of Theodor W. Adorno*. London and Basingstoke: Macmillan, 1978.

Rosenfeld. "Iowa Ethanol Production Threatened." *Daily Iowan*, 26 January 1993, 3A.

Rowthorn, Bob. "Northern Ireland: An Economy in Crisis." In *Beyond the Rhetoric: Politics, the Economy and Social Policy in Northern Ireland*, edited by Paul Teague. London: Lawrence and Wishart, 1987.

Ryan, Gregg. "Alarm at Soaring Suicide Rates." *Evening Press*, 6 January 1993, 1.

Sage, Leland L. *A History of Iowa*. Ames: Iowa State University Press, 1974.

Said, Edward. *After the Last Sky: Palestinian Lives*. New York: Pantheon, 1986.

St. Patrick's Garryowen: 1840–1990. 150th anniversary commemoration booklet. Garryowen, Iowa, 1990.

Saldívar, José David. *The Dialectics of Our America: Genealogy, Cultural Critique, and Literary History*. Durham and London: Duke University Press, 1991.

Samuels, Andrew. *The Political Psyche*. London and New York: Routledge, 1993.

Sayre, Robert F., ed. *Take This Exit: Rediscovering the Iowa Landscape*. Ames: Iowa State University Press, 1989.

Scheper-Hughes, Nancy. *Saints, Scholars, and Schizophrenics: Mental Illness in Rural Ireland*. Berkeley, Los Angeles, and London: University of California Press, 1979.

Schrier, Arnold. *Ireland and the American Emigration: 1850–1900*. Minneapolis: University of Minnesota Press, 1958.

Seekamp, Gail. "Farmers Go Astray Over Sheep." *Sunday Business Post*, 28 June 1992, 21.

Shanahan, Ella. "How Fare the Farmers?" *Irish Times*, 13 February 1992, 11.

———. "The Impact of CAP Reform on Consumer Prices." *Irish Times*, 1 June 1992, 10.

Shover, John L. *Cornbelt Rebellion: The Farmers' Holiday Association*. Urbana and London: University of Illinois Press, 1965.

Silet, Charles L. P., Robert E. Welch, and Richard Boudreau, eds. *The Critical Reception of Hamlin Garland, 1891–1978*. Troy, N.Y.: Whitston, 1985.

Silverman, Kaja. *The Subject of Semiotics*. New York and Oxford: Oxford University Press, 1983.

Smiley, Jane. *A Thousand Acres*. New York: Fawcett Columbine, 1991.

Smyth, Sam. "The Wall of Death that Rose from the Peat Bog." *You Magazine—Mail on Sunday*, 7 December 1986, 42.

Snyder, Gary. *The Practice of the Wild*. San Francisco: North Point Press, 1990.

Spivak, Gayatri Chakravorty. *The Post-Colonial Critic: Interviews, Strategies, Dialogues*. New York and London: Routledge, 1990.

Stalley, Roger. *The Cistercian Monasteries of Ireland: An Account of the History, Art and Architecture of the White Monks in Ireland from 1142 to 1540*. London and New Haven: Yale University Press, 1987.

Strange, Marty. *Family Farming: A New Economic Vision*. Lincoln and London: University of Nebraska Press, 1988.

Suckow, Ruth. *The Folks*. 1934. Rpt., Iowa City: University of Iowa Press, 1992.

Summers, Lawrence. "The Lessons of Debt." *Financial Times*, 3 August 1992, 26.

Swann, Dennis, ed. *The Single European Market and Beyond: A Study of the Wider Implications of the Single European Act*. London and New York: Routledge, 1992.

Tansey, Paul. "We're Stuck in EC Poverty Trap." *Sunday Tribune*, 8 March 1992, 35.

Taylor, Mark C. *Altarity*. Chicago and London: University of Chicago Press, 1987.

Teague, Paul. "Multinational Companies in the Northern Ireland Economy: An Outmoded Model of Industrial Development?" In *Beyond the Rhetoric: Politics, the Economy and Social Policy in Northern Ireland*, edited by Paul Teague. London: Lawrence and Wishart, 1987.

"'Threat' to Farms." *Ulster News Letter*, 29 February 1992, 11.

Tisdall, Caroline. *Report to the European Economic Community on the Feasibility of Founding a 'Free International University for Creativity and Interdisciplinary Research' in Dublin*. 1975. Revised edition, Dublin and London: Free University Press, 1976.

To Be a Monk: an Essay on the Cistercian Vocation. Dubuque, Iowa: New Melleray Abbey, n.d.

"The Trouble with Regionalism." *Economist*, 27 June 1992, 91.

Tschumi, Bernard. "Notes toward a Theory of Architectural Disjunction." *A & U: architecture and urbanism* (September 1988): 12–15.

Twain, Mark. *Adventures of Huckleberry Finn*. Berkeley, Los Angeles, and London: University of California Press, 1985.

Tzonis, Alexander, and Liane Lefaivre. "Why Critical Regionalism Today?" *A & U: architecture and urbanism* 234 (1990): 19–33.

"U.S. Antitrust Probe of Ag Giants Unfolds." *Des Moines Register*, 11 July 1995, 1, 4A.

Varadarajan, Geetha. "Culture, Space and Colonialism." Unpublished manuscript in the possession of the author, 1986.

———. "Semiotics and Marxism." Master's thesis, University of Iowa, 1988.

Vidler, Anthony. "The Pleasure of the Architect." *A & U: architecture and urbanism* (September 1988): 16–23.

Wallace, Iain. *The Global Economic System.* London: Unwin Hyman, 1990.

Waller, Robert James. *Iowa: Perspectives on Today and Tomorrow.* Ames: Iowa State University Press, 1991.

Wallerstein, Immanuel. *The Modern World System I: Capitalist Agriculture and the Origins of the European World-Economy in the Sixteenth Century.* New York: Academic Press, 1974.

Walsh, Dick. "These Things Happen, Says Bertie." *Irish Times,* 8 May 1993, 10.

Walsh, Maurice. *The Quiet Man and Other Stories.* 1935. Rpt., Belfast: Appletree Press, 1992.

Waters, John. *Jiving at the Crossroads.* Belfast: Blackstaff Press, 1991.

The Way Forward: National Economic Plan, 1983–86. Laid by the Government Before each House of the Oireachtas, October 1982. Microfilm.

Weiss, Michael J. "The High-Octane Ethanol Lobby." *New York Times,* 1 April 1990, Business World Magazine, 19.

Whelan, Kevin. "The Bases of Regionalism." In *Culture in Ireland—Regions: Identity and Power,* edited by Proinsias 'O Drisceoil. Belfast: Institute of Irish Studies, 1993.

"When the Only Way Out Is a Shotgun." *Independent,* 23 July 1992, 18.

White, Maury. "150 Years Ago: Sports Were Different, But Never Dull." *Des Moines Register,* 8 August 1993, D1.

Why Monasteries? Mount Melleray Abbey: Cistercian Abbeys of Great Britain and Ireland, 1985.

Whyte, John. *Interpreting Northern Ireland.* Oxford: Oxford University Press, 1990.

Wilbers, Stephen. *The Iowa Writers' Workshop: Origins, Emergence, and Growth.* Iowa City: University of Iowa Press, 1980.

Williams, Raymond. *The Country and the City.* New York: Oxford University Press, 1973.

Willis, Sharon. "Spectacular Topographies: *Amérique's* Post Modern Spaces." *Threshold* 4 (1988): 62–68.

Wilmington, Michael. "'Peach': Sharp Portrait of Ireland." *Los Angeles Times,* 14 August 1987.

Wilson, Carol R. *The World Bank Group: A Guide to Information Services.* New York and London: Garland, 1991.

Wittenburg, Bonnie. *Dain Bosworth Research Report: ADM.* 1 December 1993.

———. *Dain Bosworth Research Report: ADM.* 20 March 1995.

Wolfe, Brendan. "From Kerry to Lost Nation: A Consideration of Wolfe Family History and Its Implications for the Family Today." Unpublished manuscript, 1991.

World Almanac and Book of Facts 1991. New York: Pharos Books, 1990.

The WPA Guide to 1930s Iowa. Compiled and written by Federal Writers' Project of the Works Progress Administration for the State of Iowa. 1938. Rpt., Ames: Iowa State University Press, 1986.

Wright, Elizabeth. *Psychoanalytic Criticism: Theory in Practice*. London and New York: Methuen, 1984.

Zalaznik, David. "New Melleray Abbey: Where Life Follows a Prayerful Pace." *Iowan* (Summer 1986): 26–31, 37–38.

Zielinski, John M. *Portrait of Iowa*. Iowa City: Iowa Heritage Publications, n.d.

Zizek, Slavoj. *Looking Awry: An Introduction to Jacques Lacan through Popular Culture*. Cambridge, Mass., and London: MIT Press, 1991.

———. *The Sublime Object of Ideology*. London and New York: Verso, 1989.

American dream: past erased in, 180; pursuit of, 175–79; suspension of, 181

Amin, Samir, 6, 125

Amongst Women (McGahern), 152–55

Anderson, David, 82

Andreas, Dwayne, 133–34

Angels in the Outfield (1951, film), 174

Angels in the Outfield (1994, film), 174

Annacurra (Ireland), migration from, 30

anthropology, models in, 103

Archer-Daniels-Midland Corporation (ADM): description of, 132–34, 138; and ethanol, 139–40; FBI investigation of, 140–41; and free trade agreements, 135–38; and Irish companies, 135–37; psychocultural counterpart to, 167; and sugar market, 135–37; ubiquitousness of products of, 151; and union-busting, 138, *139*

architecture: in churches, 34; and commons tradition, 118–19; components in, 15, 70, 72; composite zone in, 55–56; functional type of, 77–78; influences on, 68–69, 72, 75; inside/outside in, 76–77; and intersections with governance and economy, 80; and language, 68; local culture for, 14–17; of Middle Ages, 47; as resistant, 18; and values, 13–14. *See also* Cistercians; Haukos, Mark

archives, and Irish migration, 35

Ardagh Chalice, 75

Arendt, Hannah, 13

Arensberg, Conrad, 102–3, 160

Argentina, debt of, 126

Arkady Feed Ltd., 132

Armagh (Ireland), 75

art: and alternative space, 8–9; assemblages as found, 12; nomadic, 76

artifice versus nature, 15

assemblages: ADM as, 132; concept of lack in, 167; definition of, 8, 10–12, 28; and desire, 80; excess cohabiting in, 21; function of, 3, 171–72; immanence of, 19; jewelry as, 76; and jouissance, 168; as models for transregional linkages, 147; and *objet petit i*, 166; parliament building

design as, 71–72; utopianism as, 82; wall of death as, 186. *See also* space-between

Auden, W. H., 13

Australia: and EU subsidies, 127–28; Irish racism in, 62

autonomy, components in, 171–72

Bailey, Leon, 21

Ballyferriter (Ireland), author's visit to, 46–48, 51–52. *See also* Gallarus Oratory; "Loosestrife in Ballyferriter" (Durcan)

banking institutions: advertisement for, *88*; and farm ownership, 107–10; and Greencore scandal, 136; role in community of, 150, 153, 175–77. *See also* international financial institutions (IFIs)

Bank of Ireland, 136

Banville, John, 40

Barry, Sebastian, 40

Barry, Ursula, 125–26

Barthes, Roland, 77

baseball: in American culture, 173–74, 177–78; as atonement, 179; celebrity games of, 185; fraud in, 172–75; as panacea, 175–78. *See also Field of Dreams* (film)

Baseball Hall of Fame, 182

Baudrillard, Jean, 78, 106

Bauhaus, 77

Beckles, Hilary, 125

Belfast (Ireland), parliament building in, 69–70

Bell, Desmond, 18, 103, 198n. 5

Berman, Marshall, 155–56

Berry, Wendell, 125

Beuys, Joseph, 77–78

Bhabha, Homi, 8, 166

biographies, uses of, 36–37

Birdwell-Pheasant, Donna, 102

Birmingham Centre for the Study of Contemporary Culture, 5, 77

Black-and-Tan war, 103

Black Sox scandal, 172–75, 179, 181, 182

Blasket Islands (Ireland): description of, 46; development in, 51–52; in poetry, 42–44

Bognar, Botone, 16

Bogue, Allan G., 38, 97, 198n. 1
Bogue, Ronald, 201n. 2
Bohan, Father Harry, 157–58
Boland, Eavan, 40
Böll, Heinrich, 78
borderwork, 8
Boulez, Pierre, 197n. 3
boundaries: definition of, 14; missionary
    articulation of, 63
boycott, origin of, 100
Branstad, Terry, 185
Brazil, foreign debt of, 125–26
Breen, R., 102
Breton, André, 68
Brock, Lou, 185
Broderick, James Lonsdale, 66
Brothers of Death (monastic order), 57–58
Browne, Ivor, 78
buildings. *See* architecture
bureaucratic materialism, 156
Burlington and Missouri River Railroad,
    87
Bush, George, 127–28, 133, 139–40

Callinicos, Alex, 167
Calloway, Kathy, 40
Campbell, Brian, 121
Canada, and free trade agreements, 200n.
    4
Canavan, Francis, 68
capitalism: cross-regional perspective on,
    114–16; debt encouraged in, 125, 150;
    delinking from, 6, 141–45, 170–71; and
    free trade agreements, 128; and
    industrialized agriculture, 154–55;
    migrants' imaginary colonized by, 156–
    57, 159–60; peripheral zones versus core
    nations in, 144; responses to, 83, 154;
    society regulated by, 19. *See also*
    agricycles; colonialism; global economy;
    privatization
Cappoquin (Ireland), Melleray Abbey in,
    58–59
Capra, Frank, 104–5, 182
Captain Boycott (film), 100, 110
Carduso, F. H., 200n. 3

Carey, Brother Conrad, 62
Carey, Michael, 35
Cargill Corporation, 133, 140
Carney, Edward, 36
Carney, John, 36
Carney, Margaret, 36
Carney, Mary O'Toole, 36
Carney, T. J., 35–36
"Carrie Usher's Journal" (Calloway), 40
Carroll, David, 77
Carroll and Coen's store, 36
Casey, Kevin, 40
Catholicism: and education, 62; migration
    encouraged by, 34; outlawed, 54;
    racialization of, 63
Catholics: and conflicts with Protestants,
    47; discrimination against, 34, 117;
    emancipation for, 117; journals for, 33;
    migration of, 30, 84; visits to Melleray
    by, 59
cattle, evaluation of, 66
Cayton, Andrew, 83–86, 89, 103, 160
ceantar, 154
Celtic jewelry, architecture influenced by,
    68, 72, 75
cemeteries, as documents, 30–32
census, definitions in, 198n. 1
centennials, publications for, 35–37
center/elite, missionary articulation of, 63
Center for Rural Affairs, 122
Central America Week, 131
centralization: resistance to, 65; support
    for, 55
chaos theory, 71
Chicago White Sox, 172–73, 175. *See also*
    Field of Dreams (film)
childrearing, regional mapping of, 198n. 4
China, collectivization in, 199–200n. 1
cholera, 60
Chomsky, Noam, 17, 125
churches, construction of, 34
Cistercians: architectural style of, 54–55,
    62; burial of, 59–60; conditions for, 59–
    61; depictions of, 55–59; early role of,
    54; farming concerns of, 65–67;
    migration of, 53–54, 60–61; regions

East Dubuque, name of, 34

Eat the Peach (film): compared to *Field of Dreams*, 187–88, 192, 194–95; criticism on, 190–91; description of, 186–92; illustration from press-pac for, *187*; stills from, *193*; success of, 186–87

economic development: agriculture's integration into, 124; critique of, 141–43; and family farms, *107*; and missionaries, 62; opposition to, 51; versus personal development, 155, 159

economy: global manipulation of local, 170–71; inflation in, 116; intersections with architecture and governance, 80; needed analysis of, 144; recessions in, 105–10, 141–42, 186, 96099. *See also* agricycles; global economy

Edwards, Eoin, 187

Eight Men Out (film), 173, 180

Eliot, T. S., 192, 194

Elizabeth I (queen of England), 47, 117

Emmet, Robert, 32, 78

Enclosure Acts, 115–19

England. *See* Great Britain

environment: attitudes toward, 99; and climate, 67, 87, 199n. 4; descriptions of, 61–62, 93–94; and economic development, 142–43; and soil conservation, 143; and topography, 15

ethanol, 133, 139–40

ethics: of aesthetics, 17–18; of cultural inquiry, 5; of psychoanalysis, 27

ethnicity, racialization of, 63

European Union (EU): agricultural advances in, 124; agricultural policy of, 119–22, 126–32, 137, 194; impact in Ireland of, 126–27, 130; imports and exports from, 130, 134–35; Ireland's role in, 120–21, 126–27; landowners in, 89; overspecialization in, 77; regional development funding from, 51, 191; regions defined in, 3; university proposed to, 77–78. *See also* Common Agricultural Policy (CAP, for EU)

Fabians, 99

Fairleigh, John, 202n. 14

Faith Healer (Friel), 45–46

Fallon, Peter, 40

familism, 160

family: colonization of, 160–61; constitution of, 163; ideal view of, 102; Iowa as metaphor for, 106; protection of, 167–68; and queer desire, 161–62; resistance to, 162; and suicide rate, 157–59; values in, 98–99

family farms: alternative systems for, 143–44; commercialization of, 160–63; cyclical interruptions in, 96; declining number of, 100, 114, 119–24; definition of, 64, 101, 116, 123; depictions of, 89–94, 98–99, 102–3, 147–55; dispossession of, 104; and economic development, *107*; foreclosures on, 108–10; function of, 167–68; and heartland values, 105–6, 143; ideological claims for, 91–92, 99, 102, 143; monastery compared to, 67–68; mythology of, 85–86, 151–52, 170; and 1970s crisis, 107–10; reconstitution of, 170–71; regional links between, 103, 108, 146–47

famine: anniversary of, 1, 29; causes of, 117, 124; Great Depression compared to, 81; literature on, 29–30; shortage of coffins during, 60. *See also* migrants; migration

farmers: alternatives for, 158–59; incomes for, 114–15, 121–22, 130; marginalization of, 153–55; motives for, 32; organization of American, 99–101; production quotas for, 129–30; as source of democracy, 105–6; suicides by, 156–59; third-worlding of, 124; versus wage laborers, 101, 120

Farmers' Holiday Association, 98

"A Farmer's Wife" (Garland), 93–94

farmhouse, idealization of, 104

father: absence of, 161; and children's migration, 152–53; death of, 82–83, 152,

163; dispossession of, 147–48, 156; function of, 167–68; as image of farm crisis, 154; meditations on, 64–65; recovery of good, 169–70; sexual abuse by, 148–49; silencing by, 155; son's reclamation of, 178–79; surplus value desired by, 164; as symptom of consolidation, 159

FBI (Federal Bureau of Investigation), 140–41

Feller, Bob, 185

The Field (film), 110, 153–55, 201n. 9

Field of Dreams (film): compared to *Eat the Peach*, 187–88, 192, 194–95; criticism on, 180–82; description of, 173–79; effects of, 182–83, 185; site of, 183, *184*, 185; success of, 183

Field of Dreams site, 183, *184*, 185

The Field (play), 153–55

film and videos: on agricultural reform, 199n. 3; on baseball, 173–79, 201n. 5; as critical regional artifacts, 170; on farmlife, 146–47, 153–55, 162–63, 175–76; on heartland values, 104–5; imitation of, 186, 188–89, 191; on Ireland, 103–4, 186–95; Ireland depicted as Iowa in, 68; on Irish migration, 32; on 1930s farm crisis, 99, 100, 103, 109; perception in, 179–80; role of, 2–3. *See also names of specific films*

Finn, Patrick, 31

Fiske, John, 5

Fitzgerald, Gretchen, 62–63

Fitzpatrick, Joan, 158

"five seasons," 79

Flannagan Brothers, 35

Foley, Dan, 155

The Folks (Suckow), 98–99, 199n. 5

forced symmetry. *See* symmetries

Ford, John, 32, 99, 103–4

Frampton, Kenneth: on critical regionalism and architecture, 3, 13–17, 118; criticism of, 17; stereosensory method of, 20

France: 1968 student protests in, 164, 167; and oilseed production, 138

Frankfurt School, 13

free trade agreements: impact in Ireland of, 127–32; implications of, 200n. 4; level-down impact of, 141. *See also* General Agreement on Tariffs and Trade (GATT); North American Free Trade Agreement (NAFTA)

Free University, proposal for, 77–78

Friel, Brian: and alternative university, 78; on artists, 45–46; Durcan's poem for, 41–43, 45, 64; on language, 43

frontier (U.S.), 86, 89, 93–95

fuels, taxation on, 142

Gadamer, 13

Galbraith, John Kenneth, 125

Galena (Illinois), settlement of, 34

Gallarus Oratory (Ireland): description of, 47–48, 50; influence by, 48, 50; photographs of, *44, 45, 49*; in poetry, 41–44; role of, 54

Garland, Hamlin, 90–94, 96, 99

Garrity, Sarah, 35

Garryowen (Iowa): sesquicentennial of, 65; settlement of, 34

GATT. *See* General Agreement on Tariffs and Trade (GATT)

Gehrig, Lou, 173

General Agreement on Tariffs and Trade (GATT): and ADM, 138; debates on, 131–35; and EC subsidies, 127–30; effects of, 128; goals of, 130; psycho-cultural counterpart to, 167; structural adjustment in, 125; and suicide rate, 158

George, Henry, 99

Gere, Richard, 109, 175, 179, 194

Germany: migration from, 29, 32; oilseed plants in, 138; as series of units, 3

"Ghost Stories" (Boland), 40

Gibson, Bob, 185

Gillis, Alan, 129

Gleick, James, 71

global economy: concept of region in, 3; effects of, 143–44, 163–64, 188; and farm life, 149–55; and free trade agreements, 128–31; marginality in, 77; migrants as vehicle of, 83–84; resistance to, 185; tactics in, 140–41; and unemployment, 190–91. *See also* agricycles; economy; marketing strategies; multinational business

globalization: of agriculture, 132–34, 138; alternative experiences to, 16; boredom with, 161; and disengagement, 144; and homogenization, 4–5, 18, 28; and interior/exterior views, 22–24; and regions, 3–6; and vertical administration, 124. *See also* Archer-Daniels-Midland Corporation (ADM)

Gómez-Peña, Guillermo, 8

Government of Ireland Act (1920), 69

Grant, Ulysses S., 34

The Grapes of Wrath (film), 99, 103

The Grapes of Wrath (Steinbeck), 98–99

Graves, Charles, 58–60

Great Blasket Visitor Centre, 51

Great Britain: economic development policies of, 115–19; rural population of, 117; suicides in, 157

Great Depression: famine compared to, 81; farm crisis during, 96–98; values in, 98–99

Greencore scandal, 135–37, 141

Grey, Lord, 47

Grossberg, Lawrence, 5–6

groundwater contamination, 66

Group of 7 (G7), 131

Guattari, Félix: on assemblage, 11–12, 80; on collectivity, 170–71; critique of, 169; on jewelry, 76; on nomadic analyses, 7, 9–10; on smooth space, 16

GUBU, definition of, 201n. 3

Gwynn, Stephen, 47

Habermas, Jürgen, 13–14

Hall, Stuart, 5

Hammer, Armand, 133

Hannan, D. F., 102

Haraway, Donna, 6, 17, 166

Harris, Wilson, 8–9

Hartnett, Michael, 146

Haukos, Mark: architectural drawings by, 73, 74, 75; influences on, 68–69, 76; parliament building designed by, 71–72, 75–77

Heaney, Seamus, 48

heartland: and agricultural policy, 105–6, 143; baseball as representative of, 173–74, 177–78; and desire, 185; factitiousness of, 165; as frame of Irish reference, 114; invention of, 104–5; magic realism in, 180; realities in, 109–10; and structural adjustment policy, 125; utopian desire enacted by concept of, 185; values of, 105–10, 143. *See also* American dream

Hegel, G. W. F., 21

Heidegger, Martin, 13–14, 23

Heineken, Freddie, 3, 7

Henry VIII (king of England), 116–17

hermeneutics, postcolonial, 8–9

heterogeneity, resistance to, 84–85

Hill, John, 100

history: and architecture, 68–69; erasure of, 180; malleability of, 181; perspective of, 20–21; role of, 2–3

Hogan, Dick, 51

Hogan, Patrick, 100–101

Holbrook (Iowa): cemetery near, 31; migration to, 36

"Holiday" strike, 96

Holy Cross monastery (Ireland), 62

homogenization, 3–5, 18, 28

homosexuality, 162–63

Hore, Father Thomas, 29–31

horizons, types of, 10

Horton, Loren, 28

Howe, Daniel Walker, 84

Humphrey, Hubert, 133

identification, as trap, 11

identity, 165–68

identity-thinking, 21
IFIs. *See* international financial institutions (IFIs)
IGTWU (Irish General Transport and Workers Union), 101
Illich, Ivan, 77
Illinois, migration to, 34
imaginary: of agrarians, 180–83, 185; of migrants, 156–57, 159–60
immigration. *See* migration
Imogene (Iowa), migration to, 35
imperialism, and heartland values, 106
inappropriate/d other, 6
in-betweenness, definition of, 10. *See also* space-between
independence versus sovereignty, 127
India: and colonialism, 8–9; Irish racism in, 62
"In Gallarus Oratory" (Heaney), 48
inside versus outside: in architecture, 76–77; contradictions between, 48; definitions of, 2, 7; function of, 19–20, 166–68; and objectivity, 1–3; as part of whole assemblage, 164; and projections of utopian past, 103; zone between, 21–23, 76
interbeing, 10. *See also* space-between
international financial institutions (IFIs): delinking from, 142, 170–71; encoded in heartland, 106–7; hegemony of, 160, 188; hierarchy of, 113; role of, 12, 164; as transcendental signifier, 159–60. *See also* International Monetary Fund (IMF); World Bank
International Monetary Fund (IMF), 125–26, 128
International style, 14
International Writers Program (University of Iowa), 39–40
interspace, aesthetics of, 7–12
intuitive creativity, 164–65
Iowa: childrearing in, 198n. 4; creed of, 133; descriptions of, 86–87, *88*, 89, 97; farm crisis in, 109–10; film depictions of, 68, 105, 109, 175–79; and GATT talks,

131–32; Ireland's links with, 27–29, 83, 95–96, 106–7, 109–10, 195; literature depictions of, 91, 94; as metaphor, 106; migration to, 29, 34–35, 38–39, 86; as place and as word, 50; place-names in, 65; WPA's guide to, 97. *See also Field of Dreams* (film); Iowa towns
Iowa, O Iowa! (Garland), 93–94
Iowa Board of Immigration, 29, 86–87, 199n. 4
Iowa Catholic Historical Review, 33
Iowa City (Iowa), and Field of Dreams site, 183
Iowa Department of Natural Resources, 66
Iowa Farm and Rural Life Poll, 143
Iowa Heritage Series, 96
Iowa State University, 96, 143–44
Iowa towns: Cedar Rapids, 79; Cosgrove, 31–32; Council Bluffs, 66; Dubuque, *61*, 66; Dyersville, 183, *184*, 185; Garryowen, 34, 65; Holbrook, 31; Imogene, 35; Iowa City, 183; list of, 65; Lone Tree, 157; Lytle City, 35, 37; Parnell, 31–32, 35–37, *37*; St. Patrick, 32; Windham, 31
Irace, Fulvio, 13
IRA (Irish Republican Army), 185
Ireland: agricultural policies in, 100, 117–21; bog in, 190; conditions in, 37, 64–65; conflicts in, 46–47, 185; critical studies in, 198n. 5; "dependent" development of, 115–16; and enclosure movement, 117; family farms in, 100–104, 194; foreign debt of, 125; and free trade agreements, 127–32; Greencore scandal in, 135–37, 141; Iowa's links with, 27–29, 83, 95–96, 106–7, 109–10, 195; marginality of, 77; migration from, 28–33, 84; nationalism in, 100, 117; outsider expectations for, 104; regionalism in, 124; rural fundamentalism in, 105–6; rural population of, 121, 142; suicides in, 157–59; as third-world country, 120, 124, 200n. 3; tradition in, 60, 160; unemployment in, 158, *158*,

Meagher, Thomas F., 34
meanings, vertical versus horizontal
    connections in, 113
Melleray Abbey (Ireland): depictions of,
    55–59; establishment of, 54, 58–59; as
    icon for monasticism, 64; migration
    from, 53–54, 60–61. *See also* New
    Melleray Abbey (Iowa)
Metropolitan Federal Bank, advertisement
    for, *88*
Mexico: debt of, 126; and free trade
    agreements, 200n. 4
Michael Joe (Murray), 40
middle passage, 8
Middleton, Neil, 125
Midwest Center for Developing Artists,
    advertisement for, *123*
Midwest (U.S.): consumer culture in, 38;
    contradictions in, 90–94, 98–99; cyclical
    recession in, 96–99; depictions of, 90–
    94; and free trade agreements, 131–32;
    geopolitics of, 83–95; migration to, 34–
    35; mythmaking in, 85–86, 151–52;
    promotion of, 86–87, *88*, 89, 119; sense
    of time as space in, 79; suicides in, 156–
    57; and values, 85, 91–92, 104–10, 143,
    180. *See also* heartland
migrants: attitudes toward, 84–85; and
    baseball, 173–74; Cistercians as, 60;
    colonized imaginary of, 156–57, 159–60;
    diseases of, 60; motives of, 30, 32–33,
    64, 83–84, 92–93; names of, 31; origins
    of, 31–32; recommendations to, 86–87,
    89; socialization of, 160; stereotypes of,
    37–38; success of, 38; women as, *85*
migration: assumptions underlying, 64;
    causes of, 117; by children, 152–53;
    conditions in, 50; denunciation of, 101–
    2; effects of, 38–39, 155; and host
    populations, 84–85; from Ireland, 28–33,
    84; literature on, 39–41; Midwest
    promotion of, 86–87, *88*, 89, 92;
    perspectives on, 28–29; restrictions on,
    84; songs about, 92
Miles, Sarah, 192

Miles from Home (film), 109, 175, 179, 194
Milltown (Ireland), film sited in, 190
Milwaukee Railroad, 35
Minh-ha, Trinh T., 6
Minnesota, promotion of migration to, 86
mirroring, 170–72, 181, 195
missionaries, goals of, 62–63
Mississippi River, 34, 82
Missouri, Cistercians in, 61
modernism, critique of, 13–14
modernization, 66, 155–56
monasteries: architectural connections
    between, 62; early organization of, 54–
    55; family farms compared to, 67–68.
    See also Cistercians; Melleray Abbey
    (Ireland); New Melleray Abbey (Iowa)
Monastery Seasons (newsletter), 65–67
monasticism: celebration of, 62; compared
    to family farming, 67–68; in Joyce's
    fiction, 64
Moore, Moss, 155
Morris, John, 33
Morrow, Addie, 122
Morton, H. V., 59
Moten, Fred, 8
Mount Melleray. *See* Melleray Abbey
    (Ireland)
Mr. Smith Goes to Washington (film), 104
Mullaney, Brother Kieran, 60–61
Mullarkey, Gabrielle, 32–34
multinational business: alternative
    experiences to, 16; critique of, 131;
    influence by, 115; and regionalization,
    4–5; and subsidization, 121; tactics of,
    140–41; and unemployment, 190–91. *See
    also* Archer-Daniels-Midland Corpora-
    tion (ADM); capitalism; globalization;
    international financial institutions (IFIs)
Munck, Ronnie, 115, 117, 120, 124
Murphy, Bridget, 31
Murphy, Tomás, 40
Murray, John J., 89
Murray, William, 40–41, 199n. 5
Murray, William C. 102
myths, of family farms, 85–86, 151–52, 170

"My Wall of Death" (Ormrod), 188–89

NAFTA (North American Free Trade Agreement), 128, 200n. 4
National Brotherhood of Professional Players, 172
nationalism, 12, 100, 117
National Museum (Ireland), 75
nations, definition of, 6–7
nativists, attitudes of, 84–85
nature versus artifice, 15
Navan Fort (Ireland), 75
Nebraska: farmers' protests in, 95; farm women in, 94–95; promotion of migration to, 86
Nebraska Farmers' Alliance, 94
negative dialectic: Adorno on, 3, 18–19, 53, 113; and discovery of alternatives, 53; framing of, 18–21; role of, 3, 21–23
Nelson, Cary, 6
neomodernism, 14
Netherlands, migration from, 29
Nevin, Brigid, 120–22
New Age consciousness, 8
New Deal: and farm crisis, 97–98; and film, 199n. 3
Newhall, Maj. John B., 87
New Melleray Abbey (Iowa): cemetery at, 31; farming at, 65–67; history of, 60–61; and Irish migration, 30, 33; postcard of, *63;* sacred and commercial economies of, 113
New World Order, 2
nitrates, 66
nomadism: and art, 76; and baseball, 173–74; elements in, 12, 167; and literature, 9
nomadologies (nontraditional histories), 7
North American Free Trade Agreement (NAFTA), 128, 200n. 4
North Dakota: depictions of, 91; migration to, 93
Northern Ireland: administration of, 69–72; agriculture in, 120, 122, 127, 130; and colonialism, 8–9; and European

unification, 3; visitors to Iowa from, 185
Northern Ireland Parliament Building: description of, 69–72; plans for, *73, 74, 75*
Norway, migration from, 29

objectivity, 1–3, 5
objet a, 164–65
objet iowa, 166
objet irlandaise, 166
objet petit i, 165–67
O'Casey, Sean, 101
Ó Cearna, Sean Pheats Tom, 51
O'Connor, Father James, 60–62, 67
O'Connor, T. P., 35
O'Donoghue, Michael, 186
oil crisis, 108
oilseed, and free trade agreements, 134–35, 138
Old Northwest Territory ordinance (1787), 82
Oliver, Kelly, 169–70
O Muirthile, Liam, 51–52
O'Neill, Tip, 133
Onibaba (film), 161–63
Onuf, Peter, 83–86, 89, 103, 160
oppression, 28–29, 167
Ordinance of 1787 (U.S.), 82
O'Regan, Michael, 155
Ormrod, Peter, 185–86, 188–90
ornamentation, religion conflated with, 75
O'Ryan, Father Vincent, 58–59
other, construction of realities for, 23–24
Otomo, Kohei, 183
O'Toole, Fintan, 154–55, 181–82
O'Toole, Mary, 36
outsiderness: definition of, 2, 7; thinking in, 19–20. *See also* inside versus outside

Packard, Norman, 71
pamphlets, Midwest promoted in, 86–87, *88,* 89. *See also* advertisements
Paolozzi, E., 7
parents: and connections with children, 169–70; meditations on, 64–65. *See also* father

Parker, Stewart, 190–92, 194, 201n. 12, 202n. 12
parliament building: construction of, 70; influences on, 68–69, 72; plans for, 73, 74, 75
Parnell, Charles, 35
Parnell (Iowa): cemetery at, 31; history of, 32, 35–37; postcard of, 37
Parnet, Claire, 10–11
participant observation, 1
Partridge, John, 115
patriarchy: delinking enabled by, 171; effects of, 161–63, 165. See also father
pattern language, 68, 72
Patterson, Eric, 172–73
payment-in-kind (PIK) program (U.S.), 66–67
peasant proprietors, 118
Pepitone, Joe, 185
Peterson, Ed, 114
Pett, Joel, 128
Pfizer's Corporation, 132
Philadelphia, Here I Come (Friel), 45
PIK (payment-in-kind) program (U.S.), 66–67
The Plow that Broke the Plains (film), 199n. 3
"P.M." (program), 185
political economy, cross-regional perspective on, 10, 114–15
politics, agribusiness influence on, 133–34
potato, Irish import of, 122
Poulantzas, Nicos, 200n. 3
Powers, Elmer G., 96–97, 156–57
PrairieFire organization, 157
Prairie Home (newspaper), 94
prairies, descriptions of, 61–62, 93–94
Presbyterian Assembly's College (Belfast), 69
Presley, Elvis, 186, 188–89
price-fixing, 139, 140–41
privatization: versus collective behavior, 172–74, 177–78; versus commons tradition, 118–19; legacy of, 117, 135–36
production: conditions for cheaper, 197n. 2; cycles of, 190–91; rationalized in tandem with craft, 14

progress, 14, 142–43, 151
Project Children program (Irish), 185
Protestants: and conflicts with Catholics, 47; and cultural values, 84–85
psychoanalysis: in cultural studies methodology, 23–24; ethics of, 27; goal of, 22
Psychological Society of Ireland, 157
Pulitzer Prize, 147

The Quiet Man (film), 103–4

racism, church's complicity in, 62–63
Radio Telefís Eireann (RTE), 185–86, 189
Ragland-Sullivan, Ellie, 200n. 3
railroads, 35, 84, 86–87, 95
Raleigh, Sir Walter, 47
rapeseed, and free trade agreements, 138–40
rationalization, 27–28
Reagan, Ronald, 133, 135
Reamore (Ireland), land dispute in, 155
recessions: as cyclical, 96–99; economic role of, 141–42, 186; media reports of, 191
Reed, Donna, 105
Rees, Jim, 29–31
reflexive viewing, 1
regionalism, 18, 124
regional studies, focus of, 2–3. See also critical regionalism; regions
regions: definition of, 3–4, 6–7; dialogue among, 9; dynamic instability across, 21; and globalization, 4–6; links among, 7, 12, 81; and space-between, 48, 50; symmetry among, 8; theorizing in, 28
reification, 22
religion, conflated with ornamentation, 75. See also Catholicism; Catholics; Cistercians; Protestants
Reno, Milo, 98
Republican Party, values of, 84–85
Ricoeur, Paul, 13
Riley, Glenda, 38, 198n. 1
The River (1937, film), 199n. 3
The River (1984, film), 110

subjectivity: heterogeneity in, 46; and
    intercultural explorations, 2, 5–6;
    structural redefinition of, 171
subject/object relations, 2, 5–6, 21. *See also*
    inside versus outside
subsidization: of crops, 133, 137; by EC,
    127–30, 137, 138; effects of, 120; and
    ethanol, 133; regulations on, 121; as
    regulator of overproduction, 126
success, as Midwest ideal, 91–92
Suckow, Ruth, 98–99, 199n. 5
sugar: as commodity, 135–37, 141; and
    multinational companies, 137–38;
    subsidies for, 133
suicides, 156–59
Sutton, Nina, 78
Sweden, migration from, 29, 32
symmetries: among regions, 8, 29; function
    of, 21, 23, 147; perception of, 7–8
synchronicity, 9

Tafuri, Manfredo, 13
Tanzania, village cooperatives in, 199–
    200n. 1
Taormina Film Festival (1986), 186
Tara Brooch, 75
Tate and Lyle PLC, 137, 140
tenant farmers: eviction of, 100; freedom of
    contract for, 117; increased number of,
    97–98
territorialization, and nomadic space, 9
Texas, migration to, 30
Thatcher, Margaret, 135
third space, 8
third-world countries: and agricultural
    policies, 124–25; American farmers'
    links with, 108; and free trade agree-
    ments, 141; Ireland as, 120, 124, 200n.
    3; recolonization of, 115; self-reliance
    for, 144
Thornely, Sir Arnold, 70
A Thousand Acres (Smiley): comparisons
    with, 155, 159; description of, 147–52; as
    summary statement, 154–55
Tipperary County (Ireland), migration
    from, 32

Tisdall, Caroline, 77–78
Toibin, Niall, 191, 202n. 13
topography, 15
Translations (Friel), 43
Trecy (Tracy), Father Jeremiah, 33–34
Treichler, Paula, 6
Tschumi, Bernard, 68, 76–77
Turner, Graeme, 5
Twain, Mark (Samuel Clemens), 82–83,
    199n. 2
twins, mirroring of, 181
Twohig, Catherine Jones, 33–34
Tzara, Tristan, 68
Tzonis, Alex, 198n. 5

Ulster (Ireland), migration from, 84
Ulster Farmers' Union, 130
Ulster Volunteer Force, 185
unconscious, and thinking as outsider, 19–
    20
underdevelopment, 6, 77
unemployment, in Ireland, 158, *158*, 186,
    188, 190–91
UNICEF, 125
unions, class nature of, 101
United International Pictures, 187
United Nations, conferences held by, 142
United States: agricultural policy of, 66–67,
    109, 114–15, 127–28; dreams betrayed
    in, 99; as extension of Ireland, 181–82;
    farm crisis in, 122–23; and free trade
    agreements, 127–29, 134–35, 200n. 4;
    and frontier, 86, 89, 93–95; and Ireland's
    foreign debt, 126; Irish population in,
    38–39; Irish racism in, 62; symbol for,
    106, 183. *See also* American dream;
    heartland; Iowa; Midwest (U.S.)
U.S. Department of Agriculture, 66–67,
    114–15
U.S. Supreme Court, 172
universalism versus rootedness, 15
University of Iowa, 39, 66
utopianism: as assemblage, 82; and desire,
    185; and Midwest promotion, *88*, 89;
    projected onto past, 103

values: in agriculture, 122–23, 143; and
architecture, 13–14; articulation of,
176–78; baseball as representative of,
173–74, 177–78, 180; of community,
148, 153; contradictions in, 106; and
family farms, 105–6, 143; in Great
Depression, 98–99; marketing as core
of, 180; of middle class, 85; of Midwest,
85, 91–92, 104–10, 143, 180; in politics,
84–85; resistance to, 162. *See also*
American dream; progress; utopianism
Venturi, Robert, 14
vernacular populism, 14
Vidler, Anthony, 77
visuality, movement beyond, 16

wage laborers: versus farmers, 101, 120;
and global economy, 144; and multinational union-busting, 138, *139*. *See also*
unemployment
Wallace, Henry, 98
Wallace, Iain, 116
Waller, Robert James, 66, 142–43
Wallerstein, Immanuel, 6, 7
wall of death (Ireland): as assemblage, 186;
description of, 188–89; impetus for, 186;
still from film, *193*. *See also Eat the Peach*
(film)
Walsh, Dick, 137
Walsh, Maurice, 103–4
Ward, Alan J., 68
weaponry, jewelry as affects corresponding
to, 76
Weiss, Michael J., 38
wells, contamination of, 66
westward movement, emotional effects of,
93–95

Whelan, Kevin, 124
Whig Party, values of, 84
Whitacre, Mark, 140
Whitt, Laurie Anne, 5
Wilbers, Steven, 39
Willis, Sharon, 78, 106
Windham (Iowa), cemetery near, 31
Wisconsin: depictions of, 91; promotion of
migration to, 86
Wittenburg, Bonnie, 135–36, 138
women: film depictions of, 161–63;
literature depictions of, 93–94, 148–50;
marginalization of, 162–63; as migrants,
85; recollections by, 94–95
Works Progress Administration (WPA), 97
World Bank: agricultural policies of, 124–
25; interest rates of, 108; role of, 125–
26, 128
World Family Farmers' Summit (1993),
131
World Series of baseball (1919), 172–75
world system theory, 6
World Trade Organization (WTO), 131,
140
World War II, propaganda films for, 105
WPA (Works Progress Administration), 97
Writers' Workshop (University of Iowa),
39–40
writing, metatext composed of, 39
WTO (World Trade Organization), 131,
140

X (Mr.), 68

Yeats, William Butler, 68

Zizek, Slavoj, 10, 16–17, 78, 165–66